PREFACES TO ENGLISH
NINETEENTH-CENTURY THEATRE

PREFACES TO ENGLISH NINETEENTH-CENTURY THEATRE

Michael Booth

*Manchester
University Press*

From *English Plays of the Nineteenth Century*
edited by Michael Booth
© Oxford University Press

Reprinted by permission of Oxford University Press

Published by
Manchester University Press
Oxford Road, Manchester M13 9PL
1980
Distributed in North America by
Humanities Press Inc
Atlantic Highlands
N.J. 07716, U.S.A.

British Library Cataloguing in Publication Data

Booth, Michael Richard
    Prefaces to English nineteenth-century theatre.
    1. English drama—19th century—History and
    criticism
    I. Title
    822'.7'09   PR721

    ISBN 0-7190-0813-1

Printed and bound by
Clark Constable Ltd, Edinburgh

CONTENTS

LIST OF ILLUSTRATIONS

FOREWORD

T H E purpose of these prefaces is to make available in one volume the separate introductions to my edition of *English Plays of the Nineteenth Century*, which appeared in five volumes between 1969 and 1976. Each of these essays prefaced a selection of plays from a particular dramatic genre, or more than one genre, so that references to the plays themselves would illustrate points made in the prefaces. However, they can, I think, stand on their own as offering historical information on and critical interpretations of virtually the whole range of nineteenth-century drama except for light opera, musical comedy, and the plays of Shaw and Wilde—omitted from selection because of the musical character of the first two and the general availability of the last.

Historians of drama and theatre are not often given the chance to attach a reconsideration of their own opinions to the work originally containing these opinions. As the writing of these prefaces was begun in 1967, the interval of years since then has afforded the opportunity of looking back at earlier judgments. One significant change in critical opinion of nineteenth-century drama and theatre is that there is a lot more of it now than there was then, and a full re-examination of this drama and theatre would have to take place in the context of significant new commentary. In 1967, with a few notable exceptions, the subject was taken far less seriously than it is now; history and criticism, if it existed at all, was frequently dismissive and sometimes contemptuous. The struggle to establish nineteenth-century drama and theatre as a respectable and important part of English theatrical history still goes on, but opponents on the other side of the battle lines—mostly now to be found in the literary fastness of Departments of English—at least cannot complain of a lack of information and interest.

Were I to write these five prefaces again, there would inevitably be adjustments of emphasis. Since, inescapably, a consideration of the drama of the period is inseparable from a consideration both of the audiences who saw it and the theatres they saw it in, I would now provide more information on theatrical context, although the use of that word 'context' implies, wrongly, that the plays come first and the theatre that gave them life can be relegated to a subordinate background. In the original edition information of this kind was largely confined to appendices, but more needed to be said in the prefaces themselves about the composition of audiences, acting styles, production methods, the deep social and cultural roots of the contemporary drama, and the particular relation between a play and the theatre that first performed it.

The question of the audience, or, rather, audiences for nineteenth-century drama is a crucial one. No theatre audience over a hundred-year period can possibly remain homogeneous, and in the nineteenth century the composition of any audience varied according to decade, district, theatre, and repertory. Class and income level, housing, means of transportation to the theatre, safety of the streets, and cultural tastes developed outside the auditorium are obviously significant factors in audience analysis. Such information is available from many scattered sources, but has attracted little attention because historians of the stage are not commonly social, economic, and cultural historians as well—although they should be, since theatre is inevitably a part of society, economics, and culture. Without a proper understanding of these matters, and of the nineteenth-century audience, there can be no proper understanding of the drama and theatre. It is right that the predominant emphasis of the play selections and prefaces of the volumes of *English Plays of the Nineteenth Century* was on the drama of the West End, as the West End play was in the mainstream of dramatic writing. Nevertheless—and here is where class, audience, geography, economics, etc., are important—there is much evidence to suggest that for a considerable part of the century the working and lower middle-class audience of the East End and other working-class districts constituted a majority of the theatre-going population in London, and that this audience was also of major significance in the provinces. Thus I would now further amend the earlier emphasis on the West End with qualifications of this kind; such amendment might also lead—were the play selections to be done over again—to a greater variety of geographical choice.

The economics of theatre was a topic touched on perhaps too briefly when the prefaces were written; like the matter of the audience (itself closely linked with economics) the matter of theatre as a business, and to what extent that business determined the content of drama and the style of its performance, are questions deserving space in any investigation of the drama of any period. Nineteenth-century theatre was not subsidized, and every one of the thousands of plays written for public performance in the professional theatre was on its own at the box office. The manager's total dependence on public favour naturally determined his choice of actors, authors, production methods, and pricing policies, and of course very much affected the kind of drama he offered. The connection between business depressions and theatrical bankruptcies is an obvious one, but it has not previously been associated with the state of the drama itself. Less obvious is the relation between theatrical hard times and changes in repertory policy and seat prices designed to bring in a different audience with different tastes. Similarly, in the period of national prosperity ensuing from the 1860s, the economic well-being of many managements was clearly reflected in—indeed, to a considerable extent determined—not only the health of the theatre but also the content and style of the drama written, at least in the West End, for a more prosperous audience whose ways of living had substantially changed. These things are all part of 'context' at the very least, and ought at the very least to be acknowledged.

Contextual in the same sense and in the same degree of importance are acting and production style. As to the former, nobody has written anything like a satisfactory account of the development of the acting styles appropriate to the different nineteenth-century dramatic genres and their relationship to each other; the whole matter is complex and difficult and could hardly be comprehended in prefaces to a series of play selections. However, although three of the appendices touched upon aspects of acting, it might have been useful to have said something in the prefaces about melodramatic acting, tragic acting, light comedy, low comedy, and burlesque acting in preparation for the reading of plays containing a range of parts meant to be acted in highly individual styles which gave theatrical meaning and life to the scripts themselves. An appreciation of how these styles worked on stage illuminates speeches and character types which in a purely literary sense may appear merely bizarre. The changes in acting style required by a changing audience are also factors to be taken into account, as is the relation of scripts to performance in—until the end of the century—an actors' rather than a writers' theatre. One might also have said more in the first instance of the way in which much nineteenth-century drama was written for a pictorial stage that emulated painting and that, with increasing care and painstaking research methods, attempted to give archaeological reality to plays with a historical setting. The same meticulousness was applied to drama with a contemporary setting, and the principles of realism and pictorialism were applied to all stage settings of any scale no matter what the chronological period of the play performed. Lighting, costuming, properties, and all the stage arts served these principles, and it is interesting to note how technological developments made certain kinds of theatre possible, especially sensation drama and the fully-blown Victorian pantomime. The increase in the number of scenes written to embody innovations in lighting and stagecraft, for instance, is remarkable.

On reflection, to make these desirable adjustments in emphasis to the original prefaces might take as much as writing again. A preface is, after all, a preface, and the intention of the prefaces was to introduce in a general way the plays to follow. These subjects are all large ones and deserve thorough exploration on their own account; nevertheless, some indication of their existence and their relation to the drama might have been made without taking up too much space.

When it comes to the drama, there is little I would wish to alter, except—as already suggested—to take more account of working-class drama from outside the West End, since there was so much of it and so many people went to see it. I still believe, contrary to generally received opinion, that drama did not so much 'decline' in the nineteenth century as transform its character in response to significant cultural, social, economic, and theatrical changes. Just to note three examples, the immense popularity of melodrama and the Regency harlequinade, and the great success with audiences of early nineteenth-century comedy of the Holcroft–Dibdin–Reynolds school, make no sense whatever unless initially approached from the point of view of these changes. It was undoubtedly true that the theatrical product of such changes was less satisfying from a literary perspective, but that is 'decline' of another kind. Almost until the end nineteenth-century drama never pretended to the status of literature, and it would be a serious mistake to judge it primarily from a literary standpoint. Of all periods of English dramatic history, it is the nineteenth century which most loudly proclaims what ought to be a truism, that drama written for performance is never literature pure and simple; to me that is one of the most interesting aspects of nineteenth-century drama and, indeed, one of its great virtues.

The sense of evolution in this drama, a major theme in the original prefaces, also needs reiteration. The tendency in some academic circles is still to believe that English drama was reborn in the 1890s with Pinero, Jones, and Shaw, and later Granville-Barker, with Tom Robertson in the 1860s playing the role of an Evangelist pointing to the light to come. However, any close examination of the complex fabric of the drama, of the inter-woven strands of early work comprising an essential part of the pattern of later years, convinces one beyond doubt that the playwrights of the nineties were indebted for most of their thematic material and much of their style to previous generations of dramatists, that Shaw would not have written as he did had he not been able to lay iconoclastic hands on the inherited wealth of Victorian melodrama and comedy, that Robertson's society comedies drew on Boucicault's and Bulwer-Lytton's before him, that Boucicault and Bulwer-Lytton adapted for their own purposes the vigorous, class-oriented, melodrama-ridden comedy of Holcroft and Reynolds at the beginning of the century. And so it goes with all the genres. The Gilbert and Sullivan operas were built on the fairy extravaganzas of Planché; Pinero's Paula Tanqueray comes from a long line of Victorian adventuresses dwelling outside the social pale; the comic characters in Henry Arthur Jones are refinements of the cruder comic men and women of earlier melodrama. Every-where there was development and change; nowhere a break in continuity, a fresh start, or a New Drama.

The strong moral idealism and domestic sentimentality of almost all nineteenth-century drama, even of light entertainments like pantomime openings and farce, are no longer marked features of modern drama, but twentieth-century drama was shaped by its predecessor in ways that once again emphasized continuity and evolution. Class antagonism, urban environmentalism, working-class settings and characters, social problems, social protest, social and scenic realism, comic and philosophical absurdism were all bequests from the nineteenth- to the twentieth-century stage, The fact that much of this matter was available—in contrast to the twentieth-century experience—in a truly popular theatre appealing to all classes enhances rather than diminishes its value and significance. Since nineteenth-century drama was a popular rather than a coterie art, this appeal both extended and limited its nature: extended by a considerable range of subject matter, dramatic style, and theatrical technique immediately accessible to and readily understandable by a wide variety of audiences; limited because this very accessibility meant keeping to tried and true paths, to a common denominator of the understanding, to an avoidance of intellectual and aesthetic subtlety. Thus the drama of the nineteenth century must be accepted on its own terms, not ours. This is not to say that it is inaccessible to us or remote from our own experience of life and art, and therefore neither of interest nor consequence. On the contrary, with a little necessary historical perspective and theatrical knowledge we soon find our way into one of the most stimulating, entertaining, and valuable periods of the English drama. The development of this drama and the benefits that come from reading it are outlined in the following prefaces; so I shall not repeat myself here. Of course it is much better to read the plays themselves than any writing about them, but at least these prefaces can be offered as possibly helpful reference points on a crowded dramatic map.

Virginius. Macready as Virginius: 'Thou seest that hand? It is a Roman's, boy.'
Act One, scene two.

I. DRAMA 1800-1850

There has been no period, for the last two centuries, in which invention and activity have been more conspicuous in the dramatic field than during the thirty or forty years which include the epoch of such dramatists as Miss Mitford, Sheridan Knowles, Bulwer Lytton, James White, Jerrold, Browning, G. Darley, Searle, Marston, Horne, Lovell, Troughton, Bell, Mrs. Gore, Sullivan, Peake, Poole, Hook, Planche, Charles and George Dance, the Mortons, Mark Lemon, Buckstone, Selby, Fitzball . . . Bernard, Coyne, Oxenford, Shirley Brooks, Watts Phillips, and those peculiar products of our own time, the burlesque writers, like the Brothers Brough, and Messrs. Byron and Burnand.[1]

THE modern reader interested in the history of English drama can only gaze in amazement at a list resembling a catalogue of obscure warriors in a long-forgotten minor epic. He would be more inclined to agree with William Harness, who in 1825 declared in an open letter to Charles Kemble and William Elliston, managers respectively of Covent Garden and Drury Lane, 'Your stages have fallen into the hands of the most contemptible of the literary tribe; and your admirers, both in number and in consequence, have been worthy your play-writers. Who are your successful authors? Planche and Arnold, Poole and Kenney; names so ignoble in the world of literature that they have no circulation beyond the green-room.'[2]

So ignoble has the drama of the nineteenth century been considered that only now is it emerging from that arid wasteland of indifference and contempt to which opinion has consigned it, but its steps are slow and painful. Generally, historians and critics who have bothered with the subject at all have said that the drama of about 1800 to 1890 is a formless mass of mediocrity, dull and repetitive, lacking literary quality and

---

[1] Tom Taylor, Introduction to *The Ticket-of-Leave Man*, 1863.
[2] 'A Letter . . . on the Present State of the Stage', *Blackwood's Magazine*, xvii (June 1825), 730.

thematic significance, a vast sea of theatrical trivia and down-right badness, a drama that slumbered fitfully for a hundred years while the glorious dawn of Shaw and Oscar Wilde waited in an East pregnant with momentous art.[1] This is still the common view, and the student of drama usually takes a colossal leap over the dark abyss yawning dangerously between Sheridan and Shaw, and lands thankfully on the other side.

No one can claim that the nineteenth century was an age of dramatic excellence; it was the opposite. Yet one cannot ignore a century of development in which the theatre abandoned traditional modes of expression and came haltingly into modernity. In 1800 the English theatre was a theatre of illusion still. Staging was symbolic rather than realistic. Scenery with conventional designs of wood, castle, chamber, palace, and street, painted on the flat surfaces of wings and shutters that changed in grooves, moved on and off stage in full view of the audience, as it had since 1660. Players entered and exited through proscenium doors opening and shutting upon library and forest alike, and they made their most effective 'points' downstage dead centre. Acting, whether in tragedy, comedy, farce, or melodrama, was considerably larger than life: stylized, energetic, and highly emphatic. Costume was sometimes vaguely suggestive of period, sometimes traditional, sometimes exaggerated for comic effect, sometimes contemporary even in classical drama. Both stage and auditorium were lit throughout the performance by candles and oil lamps, and pit and gallery audiences were, in the event of a full house, desperately over-crowded on hard, backless, unreserved benches.

By 1900, for better or worse, the theatre was a theatre of realism: realism in staging, acting, costuming, and all aspects of production. The box set, built-up scenery, and elaborate imitation of the settings of modern and ancient life replaced the simple wing, shutter, and groove system. The art of stage management had developed enormously, and styles of performance had become steadily more restrained and natural; for

---

[1] The authors of special studies of nineteenth-century theatre have, of course, been much more careful and detailed in their judgements. Notable among these studies are Ernest B. Watson, *Sheridan to Robertson* (1926); George Rowell, *The Victorian Theatre* (1956); and Allardyce Nicoll, *A History of English Drama*, iv–v, 2nd edn. (1955–9). To Nicoll's work in particular all historians of the nineteenth-century stage are greatly in debt.

perhaps the first time in theatre criticism underplaying and not overplaying was complained of. Costume and furnishings were exactly appropriate for a play with a contemporary setting, archaeologically correct for a play set in the past. Well-behaved middle-class audiences sat comfortably on reserved seats in darkened auditoriums, watching stages illuminated by the latest electric lighting.

Thus traditionalism slowly broke down under the impact of changes in a theatre anything but stagnant and backward. The nineteenth century has not generally been regarded as a period of theatrical experiment and innovation, but it was, and struggling underneath the apparent tyranny of conformity and convention was the rebellious spirit of reform. It is not my purpose here to examine the many changes in theatrical practice briefly summarized above—they are fully described by Watson, Nicoll, and Rowell—but it is important to remember that in the nineteenth century theatrical change preceded, and had to precede, changes in the content of drama, that dramatic reforms would not have occurred without theatrical reforms preparing the way. The work of Madame Vestris at the Olympic (1831-8), of Macready at Covent Garden (1837-9) and Drury Lane (1841-3), of Samuel Phelps at Sadler's Wells (1844-62), of Charles Kean at the Princess's (1850-9), and of the Bancrofts at the Prince of Wales's (1865-79), was collectively responsible for much improvement in standards of acting and production, as well as providing the theatre with considerable impetus to travel further along its already chosen road to realism. The end of this road was reached before the twentieth century began, and the climax and perfection of earlier developments was attained by the managements of Henry Irving at the Lyceum (1878-1902), John Hare at the Garrick (1889-95), George Alexander at the St. James's (1891-1918), and Herbert Beerbohm Tree at the Haymarket and Her Majesty's (1887-1915).

Where the theatre went the drama followed. A drama realistic in characterization, theme, and dialogue became possible only when acting, staging, and costuming had themselves become more realistic, and a good deal of theatrical spadework had to be done before a quality drama in the realistic mode could emerge in the 1890s and the pre-war years of the next century. The return of Society and the more intellectual playgoer to the theatre was of the greatest importance, for it changed the drama and was responsible for the upper-middle-class settings and themes of Jones, Pinero, Wilde, and Shaw. Thus the theatrical legacy of the nineteenth century seems more significant than the dramatic. Yet the realistic stage observation of the daily life of ordinary people is nineteenth century in origin. The domestic conflict and suffering that mark the work of many modern British playwrights goes back to the agonies of domestic melodrama. Prose drama with working- and middle-class settings, and dialogue with regional working-class dialects and accents, are nineteenth- and not twentieth-century creations. The vigorous and varied creativity that bridged the vast gulf of conception and style between *Virginius* in 1820 and *Mrs. Dane's Defence* in 1900 can only be fully understood in relation to its theatrical and social context, but it cannot be understood at all without a reading of the plays themselves. The personality and taste of an age can be studied in the drama of that age as well as in its fiction, painting, poetry, music, and architecture. There is no doubt that on the whole the nineteenth century got from its dramatists the plays it wanted and refused the plays it did not want; and that what it got suited it admirably.

Whatever their opinion of the merit of nineteenth-century drama, critics have been unanimous in pronouncing it lower than ever before. 'Why has the drama declined?' was a perennial question, a question discussed endlessly in the press, in theatrical memoirs, and even posed to witnesses before Select Parliamentary Committees. Nobody could agree on the causes of this decline; they are still argued over, and when added together make a list of formidable length. It was said that theatres were in a bad way because of too much competition (and because of too little); that star actors received immense salaries and authors not nearly enough; that actors and managers treated authors abominably; that the later dinner hour kept fashionable people away; that such people did not attend theatres because the lower classes were too noisily in evidence; that anyway they preferred exhibiting themselves at the opera and at the visits of French companies; that the solid middle class did not come because of increased evangelical hostility to the theatre and because of the presence of their inferiors who corrupted the

drama because they *did* come and liked mere entertainment and
vulgar show; that Drury Lane and Covent Garden were too
big to see and hear in properly; that these two theatres were
overburdened with the expense of providing virtually separate
companies for tragedy, comedy, opera, and pantomime; that
good authors were not to be found; that too many new amuse-
ments were competing for public attention; that people preferred reading novels to going to plays. Poets did not choose,
or were unable, to write well for the stage. Managers were
incompetent and tyrannical, stars jealous and selfish. Times
were hard. The drama was separate from literature. As to the
plays themselves, if they were comedies or farces they were
frivolous and inane, if tragedies dull or extravagant, if melodramas crude and sensational. Whatever they were they might
well be French in origin and thus unworthy of the consideration
of a true Englishman.

Whether such allegations, all made before 1840 and all
supportable by facts or a body of contemporary opinion, or
both, name factors actually or substantially contributory to
'the decline of the drama', ascertainable conditions—apart
from the constantly iterated complaints of managers, dramatists,
actors, and critics—testify to one fact of decline. From the
financial viewpoint alone, Drury Lane and Covent Garden
suffered as badly before the abolition of their monopoly on the
legitimate drama in 1843 as after it. By 1818 Drury Lane's
debts amounted to £80,000, and the receipts of the new theatre
had fallen from £75,584 in its first season of operation, 1812-13,
to £41,066 in 1817-18, or from a nightly average of £370 to
one of £205.[1] The sensational attraction of Edmund Kean, who
first appeared at Drury Lane in 1814, could do nothing in the
long run to increase dwindling receipts. In the 1820s and 1830s
Elliston, Price, Lee, Polhill, Bunn, and Hammond tried to
make a success of management but were driven into retreat and
bankruptcy. Macready's management of 1841-3 also proved a
financial failure, and the theatre reverted once more to the inde-
fatigable Bunn. During a similar period Covent Garden had
as many managers—Charles Kemble, Laporte, Bunn, Osbaldis-
ton, Macready, Vestris—and fared as badly as its rival. By
1832, when Charles Kemble testified that theatres were on the

[1] *The Theatrical Inquisitor*, xiii (November 1818), 366-7.

average 'never above one half full',[1] Covent Garden's debts amounted to £160,000, and receipts had dropped from a seasonal average of £79,000 during 1809–20 to one of £55,000 during 1820–32. In 1810–11 £98,000 was taken in, in 1828–9 £41,000.[2] Drury Lane did not become a successful financial venture until after Augustus Harris took it over in 1879. Covent Garden never recovered, and became an opera house in 1847. Their competitors the minor theatres, where before 1843 only the 'illegitimate' drama containing songs and music could be staged, did not do much better. Theatrical hard times prevailed almost everywhere in the first half of the century, and the long-awaited abolition of the patent monopoly in 1843 brought relief to neither major nor minor theatres. In such conditions it is difficult to see how any kind of drama could have flourished.

To investigate all the non-financial aspects of the so-called decline of drama during this period would require much more space than this Introduction can provide, but the picture is not so black as it is often painted: it would be fairer to say that drama did not so much 'decline' as, within new social and cultural contexts, radically change its nature. If the quality of the old tragedy was low, there was compensation in the bustling high spirits and rough energy of the new melodrama, and the compromise between the 'legitimate' and 'illegitimate' determines the nature of the best serious drama after 1850.

What determined the nature of all drama was public taste as it operated in the theatre. In the first three decades of the century the Romantic spirit dominated fiction, poetry, and the theatre; audiences sated themselves on Gothic tragedy, Gothic melodrama, and dramatizations of Scott. When Romanticism exhausted itself on the stage, the most popular drama became (and remained until the end of the century) that with a strong domestic flavour. The artistic pleasures of the working and lower middle classes, who comprised the bulk of the new audiences, were entirely 'popular' and what we would term

---

[1] *Report from the Select Committee on Dramatic Literature* (1832), p. 52. Poor attendance was in spite of rapidly increasing population. London grew from about a million in 1800 to nearly three million in 1850. Of course the number of theatres increased too, from nine in 1800 to twenty-two in 1851.
[2] Ibid. pp. 101, 249.

crude and vulgar, but those of the more educated classes inclined also to the simple and unsophisticated; this lack of sophistication marks fiction as well as drama. What both the reading and play-going public looked for was a great deal of sentiment and strong pathos, domestic suffering and domestic bliss, a good story line, sensation and violence, a stern morality, much positive virtue and its reward in the almost inevitable happy ending, eccentric humour, and native English jollity and spirit. This pattern of taste established itself before the accession of Victoria as a powerful shaping force in the theatre, and dramatists had to follow the pattern if they wished their work to remain acceptable to an innately conservative public. The boundaries of this taste were clearly marked and cosily restrictive. They were made even more restrictive by the Lord Chamberlain and his subordinate the Examiner of Plays, who presided despotically over the moral and political health of the stage. The main reason why the vigorous political life of the century is not reflected in the drama, thus robbing it of much contemporary significance, is that the Examiner of Plays would not allow it; neither would he allow any serious experimentation with sexual themes. One must not conclude, however, that these officials were reactionaries damming up the tide of dramatic progress, fuddy-duddy autocrats in an age longing for bold and daring plays. Nothing of the sort: until late in the century dramatists, managers, and audiences were as conservative as the Lord Chamberlain and his Examiner, whose edicts were quite in accord with the taste of the times.

The tragedy performed in the theatres of the first fifty years of the century was *not* in accord with the new public taste, and it failed. Most of it is bad. The complaint that nineteenth-century drama was bad because it was divorced from literature was heard then and is repeated now, but the trouble with nineteenth-century tragedy is that its authors were concerned to produce 'literature' when they wrote it. Abetted by a circle of intellectual and literary critics, they scorned the base earth of the world around them and loftily fixed their gaze on the bright stars of Shakespeare and the Elizabethan drama. James Cooke typified the judgements of a score like him when he declared that the degradation of the drama was owing to the 'neglect of the great models of stage literature';[1] to repair such neglect he urged that by the publication of Elizabethan plays 'the public mind be instructed to the knowledge of what a rich mine of pure dramatic gold we have amongst us'.[2] Richard Hengist Horne objected that 'the propensity of modern times to reduce everything as much as possible to a tangible reality . . . has done incalculable mischief in its sweeping application to the ideal arts'.[3] To him drama was an ideal art, with no significant relation to contemporary society; 'whether the circumstances of modern society and civilization are eventful enough to give new incidents to the Drama, may be doubted. If not, it must and will, in future, take a more imaginative and philosophical tone.'[4] The public did not, of course, object to 'literary' tragedies, since the most popular tragic writer on the stage was Shakespeare. What they refused to see were literary tragedies with a lack of external action, or with entirely mental action substituted for stirring outward events, tragedies written without stagecraft, tragedies with introspective characters philosophizing statically in pseudo-Elizabethan blank verse.

For writers seeking dramatic models to emulate, as too many did, the fatal error of trying to write like the Elizabethans was compounded by the example of the great Romantics. Again, it has been said that because the Romantic poets could not or would not participate fully in the theatre the drama suffered and lost potentially great leaders. This argument is tenuous; it is closer to the truth to argue that the early nineteenth-century theatre would have been much better off it if had never heard of Byron and Coleridge. The Romantics modelled their plays on a dead Elizabethan mode and were prone to the faults enumerated above. They knew little about the theatre and cared less; they were primarily interested in drama for the exploration of character and ignored plot and action; they were fascinated by psychology, motive, theory, and abstraction; they tried to make their verse as Shakespearean as possible. Their genius was poetic, not dramatic, and when their tragedies succeeded on the stage—a most rare event—it was either because of spectacular production, as in the case of Coleridge's *Remorse* (1813),

---

[1] *The Stage* (1840), p. 5.   [2] Ibid. p. 12.
[3] 'An Essay on Tragic Influence', Preface to *Gregory VII* (1840), xvi.
[4] *A New Spirit of the Age* (1844), ii. 123.

or fine acting, such as Macready's in Byron's *Werner* (1830). Yet the fact that they were unsuccessful and often unacted did not prevent them from being admired and imitated. The imitation of an imitation did not go far to strengthen drama.

The Romantic influence on drama was, as I have said, strongest in the first three decades of the century, when the passion for Gothic engulfed tragedy and melodrama alike. Because of its extravagance of setting and characterization, Gothic tragedy sometimes possesses a vigour and manic excitement lacking in later tragedy. The tormented hero, the gloomy castle and dungeon, the monk and the hermit's cell, the dark forest, the persecuted heroine, and the robber band, were already familiar from earlier plays like Horace Walpole's unacted *The Mysterious Mother* (1768), Robert Jephson's *The Count of Narbonne* (1781), an adaptation of *The Castle of Otranto*, Richard Cumberland's *The Carmelite* (1784), Andrew McDonald's *Vimonda* (1787), and *The Regent* (1788) by Bertie Greatheed. In the 1790s the novels of Ann Radcliffe began their stage career and were immediately influential. There are at least ten dramatizations of her books, among them James Boaden's *Fontainville Forest* (1794), from *The Romance of the Forest*, and Henry Siddons's *The Sicilian Romance, or The Apparition of the Cliffs* (1794), from *A Sicilian Romance*.

The Gothic vogue continued unabated. Joanna Baillie's *De Montfort* (1800), written—typically of the Romantic approach to drama—to embody in dramatic form the passion of Hatred, contains a melancholy and tortured central character who hates his enemy so powerfully that finally he murders him in a forest. The directions indicate well-established acting and staging conventions for this kind of play. De Montfort '*comes forward to the front of the stage and makes a long pause, expressive of great agony of mind*'. He enters '*with a disordered air, and his hand pressed against his forehead*', and later '*gives loose to all the fury of gesture, and walks up and down in great agitation*'. The last scene of Act IV and most of Act V takes place where monks and nuns huddle together, terrified by sounds of murder in the storm outside the convent: '*The inside of a Convent Chapel, of old Gothick architecture, almost dark: two torches only are seen at a distance, burning over a new-made grave. The noise of loud wind, beating upon the windows and roof, is heard.*' The author was so

fond of this setting that she used it again in *Henriquez* (1836),
with the addition of '*a solemn Requiem for the Dead*', which '*is
heard at a distance, sounding from above*'. Henriquez enters and
delivers a meditative speech of forty-five lines; it is characteristic of this school of tragic writing that the verse should either
blaze with impossible passion or, more frequently, slacken
listlessly into decorative and protracted description. Joanna
Baillie wrote far better verse than most of her contemporaries
and successors, yet such a speech as this, by the King of Castile
in *Henriquez*, illustrates the common tendency to engage in
leisurely poetry for its own sake:

> But finding
> From wrecks of mountain torrents, or neglect,
> The straight road to Zamora was impassable,
> I took the wider compass, and proceeding
> Through these domains by favour of the night,
> Yon castle from its woods looked temptingly
> And beckoned me afar to turn aside.
> The light from every lattice gaily streamed,
> Lamps starred each dusky corridor, and torches
> Did from the courts beneath cast up the glare
> Of glowing flame upon the buttress'd walls
> And battlements, whilst the high towers aloft
> Show'd their jagged pinnacles in icy coldness
> Cloth'd with the moon's pale beam.

Hazlitt's objection is relevant here:

The modern romantic tragedy is a mixture of fanciful exaggeration and indolent sensibility . . . [it] courts distress, affects horror,
indulges in all the luxury of woe, and nurses its languid thoughts and
dainty sympathies, to fill up the void of action. . . . The unexpected
stroke of true calamity, the biting edge of true passion, is blunted,
sheathed, and lost, amidst the flowers of poetry strewed over unreal,
unfelt distress, and the flimsy topics of artificial humanity prepared
beforehand for all occasions.[1]

Fifty years after *De Montfort* tragic dramatists were still
composing in well-worn Gothic conventions. F. G. Tomlins's
Garcia (1849), set in Spain in 1488, tells the story of Count

---

[1] *A View of the English Stage* (1818), pp. 288–9.

Garcia, who at the instigation of the villain murders a Moorish refugee on his way to testify to the Inquisition that he received illicit shelter for a few hours at the mountain castle of the Garcia family. After the murder Garcia is seized with remorse and horror, and the Inquisition arrests villain and hero for the crime. Although Tomlins was a leader of the movement asserting the dramatic and literary superiority of the 'unacted drama', and although he and his cohorts heaped scorn on the acted drama, his sole stage play is lamentable, yet fully representative of a class of drama which the authors believed would save the stage and restore it to pristine glory if only their work was performed. This movement was especially strong about 1840, but we can only conclude from examining its plays that managers were wise to reject them.

The climax of Gothic tragedy was reached in Charles Maturin's *Bertram, or the Castle of St. Aldobrand* (1816), the most extreme example of its kind. Maturin, the author of a noted Gothic novel, *Melmoth the Wanderer* (1820), also wrote *Manuel* (1817) and *Fredolfo* (1819), the former set in medieval Switzerland on Mount St. Gothard and the latter in feudal Spain; neither had the success of *Bertram*. The exiled Bertram, shipwrecked under the cliffs of the priory of St. Anselm, finds his beloved Imogine married to his enemy Aldobrand. Bitter and tormented, he leads a desperate band of outlaws and at their head murders the good Aldobrand. Imogine runs mad and dies; Bertram stabs himself. A summary conveys no idea of the intense ferocity of Bertram's passions and Imogine's despair, or of the wild extravagance of Maturin's tragic conception. *Bertram* is a bad play, but it is sensationally bad, and audiences were swept into rapture for twenty-two nights by Kean's Bertram. The acting was thoroughly melodramatic, as a look at the stage directions will show. At different times Bertram *'meditates in gloomy reflection'*, and *'looking round ghastlily'*, *'bursting into ferocity'*, expressing himself *'with frantic violence'*, is the complete Gothic hero-villain. The first scene of Act IV is *'a dark night under the Castle Walls*; BERTRAM *appears in a state of the utmost agitation; he extends his arms towards a spot where the Moon has disappeared'* and speaks. We find Imogine *'throwing herself vehemently on her knees'*, *'sinking down'*, *'recoiling'*, *'shrieking'*, and rushing in *'with her child, her hair dishevelled, her dress stained with blood'.* Over thirty years later one writer still vividly remembered the acting:

Who can forget the terrific effect produced by Kean: the agonised glare he threw on the dead Imogen [*sic*], the rapidly-changing features, fiercely agitated by the storm of passion within, and finally the desperate energy with which he plunged the fatal weapon, to the very hilt, into his bosom, caused a thrill of horror, and almost awakened a transient emotion of pity.[1]

It was Kean, too, who raged and suffered as Brutus and drew crowded houses to J. H. Payne's indifferent *Brutus, or The Fall of Tarquin* (1818), delivering speeches like the following denouncing Sextus Tarquin:

[*With a burst of frenzy.*] The furies curse you then! Lash you
     with snakes!
When forth you walk may the red flaming sun
Strike you with livid plagues!
Vipers that die not, slowly gnaw your heart! *etc.*

The Gothic past, ancient Rome, the Italian Renaissance, medieval Spain, sometimes the England of history or feudal Scotland—these were the commonly employed settings of tragic dramatists. Occasionally a play of this sort achieves a certain distinctive quality. One such is Douglas Jerrold's *Thomas à Becket* (1829), in vigorous rhetorical prose rather than verse, an unusual choice of form, but then Jerrold was writing for the melodrama-loving audience of a minor theatre, the Surrey. It was not a success, and William Moncrieff commented in the preface to Richardson's acting edition that 'it wants the domestic charm that appeals to men's business and bosoms: the struggles of church and state are "caviare to the million" '. Another better-than-average tragedy is *Feudal Times* (1847), by James White, set in Scotland in the reign of James III and depicting a fatal enmity between the Earl of Mar and the Douglas. The plot is simple, not overburdened with history, and the verse, though often over-poetic, is relatively natural and easy. For instance, the Douglas dismisses a bishop's hint that Mar should be assassinated:

I know the sort of slaying pleases best
Our holy mother Church; a quiet stab

---

[1] An Old Playgoer, *Desultory Thoughts on the National Drama* (1850), p. 48.

Where no one sees; a sleeping draught too strong;
An eyeless dungeon in some hidden tower:
I'll have no deed like this to please the Church.
This Cochrane is a Man, and as a man,
And by a man, he shall be slain.

Nevertheless, *Feudal Times* suffers badly from the general
nineteenth-century tendency to idealize innocence and goodness
and love to the point of incredibility; Mar is such a noble, good-
hearted man, with no discernible faults, that he is quite unfit
for the role of tragic hero. The same tendency enervates *Virginius*
and *Richelieu*, especially in their portrayal of womanhood, and
imparts an essential lifelessness to the serious drama of the day.

All the faults of contemporary tragic practice are present in
one of the most admired tragedies of its time, Thomas Noon
Talfourd's *Ion* (1836). Set in classical Greece, it shows an Argos
instructed by the oracle of Apollo that the curse of pestilence
upon it will not end until the tyrant Adrastes and his race are
eliminated. A gentle, noble-spirited foundling, Ion, goes to
kill Adrastes, but discovers that the latter is his father. Another
conspirator murders the king; Ion assumes the throne in a
public ceremony and then kills himself; the pestilence ends.
Prolonged love scenes between Clemanthe and Ion weaken the
dramatic structure, and the verse is characterized by a speech of
Ion's when he asks Adrastes if he has ever loved:

> Think upon the time
> When the clear depths of thy yet lucid soul
> Were ruffled with the troublings of strange joy,
> As if some unseen visitant from heaven
> Touch'd the calm lake and wreath'd its images
> In sparkling waves; recall the dallying hope
> That on the margin of assurance trembled,
> As loth to lose in certainty too bless'd
> Its happy being; taste in thought again
> Of the stolen sweetness of those evening walks,
> When pansied turf was air to winged feet,
> And circling forests by etherial touch
> Enchanted, wore the livery of the sky
> As if about to melt in golden light
> Shapes of one heavenly vision; and thy heart
> Enlarged by its new sympathy with one,
> Grew bountiful to all!

Ion is a recitation rather than a play; an icy coldness deadens verse, character, and situation alike, and it would seem that only the skill of Macready and later of Ellen Tree in the part of Ion ensured success. In his preface to the fourth edition (1837) Talfourd admitted as much in praising Macready:

By the graces of beautiful elocution, he beguiled the audience to receive the Drama as belonging to a range of associations which are no longer linked with the living world, but which retain an undying interest of a gentler cast. . . . The consequence of this extraordinary power of vivifying the frigid, and familiarising the remote, was to dissipate the fears of my friends; to render the play an object of attraction during the short remainder of the season.

The more acute contemporaries of the tragic dramatists well knew where the weaknesses lay. Blaming the intellectual milieu, the *London Magazine* said that 'if a bias to abstraction is evidently, then, the reigning spirit of the age, dramatic poetry must be allowed to be most irreconcilable with this spirit; it is essentially individual and concrete both in form and in power'.[1] John Lacy condemned the love of poetry for its own sake:

All our modern tragedists indulge in a similar liberal effusion of the talking-principle within them: the same indolent dicacity, the same proneness to disburse copious harangues and monotonous dissertations, characterize the poetic school of the drama in general. A verbal diarrhoea is the epidemic disease which afflicts the whole tribe. . . . It seems to be forgotten . . . that the end of tragedy is not to tranquillise, but to rouse.[2]

In another article, referring to *Bertram*, Lacy thought that 'if we are to choose between Tom o'Bedlam and Sir Velvet-lungs, give us the madman rather than the poet. It requires no great depth of penetration to see which will best succeed upon the stage.'[3] He was not therefore surprised at the popular failure of modern tragedy, an instance of which he graphically described:

Another tragedy is produced: three acts are suffered to pass over in noiseless tranquillity; no sound whatever, but the drawing of an occasional cork, or the blowing of a solitary nose: but at the close of

[1] *The London Magazine*, i (April 1820), 433.
[2] 'A Letter to the Dramatists of the Day', *The London Magazine*, viii (September 1823), 281.   [3] Ibid. ix (January 1824), 62–3.

the fourth, the audience begins to yawn, gape, sneeze, cough, and throw orange-peel at the musicians: in the fifth some fall fast asleep, others retire to the lobbies, the pit begins to squabble, the boxes to chatter, and the galleries grow noisy, boozy, and amorous: nothing like interest, attention, or enjoyment—till the horses or the dancing-girls enter! Why? Why because the people (blockheads and barbarians as they are!) cannot perceive the excellence of the piece.[1]

Writing in 1850, George Henry Lewes generalized usefully on the principal defect in the dramatists of the past fifty years, from which other defects arose:

If they had never known this Old Drama, they must perforce have created a new form, and instead of the thousand-and-one imitations of the old dramatists . . . we might have had some sterling plays. Who are the successful dramatists of our day? Precisely those who do *not* imitate the Elizabethan form! . . . We do wish that the dramatist should not be an archeologist, that he should not strive to revive defunct forms, but produce a nineteenth century drama: something that will appeal to a wider audience than that of a few critics and black-letter students.[2]

Preferring historical settings and themes of rebellion, conspiracy, and love, dramatists turned their backs on their own century and tried to bring history and ancient tragic subject matter to life. Sometimes it appears that their main concern was history rather than drama. Charles Kean's declaration in 1859 that he had never permitted historical truth to be sacrificed to theatrical effect might be removed from its context of his management of the Princess's and applied to the composition of historical tragedies and dramas. In his preface to *The Earl of Gowrie*, published in 1845 and acted at Sadler's Wells in 1852, James White remarked that 'whether this is a fit subject for dramatic treatment I am no judge, but it will be seen that I have followed the historical narrative with very little alteration'. Browning, in the preface to the unsuccessful *Strafford*, done by Macready at Covent Garden in 1837, admitted the Romantic weakness of 'Action in Character rather than Character in Action. To remedy this, in some degree, considerable curtailment will be necessary.' However, he was proud of his history.

---

[1] 'Theatricals of the Day', *The London Magazine*, x (December 1824), 641. These articles under John Lacy's name are attributed by Nicoll to George Darley.

[2] *The Leader*, 3 August 1850.

'The portraits are, I think, faithful; and I am exceedingly fortunate in being able, in proof of this, to refer to the subtle and eloquent exposition of the characters of Eliot and Strafford, in the Lives of the Eminent British Statesmen, now in the course of publication in Lardner's Cyclopaedia.' Yet faithfulness to the 1630s clogs *Strafford* with events obscure to a nineteenth-century audience, and tragedy suffocates in the airlessness of historical reference.[1]

Only a few attempts were made to construct tragedy out of the materials of modern life, and these are failures because their traditionally minded authors could not satisfactorily adapt new subject matter to antique methods of treatment. *A Blot in the Scutcheon* (1843), written by Browning for Macready's Drury Lane management, was a worse failure than *Strafford*. Although he set it in the eighteenth century Browning did try to shape his material according to the melodramatic and increasingly domestic taste of the times. Lord Mertoun obtains Lord Tresham's permission to ask for the hand of his sister, Mildred. But Mertoun and Mildred are already lovers, and he climbs nightly to her window. Tresham discovers all, kills Mertoun in a duel, and abuses his sister. She dies of a broken heart and the remorseful Tresham takes poison. The play is obscured, not by history, but by 'Action in Character' and a style of verse-writing the opposite of the 'indolent sensibility' Hazlitt complained of. Tresham asks for an opinion about Mertoun:

> How seems he?—seems he not—come, faith, give fraud
> The mercy-stroke whenever they engage!
> Down with fraud, up with faith! How seems the Earl?
> A name! a blazon! if you knew their worth,
> As you will never! come—the Earl?

Guendolen speaks to Mildred of Mertoun:

> Ask and have!
> Demand, be answered! Lack I ears and eyes?
> Am I perplexed which side of the rock-table

---

[1] 'In all the historical plays of Shakespeare, the great poet has only introduced such events as act on the individuals concerned, and of which they are themselves a part; the persons are all in direct relation to each other, and the facts are present to the audience. But in Browning's play we have a long scene of passion—upon what? A plan destroyed, by whom or for what we know not. . . .' (*The Diaries of William Charles Macready*, ed. William Toynbee (1912), i. 390.)

The Conqueror dined on when he landed first,
Lord Mertoun's ancestor was bidden take—
The bow-hand or the arrow-hand's great meed?
Mildred, the Earl has soft blue eyes!

Actors must have found such lines difficult, but one pities audiences more.

A dramatist who made a deliberate effort to use modern life for tragic purposes was Westland Marston. In the preface to *The Patrician's Daughter* (1842), Marston writes:

> The following pages originated in the desire of the Author to write a Tragedy indebted for its incident, and passion, to the habits and spirit of the age. It is well that an attempt of this kind should be made. . . . The elevated and gifted Spirit sees the sublime in The Present, recognizes the Hero *in undress*, and discovers greatness, though it be divested of pomp. . . . To limit to the past, the dramatic exhibitions of our nature, is virtually to declare our nature itself radically altered.

The theory is excellent, but the practice falls somewhat short. Mordaunt, a radical politician, is invited to stay in the country with his chief political opponent, the Earl of Lynterne, a cabinet minister, and falls in love with Lynterne's daughter Mabel. Fooled by her proud aunt into believing that the true-hearted Mabel scorns him because of his humble birth, Mordaunt seeks revenge by betrothing himself to Mabel and then publicly denouncing her on the eve of the marriage. Some months later the grief-stricken Mabel expires in the arms of the now undeceived and repentant Mordaunt. At first sight it seems that the political overtones of *The Patrician's Daughter* might make the play a genuine modern tragedy of political life and satisfy Bulwer-Lytton's complaint of some years earlier:

> We banish the Political from the stage, and we therefore deprive the stage of the most vivid of its actual sources of interest. At present the English, instead of finding politics on the stage, find their stage in politics. . . . In these times the public mind is absorbed in politics, and yet the stage, which should represent the times, especially banishes appeal to the most general feelings. To see our modern plays, you would imagine there were no politicians among us.[1]

---

[1] *England and the English*, 2nd edn. (1833), ii. 141–2. Bulwer-Lytton was, however, forgetting the Lord Chamberlain, and perhaps Marston was not.

In reality, *The Patrician's Daughter* has nothing whatever to do with politics (the political reference is extremely vague), and its only claim to modernity is the theme of class enmity between the low-born radical and the conservative aristocratic family, a theme only made relevant to the plot by an extraneous piece of trickery. Furthermore, Marston's experiment did not extend to the use of a medium other than blank verse, which he wrote as badly as his contemporaries.[1] After reverting to a conventional historical background for *Strathmore* (1849), a tragedy set in Scotland in 1679, Marston essayed the contemporary once again with the verse drama *Anne Blake* (1852), specifically located '*near the middle of the nineteenth century*'. Anne Blake, embittered by dependence on her heartless and snobbish uncle and aunt, Sir Joshua and Lady Toppington, loves the poor artist Thorold, although uncle and aunt try to force her by threats and subterfuge into a match with the heir to a peerage and a fortune. The play is mostly taken up by misunderstandings caused by superficial tricks of plot. Finally Thorold, suddenly rich from a fortune in newly prosperous Indian mines, wins Anne, also enriched by her dead father's share in the same mines. Here again, except for a general sense of class hostility, *Anne Blake* draws nothing from the life of the mid nineteenth century.

When one examines the stage career of tragedy and the serious legitimate drama in the last century, one is surprised— bearing in mind their too common failure to please—that they lingered so long and that many plays passed into the standard repertory for fifty years or more. However, such plays were often first-class acting vehicles, and in any consideration of nineteenth-century drama we must never forget the skill of the great actors in transforming what today seem pages of lifeless and unreadable text into *tours de force* which electrified audiences and stirred memories years after the event. I have already instanced Kean's Bertram and Macready's Ion; Marston's

---

[1] *The Patrician's Daughter* was also done by Macready, who is extolled by historians for his exacting standards of production and his courage in making a stand, against hopeless financial odds, in defence of the legitimate drama. This is true, but it must also be realized that because of his abhorrence of the popular and domestically melodramatic—the true taste of the age—Macready, in his otherwise admirable search for new serious authors, would accept only the 'legitimate' work of writers like Talfourd, Browning, and Marston, and rejected, for instance, *Oliver Twist* when Dickens offered it to him for the stage. In this respect Macready was a reactionary figure.

description of Macready's Richelieu is also relevant,[1] but perhaps the point can be made more fully—and it is an important one—by contemporary impressions of actors at work on seemingly intractable material.

Henry Hart Milman's tragedy *Fazio* (1816) has a setting of Renaissance Florence and presents Fazio's theft of the miser Bartolo's gold after Bartolo has been stabbed by robbers, Fazio's betrayal, out of jealousy, by his wife Bianca, and Bianca's remorseful and unavailing efforts to save him from execution for Bartolo's murder. Milman said in a note to the play, which was published before it was acted, that *Fazio* was 'written with some view to the stage', but speeches are verbose and scenes follow each other without a change in speaker: for example in Act I Fazio utters four consecutive speeches totalling ninety lines in four scenes, and in Acts IV and V Bianca speaks a despairing soliloquy of over seventy lines extending through three scenes. However, *Fazio* contains two fine acting parts, especially that of Bianca. About 1847 John Coleman saw Charlotte Cushman as Bianca in Edinburgh. From the time Bianca came on to denounce her husband to the Duke,

I had eyes and ears only for the poor demented creature whose face was transformed into the mask of Medusa, and whose eyes . . . glittered with infernal fire; whose hair, like a mantle of flame, streamed over her fair shoulders, while from the simple tunic of white muslin, which fell from head to heel, gleamed forth a pair of statuesque arms and a superbly moulded bust which rose and sank tumultuously as though about to burst with the agonies of a tortured, despairing heart.[2]

Later in the play Bianca, pleading to the Duke for her husband's life when Fazio is about to be executed, says,

> Ha! ye've been dancing, dancing—so have I:
> But mine was heavy music, slow and solemn—
> A bell, a bell: my thick blood roll'd to it. . . .

Coleman recalled the delivery of these lines:

The words are commonplace enough, but the tone, the look, the action, as she clutched at the great tumbling masses of hair as if about

---

[1] See the Appendix on Macready's Richelieu.
[2] *Fifty Years of an Actor's Life* (1904), i. 294.

to tear them up by the roots, were awe-inspiring! Then, pausing, she
rubbed her temples, rubbed, and rubbed again, as if trying to expunge
some damned spot, to exorcise the remorse, the agony of the demented
brain. A mist arose before my eyes; a thrill, half-pleasure, half-pain,
passed through the spinal column; a lump arose in my throat; and I
sat shivering and shuddering till the fatal bell, which heralded the
death of Fazio, sounded the death-knell of his hapless wife, and she,
collapsing, fell an inert and helpless thing, dead ere she reached the
earth.[1]

Charlotte Cushman's most famous part was Meg Merrilies
in an adaptation of Scott's *Guy Mannering*. In the text of the
adaptation, Meg seems merely a stock melodramatic creation of
the 'weird woman'; Cushman turned her into a figure of terror
and tragic pity. From the wings, Coleman watched her initial
entrance the first time she played Meg in Edinburgh:

There swept on like a whirlwind a great, gaunt, spectral thing, clad
from head to heel in one, and only one, loose flowing garment, compact of shreds and patches in neutral colours. Its elf-locks were of iron
grey; its face, arms and neck were those of a mummy new risen from
the sepulchre, while its eyes, aflame with living fire, were riveted on the
lost heir of Ellangowan, who gasped and remained speechless. . . .
The audience were breathless and dumbfounded. . . . The creature
spoke, or rather croaked, in a low guttural voice; then she crooned
forth in a voice of infinite tenderness the sweet old melody, 'Rest
thee, babe, rest thee', and tears, despite myself, rolled down my cheeks.[2]

In 1847 Fanny Kemble reappeared on the English stage and
Coleman saw her play Julia in Knowles's drama *The Hunchback*,
a part she created in 1832. In Act V Julia implores the mysterious
Master Walter, her seeming-guardian, to break off her coming
nuptials with a man she does not love. The speech does not
inspire when read; it concludes:

> Thou canst save me.
> Thou ought'st! thou must! I tell thee at his feet
> I'll fall a corse—ere mount his bridal bed!
> So choose between my rescue and my grave:—

---

[1] *Fifty Years of an Actors' Life*, i. 295.   [2] Ibid. i. 302–3.

And quickly too! The hour of sacrifice
Is near! Anon the immolating priest
Will summon me! Devise some speedy means
To cheat the altar of its victim. Do it!
Nor leave the task to me!

This is how Coleman saw Fanny Kemble play it:

Tortured, despairing, maddened, she sprang to her feet erect and terrible. With fiery eyes and dilated form she turned at bay, even as a wounded hind might turn upon the hunter's spear, then with quivering lips she commenced the famous speech, extending over some thirty lines. As it proceeded her voice gained strength, changing from the flute to the bell—from the bell to the clarion. Then upon a rising *sostenuto* of concentrated agony and defiance, she smote and stabbed Walter with that awful 'Do it! Nor leave the task to me!' Even as the last word left her lips, she strode down to the right hand corner, returned to the centre, and then came to anchor, her right hand clutched on the back of the great oaken chair, her left thrown out towards Walter, her blazing eyes fixed on him in an attitude of denunciation and defiance. Then it was, and not till then, that the breathless and enthralled auditors rose in such an outburst of wild enthusiasm as I have never heard equalled before or since.[1]

In such ways the great figures of the nineteenth-century stage overwhelmed audiences with a rhetoric and passion that made many an indifferent tragedy and melodrama acceptable and even popular.

The fall of the mighty is never without significance for the spectator. The Victorian theatre witnessed the death of English classical tragedy, a form exhausted and in ill health all through the eighteenth century, but whose conventions and styles had persisted on the stage for over two hundred and fifty years. As has been suggested, its demise occurred largely because its authors looked back to a former age and were cut off from the mainsprings of modern English life and thought; no purely imitative drama or one so detached from its society and culture has been successful or significant. However, the causes of this failure are philosophically and socially interesting. The larger-than-life world, the metaphysical matrix and values of classical

---

[1] 'Fanny Kemble', *The Theatre* (March 1893), p. 143.

tragedy, were no longer within reach of playwrights living in a growingly materialistic, non-metaphysical England of bustling progress and rapidly changing values. No matter how much they kept this world out of their tragedies, they still lived in it themselves, and were no longer capable of a meaningful expression of the ideal in dramatic terms. As yet no new tragic ideas could find their way into the vacuum; dramatists were through no fault of their own suspended between two realms of tragedy, ancient and modern. The ancient, respectable and 'literary', was dead to them, no matter how hard they struggled to keep it alive, but the modern had not yet been born. Before 1850 it was too early for tragedies of environmental and psychological determinism, too early for tragedies about the war of sex, the failure of religion, and the hopelessness, futility, and emptiness of life.

In one respect tragedy came to terms with its age and evolved: it took on a strongly melodramatic emphasis and a happy ending and became the 'drama', that peculiarly Victorian form compounded of intrigue, sensation, idealism, and domestic sentiment. The period after 1850 is dominated by this form, but it developed in the first half of the century. In its purer, more 'legitimate' aspect it is represented by Knowles and Bulwer-Lytton's *The Lady of Lyons* (1838) and *Richelieu* (1839), but even here there is a definite compromise between the older literary drama and the popular 'illegitimate' types, between tragedy and melodrama. *The Lady of Lyons*, with themes of class pride, ideal and ennobling love, the perfect bliss of Home (whether real or illusory), and the merited climb to fame, social distinction, and wealth, is modern in spirit and essentially domestic in feeling, despite historical trappings. A father–daughter relationship and young, innocent love were part of the appeal of *Richelieu*; the same appeal was made in Sheridan Knowles's *Virginius* (1820). The replacement of a metaphysical with a domestic ideal and the trend toward domestic themes and domestic realism are features of early Victorian plays that operate strongly in the more popular 'drama' and melodrama. Even in tragedy there are the same signs. In Mary Mitford's *Rienzi* (1828), a story of intrigue, conspiracy, rebellion, and young love in fourteenth-century Rome, the following speech by Rienzi's beautiful and loving daughter might—except for the verse—come straight from any domestic melodrama of the next forty years:

> Father, I love not this new state, these halls
> Where comfort dies in vastness; these trim maids
> Whose service wearies me. Oh! mine old home!
> My quiet and pleasant chamber, with the myrtle
> Woven round the casement; and the cedar by
> Shading the sun; my garden overgrown
> With flowers and herbs, thick-set as grass in fields;
> My pretty snow-white doves; my kindest nurse;
> And old Camille. Ah! mine own dear home!

Before *Rienzi*, the village heroine in J. H. Payne's operatic melodrama *Clari, the Maid of Milan* (1823) was uttering the same lament in the Duke's palace, mourning her lost cottage home and singing the song written for the play, 'Home, Sweet Home'. Horne might have deplored the tendency of the stage to 'shadow forth the smaller peculiarities of an actual and every-day life domesticity',[1] but this sort of domesticity and the presentation of a domestic ideal were to become the dominant subject matter of the Victorian stage for the rest of the century.

The drama dealing with the household and family relationships, refining itself as time passed and culminating in the 1890s in the work of Henry Arthur Jones, Pinero, Wilde, and Shaw, did not grow up independently, but evolved as part of a melodrama which by 1825 had developed three closely related but distinctive branches: the Romantic, encompassing Gothic and Eastern melodrama; the nautical (partly Romantic and partly domestic), and the domestic itself, roughly in that chronological order. The third kind, the domestic, became the backbone of Victorian drama. When Bulwer-Lytton called on intellectual dramatists to be modern and use 'tales of a household nature, that find their echo in the heart of the people—the materials of the village tragedy, awakening an interest common to us all; intense yet homely, actual—earnest—the pathos and passion of everyday life',[2] he was describing a drama that already existed on a popular level. In melodrama lies the

---

[1] *A New Spirit of the Age*, ii. 99.
[2] *England and the English*, ii. 145.

fulfilment of Bulwer-Lytton's desire that 'among the people, then, must the tragic author invoke the genius of Modern Tragedy, and learn its springs',[1] and the truth of his statement, 'I doubt if the drama will become thoroughly popular until it is permitted to embody the most popular emotions'.[2] Crude, healthy, vulgar, energetic, colourful, and popular, melodrama was everything that legitimate tragedy was not, and because of these qualities and the fact that it was in touch with its age it bloomed where tragedy withered and died.

What gave melodrama impetus were Gothic novels of terror and the supernatural, and Gothic tragedies, some of them adaptations of the novels performed both before and after 1790. Melodrama's rigid moral pattern, character types, and much of its machinery were derived from eighteenth-century senti-mental tragedy and comedy with their excess of moral senti-ment, exaltation of virtue, exhaustive exploitation of pathos and distress, generous but erring heroes, suffering heroines, comic servants, surprising revelations, mistaken identities, long-lost orphans, and missing documents. The English sentimental drama and novel in turn influenced the French comédie larmoyante and drame bourgeois; indeed, there was con-siderable interaction between these forms and current English drama on the one hand and English Gothic, German Gothic, and French boulevard melodrama of the post-Revolutionary period on the other. This Parisian melodrama, supplied in vast quantities to an avid public by Guilbert de Pixérécourt and his followers, possessed the same ingredients of violence, show, moral simplicity, emotional distress, rhetoric, and music as early English melodrama, which of course it strongly influenced. Yet Parisian melodrama was in turn derived from English Gothic, and it would be wrong to say that English melodrama was a French product. By 1800 the pattern of melodrama was set, and the rest of the century made additions and variations only. French plays continued to supply plots for melodramatists, and the novel proved fruitful for the adapter. The tendency of much nineteenth-century fiction is to the same extremes of vice, virtue, sensationalism, and pathos that one finds in melo-drama. Scott's romantic Gothicism and Dickens's domestic sentiment were enormously popular on the stage, and from The

---

[1] England and the English, ii. 150.   [2] Ibid. ii. 142.

Castle of Otranto to *East Lynne* and *Trilby* the melodrama of the
novel provided melodrama for the theatre.

The main features of melodrama are familiar: the concentration on externals, the emphasis on situation at the expense of
motivation and characterization, the firm moral distinctions,
the unchanging character stereotypes of hero, heroine, villain,
comic man, comic woman, and good old man, physical sensation,
spectacular effects (made possible by improvements in stage
technology), marked musical accompaniment, the rewarding of
virtue and punishing of vice, the rapid alternation between
extremes of violence, pathos, and low comedy. Melodrama
appears to represent a complete breakdown of dramatic forms
in its variety of content; yet paradoxically it is an extremely
rigid form that especially in its most popular manifestations in
the working-class theatres remained fixed for a hundred years.

The needs of spectators primarily determined melodrama's
content and style. Music and wordless physical incident were at
first dictated by the Lord Chamberlain, who originally permitted
only unspoken drama outside the patent theatres and later
allowed the spoken word accompanied by music. But in any
case these features admirably suited the taste of audiences who
were indifferent to the static poetic tragedy, genteel comic wit,
and delicate sentimentality. They were the new uneducated and
largely illiterate urban masses who lived in bleak and depressing
circumstances; what they wanted from the stage was thrilling
action, stirring emotion, spectacle, jolly farce, and an ideal
image of themselves and their own lives. All this they obtained
from melodrama, which simultaneously satisfied their desires
for escapist entertainment, for a better world where such as
they received the happiness and rewards proper to the virtuous
poor, and for a quasi-realistic presentation of the every-day
occurrences of their own domestic existence. For the first time
in English dramatic history, they themselves were the heroes
of a drama written especially for them in a language and with a
simplicity they could understand, a drama concerned with their
own lives and dreams. Even if the melodramatist offered them
history or pure romance he did it sensationally and colourfully;
not for him blank verse, long speeches, and action in character.
Audiences liked to see, in William Dimond's adaptation of
Byron, *The Bride of Abydos* (1818), the features of the heroine

Zulieka *'express the terror of her sex'* and those of the tyrant
pasha Giaffier *'ghastly with a deeper fear'*. They liked such a
climax as the *'Towers of Abydos in flames—grand tableau'*, a
'desperate conflict' between the hero Selim and Giaffier, a rescue
of Zulieka by Selim, who *'breaks with overwhelming frenzy
through all opposition and springs into the ruin'*, rushes through
the flames up the staircase of a tower, pursued by a dagger-
wielding villain about to strike him when *'a third explosion is
heard and the entire floor of the apartment gives way and sinks with
MURTEZA into the flames below. ZULIEKA by clinging to the
stone pillar is preserved'*; Selim returns triumphantly with her
'over the perilous ruin'. These audiences equally liked to hear such
speeches as Ben's in T. E. Wilks's *Ben the Boatswain* (1839),
which tells the world what an excellent fellow the common man
is:

> My father was a jolly young waterman on the Thames and rowed
> folks from Wapping to Rotherhithe for a penny a head; and as to my
> mother, why—bless her kind old heart! my mother keeps a mangle,
> and takes in a little bit of washing. And now what of all that there?
> Can't I hand, reef, and steer as well as any man in the fleet? Did any
> one ever see me show the white feather in an engagement, or a gale?
> . . . Ain't I got as pretty a sweetheart as your lordship any day? . . .
> Werry well, says I—then if that there be the case, what the devil
> does it matter who my father was, or whether my mother keeps
> a mangle, and takes in a bit of washing?

If the legitimate drama was as good as that they might go to
see it, or something like it; otherwise they had plenty of their
own kind of theatre to satisfy them. Sometimes the legitimate
drama would come to them; Shakespeare was melodramatized
within the law for the Surrey; Kean acted at the Coburg and the
City Theatre. Thomas Dibdin described the staging at the
Surrey in 1819 of Home's eminently literary *Douglas*:

> Which tragedy, without omitting a single line of the author, made
> a very splendid melo-drama, with the additions of Lord Randolph's
> magnificent banquet, a martial Scotch dance, and a glee . . . ex-
> quisitely set by Sanderson, and delightfully sung, together with an
> expensive processional representation of the landing of the Danes:
> besides all this, as a Surrey Theatre gallery audience always expects
> some *ultra* incident, I had a representative of Lady Randolph in the
> person of a very clever boy, by whose good acting and fearless

agility, the northern dame, at the conclusion of the tragedy, was seen to throw herself from a distant precipice into a boiling ocean, in a style which literally brought down the house.[1]

Although melodrama began its career in Drury Lane and Covent Garden as well as in the transpontine Royal Circus and Astley's, it soon became the staple fare of working-class theatres like the Surrey, the Coburg (later the Victoria), the Britannia, the Pavilion, the City of London, the Standard, the Effingham, and the Grecian—all of these in operation before 1850 and the six last-named in the East End. Of course melodrama was performed everywhere (its main West End stronghold was the Adelphi), but in the first half of the century it was mainly popular and proletarian in theme and treatment. Thus it was radical in tone; its heroes were peasants, workmen, and common sailors, its villains landlords, squires, peers, and factory owners. Much melodrama, particularly the domestic, is permeated with class hatred and darkened by a grim vision of a wealthy, authoritarian, repressive upper class tyrannizing over a poor suffering proletariat. Its attitudes were inherited from the democratic idealism of the romantic dramas of Goethe and Schiller, such as *Götz von Berlichingen* and *Die Räuber*, and more directly from the political sentiments of the French Revolution embodied in the fervent anti-tyrannical melodramas of Pixérécourt and his school. Naturally these sentiments could not be bluntly stated on a stage subject to control by government and magistrate, and anyway the English theatre vulgarized and played down foreign idealism. However, melodrama provides the richest material in English dramatic literature for the study of a rebellious class spirit in action, and an illuminatingly different insight into nineteenth-century social history.

Because melodrama reflected popular and radical feeling, it frequently expressed, no matter how crudely and fantastically, the social problems of the day; of all the nineteenth-century dramatic forms it has the most relevance to contemporary life and is the only one to treat of serious issues. By 1850 the subject matter of melodrama included slavery, the urban environment and a nostalgia for a lost rural heritage, temperance and the

---

[1] *The Reminiscences of Thomas Dibdin* (1827), ii. 270. At Drury Lane and Covent Garden the chances were that the more melodramatic and spectacular the legitimate tragedy, the greater the success.

problems of drink, industrialism and the life of the factory
worker, the game laws, the homeless poor, and class relationships. Melodrama had always been patriotic and militantly
nationalistic, and for the whole century proclaimed the superiority of England to any other country on earth, as well as depicting in violent physical action English triumphs in battles on
land and sea, and idealizing English military heroes. Even
Horne was forced to admit that popular melodrama, farce, and
light comedy, although simple, was closest to life:

The most simple is that which reflects the tone and temperament
of the age. This kind of Drama must not now be looked for amongst
what is sometimes absurdly called the 'legitimate'. That phrase is
foolishly applied to a form—the five-act form; and to that kind of
Drama which includes philosophical exposition of human character
and philosophical and rhetorical dissertation upon it. But the most
legitimate, because the genuine offspring of the age, is that Drama
which catches the manners as they rise and embodies the characteristics of the time. This, then, has forsaken the five-act form, and taken
shelter at what have been named 'Minor Theatres'. . . . Whatever the
amount of their ability, the truly dramatic, as far as it exists on the
modern stage at all, will be found in those comparatively neglected
writers of the minor drama.[1]

Growing upward from the sturdy root of popular melodrama
was the Victorian 'drama'; in fact one can trace a direct line of
descent from *The Miller and His Men* and *The Factory Lad* to
The Second Mrs. Tanqueray, An Ideal Husband, and *Widowers'
Houses*. All late Victorian and Edwardian serious drama was
fathered by the earlier melodrama. As sometimes happens in
life, the intellectual middle-class son despised his humble
working-class parents, but his parents they were all the same.
The melodrama, farce, and pantomime of the nineteenth century,
especially of the first fifty years, represented the last time that
the English theatre was in touch with the mass of the population
and popular sentiment, and the only time since the Middle Ages
that it has been dominated by neither the aristocracy nor the
middle class.

[1] *A New Spirit of the Age*, ii. 90–4.

The Second Mrs. Tanqueray. George Alexander and Mrs. Patrick Campbell.
Act One.

II. DRAMA 1850-1900

I N the last half of the nineteenth century the theatre's approach
to modernity was accelerated, and by 1900 both theatrical
practice and the content of drama had progressed an immense
distance from the early 1800s. In part this progress was
material. London's population rose from nearly three million
in 1850 to six and a half million in 1900, and the number of
theatres correspondingly increased, from twenty playhouses
and two opera houses open during the Great Exhibition of 1851
to sixty-one theatres and thirty-nine music-halls operating in
1900, thirty-eight of the theatres in the West End alone. The
vast extent of London was now traversed by cheap mass
transportation. The residents of the new suburbs created by the
railways could take advantage of them to go to the play in
town, as could provincials coming up to London in ever-
increasing numbers in search of pleasure and entertainment. In
1866—after which the theatre-building boom began—Henry
Morley estimated nightly attendance at twenty-five theatres
at 15,000,[1] and John Green, the lessee of Evans's Rooms,
believed that 40,000 people went to theatres and music-halls
every night.[2] Under these conditions the long run of a single
piece became possible and the objective of managers and entre-
preneurs. In 1861 Tom Taylor's *Our American Cousin* began a
consecutive run of 396 performances; in the 1870s H. J.
Byron's *Our Boys* ran for 1,362 performances, and this was
eclipsed by Brandon Thomas's *Charley's Aunt* in the 1890s,
with 1,466. Actors were therefore cast for one play at a time
and employed only for its run; the traditional repertory stock
company broke down, and London companies touring West
End hits replaced provincial companies playing in their own
theatres, sometimes with a single London star.

Other aspects of theatrical change mark the last fifty years of
the century as much more recognizably modern than the first.
By the 1880s the theatre was prospering financially to a far

---

[1] *The Journal of a London Playgoer* (1866), p. 17.
[2] *Report from the Select Committee on Theatrical Licences and Regulations* (1866),
p. 201.

greater extent than before, and successful playwrights, under a
new percentage system of royalties, could be assured once more
of a lucrative income from the stage. Domestic copyright
protection increased, and with the passage in 1891 of an American copyright law that at last prevented American managers
from seizing on a London success and playing it for nothing,
English authors could not only earn royalties from American
productions, but were no longer afraid to publish their plays for
a reading public; Jones and Pinero, for example, took advantage
of the new law immediately.

Inside the theatre changes were also being made. Charles
Kean reduced the number of items on the bill from three or four
to a curtain-raiser and a main play, and the Bancrofts eliminated
the curtain-raiser.[1] Audiences came at eight and went home at
eleven, and by late in the century sat fairly quietly in their seats,
although there might still be outbursts from the gallery. For
the first time in the history of the public theatre in England
(except on rare previous occasions), the playgoer's concentration upon the stage could remain peacefully undisturbed.
Well before 1900 he rested his feet on carpet and sat comfortably in upholstered dress circle or orchestra stall seats, which
could be reserved in advance, a practice begun before 1850. His
concentration was also improved by the total darkening of the
auditorium—Irving at the Lyceum in 1880 seems to have been
the first to do this consistently—while stage lighting had
steadily improved through a series of developments in gaslight,
limelight, and now electric light, the Savoy in 1881 being the
first English theatre entirely illuminated by electricity. The
brightness and sharpness of detail made possible by these
lighting improvements assisted the growth of an intimate and
natural acting style well suited to the quieter domesticity, more
restrained writing, and subtler character portrayal of serious
and comic drama alike. The stage changed shape as the proscenium doors disappeared (early in the century) and the
forestage retreated. In 1880 Bancroft at the Haymarket completed the process by painting a gold border in imitation of a
picture-frame around the proscenium, which was the exact
front of the stage. The old system of wings and back-shutters

---

[1] The old practice of more than one play on the bill and half-price at nine o'clock
still survived outside the West End in the 1890s.

changing in grooves gradually gave way to built-up scenery, the box set (introduced by Vestris at the Olympic in 1832), and the invariable use of the curtain to hide frequently elaborate scene changes. The concept of a controlling directorial hand in stage management was fully accepted by the end of the century; Boucicault, Robertson, Gilbert, and Pinero exercised a firm authority over the rehearsal and production of their plays, and actor-managers like Irving, Tree, and Alexander assumed complete responsibility for the artistic unity of all aspects of production.

Closely related to these changes in theatrical practice, and indeed stimulating many of them, were changes in the composition of audiences and the nature of their taste. In 1850 theatres were still suffering financially from the lack of aristocratic and fashionable patronage and the absence of a great proportion of the respectable middle class. Slowly, however, the theatre passed out of popular control and these classes returned. Queen Victoria's regular attendance at plays and her material encouragement of the drama by instituting command performances at Windsor Castle, which lasted until Albert's death in 1861, contributed in no small way to drawing higher society back to the playhouse. Charles Kean, the unofficial Master of Revels at Windsor for several years, benefited greatly from her patronage during his gentlemanly management of the Princess's from 1850 to 1859, a management that marked the beginning of the end of a drama based largely upon the support of popular audiences without the participation of the genteel and cultured sections of society. At Sadler's Wells from 1844 to 1862 Samuel Phelps was taming the hitherto unruly audiences of Islington and turning his theatre into a temple of Shakespeare where votaries came quietly and reverently to worship. In the 1860s and 1870s the Bancrofts made the Prince of Wales's not only elegant and comfortable, but also fashionable in both senses of the word. Finally the great prestige and good taste of Irving's Lyceum management, and the respectable enterprises of other actor-managers, completed the transformation of a popular into a middle-class theatre, with a middle-class audience and a middle-class drama.[1] The knighthoods received by Irving

[1] Matthew Arnold, who used to go to the Princess's in the 1840s, saw *The Silver King* there in 1882. He noticed that not only was the theatre much brighter

in 1895 and Bancroft in 1897 were the ultimate seal of Society's approval, and where Society led the Church followed. For years official Church hostility to the stage, so strong in the first half of the century, had been lessening. By the 1880s the clergyman-hero was not uncommon in strong drama and the clergy even came to the theatre.[1] This social transformation was made easier and quicker by the spread of music-halls, which siphoned off from the theatres the same elements of population attending in such numbers earlier in the century, the working and lower middle classes. These elements could still be found in the galleries of West End theatres, but there they were a relatively un-influential minority. However, they still had their own neigh-bourhood theatres, like the Surrey, the Britannia, the Standard, and the Pavilion, where until the strong local fare offered them was displaced by touring West End successes, they revelled in the same simple melodramatic verities and farcical exaggera-tions as before.

The changes in taste effected by the middle-class capture of the theatre naturally determined the content and performance of drama written for them. The displacement of the pit by expensive orchestra stalls meant that instead of rousing noisy and enthusiastic pittites with traditionally emphatic 'points' and the thunder of his rhetoric, the actor found himself con-fronting row on row of well-dressed, well-bred, undemonstrative stallholders on whom effects like these were wasted. Thus the movement toward a quieter style in acting, particularly at the smaller and more fashionable theatres like the Prince of Wales's and the Court, was perforce quickened. Similarly, the writing of strong drama, so acceptable before and still accept-able to more popular audiences, had to be toned down for theatres like these, the taste and responses of whose audiences were being more and more attended to. One reviewer noted of James Albery's *Duty* at the Prince of Wales's in 1879:

and cleaner inside, but also that 'the public was there; not alone the old, peculiar public of the pit and gallery, with a certain number of rich and refined in the boxes and stalls, and with whole solid classes of English society conspicuous by their absence. No; it was a representative public, furnished from all classes, and showing that English society at large had now taken to the theatre.' (*The Pall Mall Gazette*, 6 December 1882.)

[1] Especially to Wilson Barrett's spectacle-drama *The Sign of the Cross* (1896), which, despite a lavish banquet and orgy scene, was highly recommended from the pulpit.

If the dramatist in some of his strongest passages misses the tone of the house for which he is writing, the miniature stage is to blame for having cultivated a style with which dramatic breadth appears so completely out of keeping. Under no circumstances, if we leave the acting altogether out of the question, could a plot like that of *Duty* be unfolded to less advantage than here, where the occupants of stall and box are not prepared to digest strong meat, and where a highly strained emotional performance is not expected.[1]

As writing became less rhetorical and characterization less extravagant, settings and character types became socially more elevated. Workmen and peasants and sailors might remain the heroes of the East End and theatres like the Adelphi and the Marylebone, but in the West End their origins were usually more respectable; other *dramatis personae* were correspondingly raised in status. Dion Boucicault's *The Corsican Brothers* (1852) contains one of the new, polished, gentlemanly villains (not to be confused with the bad aristocrat of older melodrama), and the heroes of both *The Corsican Brothers* and Boucicault's *The Shaughraun* (1874) are gentlemen from old landed families. The social movement was ever upward in West End drama, and when we reach Aubrey Tanqueray and Sir Daniel Carteret at the end of the century, the ballroom, the conservatory, and the luxurious drawing-room are common settings. After 1880 the sports and pleasures of aristocratic and upper middle-class life supplied the big scenes of Drury Lane melodrama: Goodwood in *A Run of Luck* (1886), by Augustus Harris and Henry Pettit; Derby Day in their *A Million of Money* (1890) and *The Derby Winner* (1894), by Harris, Cecil Raleigh, and Henry Hamilton; the Grand National in Harris and Pettit's *The Prodigal Daughter* (1892); Rotten Row and Hurlingham in *Cheer, Boys, Cheer* (1895), by Harris, Raleigh, and Hamilton; Lords and the Military Tournament in Raleigh and Hamilton's *The Great Ruby* (1898). It is true that Drury Lane, with its great physical resources, had a policy under Augustus Harris of making a show with such scenes, but they were only the climax of a trend toward spectacular display and social elegance that had been going on for years. The hero of *The Derby Winner* is an Earl, the comic woman a Duchess. A glance at the list of principal characters in a Wilde drama discovers that over half of them are

---

[1] *The Theatre* (November 1879), p. 230.

titled and the rest moneyed and propertied. A faithful reproduction of scenes they knew about and a class they were familiar with was no more than fashionable audiences expected.

If the elevation in social setting and character status was new to drama after 1850, the addiction to realism was merely an enlargement and intensification of a previous trend. The Drury Lane dramas that dwelt so lovingly on upper-class pastimes and sporting events were also full of elaborately staged shipwrecks, train smashes, avalanches, earthquakes, and battles. Physical excitement had always been a vital part of melodrama, as witness the innumerable explosions and fires of Gothic and nautical plays. But the new sensations were staged with complicated machinery and effects, scores of extras, and a ponderous realism immensely satisfying to audiences that hungered for even more realism and even greater sensation. Such vast display could be staged only by the larger and better equipped theatres, but common to all theatres was the realism that aimed at an exact reproduction of the details of ordinary daily life, no matter on what class level it was lived. In 1855 W. B. Donne commented, 'To touch our emotions we need, not the imaginatively true, but the physically real. The visions which our ancestors saw with the mind's eye must be embodied for us in palpable forms. . . . All must be made palpable to sight, no less than to feeling; and this lack of imagination in the spectators affects equally both those who enact and those who construct the scene.'[1] Fifteen years later Thomas Purnell wrote, 'An audience no longer enjoys the representation of what is beyond its reach. The present and the near now best satisfies it. In the drama, as in prose fiction, realism is wanted. Every man judges what is laid before him by his own experience. Resemblance to what he is acquainted with is the measure of excellence. Truth to current existence is the criterion of merit he applies to a drama.'[2]

In 1838 audiences were thrilled to see a real lamplighter lighting real lamps in Charles Dance's *Burlington Arcade*.[3] So

---

[1] *Fraser's Magazine*, lii (July 1855), 104.

[2] *Dramatists of the Present Day* (1871), pp. 80–1.

[3] *Burlington Arcade* was done at the Olympic, and Vestris, at this theatre from 1831 to 1838, set both interior and exterior scenes of her burlettas with the greatest detail and fidelity to realism, and took the same trouble over costume. She was the first manager in the century to take such care with *mise en scène*.

too in 1867 they came in great numbers to see a real hansom cab driven across the stage in Andrew Halliday's *The Great City*. Before 1850 realistic metropolitan exterior settings were most common in domestic melodrama; later the same care was taken with domestic and commercial interiors, and such realism flourished. Tom Taylor's *The Ticket-of-Leave Man* (1863) put a suburban tea-garden and a workman's pub on the stage with scrupulous actuality. Boucicault's *Janet Pride* (1855) showed the Central Criminal Court at the Old Bailey in full working order for a trial. Charles Reade provided unpleasantly real prison scenes in the controversial *It's Never Too Late to Mend* (1864), one of them exhibiting a treadmill in operation. Scenes in railway stations, views of Waterloo Bridge, the Thames, and ships leaving the London docks constantly appear. Percy Fitzgerald noted:

> The most complicated and familiar objects about us are fearlessly laid hold of by the property man and dragged upon the stage. Thus, when we take our dramatic pleasure, we have the satisfaction of not being separated from the objects of our daily life, and within the walls of the theatre we meet again the engine and the train that set us down almost at the door; the interiors of hotels, counting-houses, shops, factories, the steam-boats, waterfalls, bridges, and even fire-engines.[1]

In 1881 Clement Scott found the last-act setting of George Sims's *The Lights o' London* 'a marvellous example of stage realism, complete in every possible detail', but too actual for comfort:

> The final act opens in the New Cut market. If anything, it is all too real, too painful, too smeared with the dirt of London life, where drunkenness, debauchery, and depravity, are shown in all their naked hideousness. Amidst buying and selling, the hoarse roar of coster-mongers, the jingle of the piano-organ, the screams of the dissolute, fathers teach their children to cheat and lie, drabs swarm in and out of the public house.[2]

Such realism of setting harmonized with natural acting and growing attention to detail in all aspects of costuming, furnishing, and decoration, whether of contemporary life or the historical past. In the same decade that Charles Kean mounted the

---

[1] *Principles of Comedy and Dramatic Effect* (1870), p. 12.
[2] *The Theatre* (October 1881), pp. 239–40.

lavish *Bal Masqué* and Montgiron's elegant house and rich supper table in *The Corsican Brothers*, he also 'upholstered' Shakespeare. The romantic realism of Irving's productions coincided in time with the elaborateness of Drury Lane sensation dramas. Richard Hengist Horne had attacked 'that dull curse upon Art—reality', and called for the 'reduction of theatrical paraphernalia to a scaffold and platform' in order to restore the honour and glory of the drama.[1] His voice was unheeded, and he was both behind and ahead of his time: behind because he looked back to the Elizabethans in an age of theatrical realism, ahead because at the peak of realism and stage show a new avenue was opened that would lead straight to the Mermaid Theatre and Stratford, Ontario, in the 1950s. William Poel, who founded the Elizabethan Stage Society in 1894, produced on a bare apron stage, with an approximation of Elizabethan staging conventions, not only Shakespeare, but also plays by Marlowe, Jonson, Middleton, Rowley, Ford, Webster, and Beaumont and Fletcher. Amongst the luxuriant growth of realistic theatre the seeds of reaction were already sown.

The Victorian materialism that created a stage art faithful to the surface of things also liked to see the inner workings of that materialism. Commercial life played an increasing part in Victorian drama. Although Restoration and eighteenth-century comedy had been concerned with wills, settlements, and financial intrigue, a portrayal of business life and City finance was reserved for the Victorian stage, and not only for comedy. The banker's office and the financial panics of 1837 and 1857 in Boucicault's *The Poor of New York* (1857) later *The Streets of London*, and Mr. Gibson's role as City employer of Bob Brierly in *The Ticket-of-Leave Man*, are examples of this portrayal. Many more might be given, but two from Tom Taylor will suffice. In the first act of *Payable on Demand* (1859), Reuben Goldsched, a poor Jew in Frankfort in 1792, is entrusted with 200,000 thalers by a Marquis flying from the French revolutionary army who was briefly sheltered by Goldsched, but slain attempting to escape from the city. The second act occurs in Clapham in 1814, where Goldsched is now a rich

---

[1] Introduction to A. W. Schlegel, *A Course of Lectures on Dramatic Art and Literature* (1840), xxvii–xxviii.

money-merchant in the City, his fortune built on the unclaimed thalers of Act I. By coincidence the Marquis's son is the poor music-master of Goldsched's daughter, and finally gets his inheritance as well as the daughter's hand. The chief interest of the act, however, is Goldsched's frantic financial speculations on the eve of Napoleon's abdication. His zeal is rewarded by the arrival of a carrier pigeon with advance news of the abdication, which gives him a full day's grace to buy on a falling market before the inevitable rise makes him even richer. All through the act Goldsched receives flying messengers with terse reports on the state of the market, and the dialogue is full of '200,000 on Omnium, at par', '10$\frac{7}{8}$ discount', 'advance of £50,000', 'Irish fives', 'closed at 85', 'four per cent consols', 'Lyons and Meyer', 'Lacquerstein Brothers', 'sell out 100,000 navy fives', etc.

Settling Day (1865) is entirely related to the world of contemporary finance. Returning from his honeymoon abroad, Markland finds that his bank has been brought to the verge of ruin by the rash speculations of his partner, Meiklam; £40,000 must be found immediately to save the firm. Meiklam criminally appropriates securities to pay the sum, but at the last moment Markland's sister-in-law offers the money from her own fortune, large amounts come in from notes due, and Meiklam is forced out of the business. Meiklam's nephew is a 'fast youth' speculating extravagantly on his own account, the comic man a fast-talking promoter of wild schemes. Impending ruin and financial crisis, expressed with some dramatic power, make *Settling Day* a good drama for the first three acts, but the last two collapse in improbable coincidence. Act II is set in the brokers' office of Fermor and Laxton, and the scene description indicates the trouble taken over getting the business atmosphere solidly established:

Along the R. *from the back to the first entrance, stand three clerks' desks, set across from* R. *to* L., *within a mahogany partition with rails at the top. At the ends of the partition . . . are slabs for writing at, with pads, pens, and ink. Rows of pegs on walls with stock receipts attached, and papers in bundles, and in partitions pigeon-holes for delivering and receiving stock papers, cheques, etc. . . . As the curtain rises the business of the office is seen in full activity. A* CLIENT *is writing out a cheque at the first slab, another* CLIENT *is transacting business at the upper pigeon-hole, another is handing in a bundle of stock receipts to one of the* CLERKS *who has come out of the partition to examine them. Four* CLERKS *are writing or running to and fro with books inside the partition.* FERMOR *is conversing with a person who carries prospectuses at the door of his private room.*

The dialogue also illustrates business preoccupations:

FERMOR. Mr. Martin, [*Reading off from his list.*], three hundred Venezuelans for money, fifty Confederates, forty Buenos Ayres sixes, [*Exit* CUSTOMER *who was at lower pigeon-hole, having paid a cheque.*] six hundred Spanish New Deferreds, for next account.

1st CLERK [*coming out with his hat on, and with his notebook in which he has made the entry*]. Yes sir. [*Exit.*

FERMOR. How are Buffalo and Lake Hurons?

2nd CLERK. Last business done at five, sir. [FERMOR *makes a note.*

FERMOR. We've an order for sixty when they touch four three-eights.

In an article entitled 'The Theatre and the Mob' Henry Arthur Jones said that in men of commerce Victorian drama had found new heroes:

The poor modern vamper-up of plays, searching for a general definite heroic ideal and heroic persons to embody it, finds himself able to seize nothing better than a steady, persistent glorification of money-making and industrious, respectable business life, and in place of Raleigh and Sidney is met by the eminent head of some great city firm. And as the Elizabethan drama reeks of the spirit of Raleigh and Sidney and is relative to the age of the Spanish Armada, so the Victorian drama reeks of the spirit of successful tradesmen and is relative to the age of Clapham Junction.[1]

The pressures of financial worry upon the ideally happy domestic life of the newly married couple are an important part of *Settling Day*. The idealizing of domesticity and the concentration of all types of drama upon domestic subject matter are the natural outcome of trends well developed before 1850. From tragedies with domestic interest and sentiments, like *Virginius*, and from the vast amount of domestic melodrama appearing between 1820 and 1850, the emotional presentation of household matters and family relationships, and the concerns of the daily life of homes, shops, streets, and villages in a modern society, passed into drama generally and dominated the stage for the remainder of the century. Boucicault's comment

1 *The Nineteenth Century*, xiv (September 1883), 450.

in a letter to Mrs. Bancroft that the public wants 'domestic drama', treated with broad comic character. A sentimental, pathetic play, comically rendered, such as Ours, Caste, the Colleen Bawn, Arrah-na-Pogue'[1] (one might add The Shaughraun) applied to the failure of his own comedy, How She Loves Him, in 1867, but it is relevant to over half a century of public taste. A mixture of domestic sentiment and domestic preoccupations with comic relief is just as characteristic of Pinero and Jones, with their Orreyeds and Bulsom-Porters, as it is in The Ticket-of-Leave Man a generation earlier, although the mixture is subtler and the comic relief less important in the later dramatists.

Almost every play of the time is an instance of the engulfing flood of domestic taste. The implied ideals of the Victorian home and of relationships between father and daughter, husband and wife, shine brightly even through historical settings. The plot of George Lovell's The Wife's Secret (1848) depends upon Lady Amyott's concealment of her brother, a Royalist fleeing from Roundhead soldiers, and the growing suspicion of her husband, Sir Walter, that she is hiding a lover. Much is made of the tender ties between brother and sister and between husband and wife; all comes right in the end as Sir Walter, finally informed of what is going on, protects his brother-in-law from searching soldiers and is reconciled with the wife whom he was about to drive from the house. Lady Amyott points the moral to the audience:

> But oh! let, too, the woman well beware
> Of thought or act her husband may not share.
> Love's flower that braves the fiercest storm without,
> Droops withered by the canker of a doubt.
> Implicit trust, its sacred spring of life,
> Brooks no reserve—no secret in a wife!

The involved plot of Two Loves and a Life (1854), by Tom Taylor and Charles Reade, with a background of a Jacobite uprising in Cumberland, concludes with a pardon for one of the conspirators personally obtained by his daughter from the Duke of Cumberland. Reprieved at the last moment from execution in the Tower, father is reunited with daughter in a fitting emotional climax:

[1] Mr. and Mrs. Bancroft on and off the Stage (1888), i. 245.

RUTH. Father, help me to live, help me—it is for your sake alone—

RADCLIFFE. My child! Farewell all—be happy! England, choose your king. I plot no more, I am a father! [*Draws her head to his bosom.*] I take my dove to a land of safety. [*Music.*] A father's love, tender and watchful as the love of angels, is round her and about her.

An interesting play concerned with the rightful place of a wife in society is Palgrave Simpson's *Broken Ties* (1872). The wife of the artist Warner left him years before in pursuit of her own art, singing. Now, as the famous diva La Silvia, she comes to London to sing in *Norma*. To his son, torn between honour and love for his mother, Warner says, 'From me you have already learned the sacred nature of domestic love. I have taught you to look on it as the banner in defence of which it is our duty to die, if need be.' Early in the play La Silvia declares that the 'perpetual struggle for success is the sole life worth living for'. However, a visit to Mrs. Sherwood, an old friend and formerly a noted singer, opens her eyes to a Great Truth. Mrs. Sherwood admits that in her first year of marriage she yearned for the stage, and the following dialogue ensues, the length of which in quotation may be excused for its doctrinal value:

MRS. SHERWOOD. But one day, I was a mother, and since that day I have only dreamed of cradles, little frocks, and baby eyes.

LA SILVIA. And you have no regrets?

MRS. SHERWOOD. Regrets? Why should I? When I see stretched forth those little hands which have so tight a hold on every fibre of our hearts, when I hear those lisping voices striving to murmur the first word of childish endearment, 'Mamma!' [SILVIA *makes a movement.*] I forget the world and all its gilded toys. All pleasure, happiness, excitement, lie in those eyes which gleam to mine—in those rosy lips which smile responsive to my smile. Ah! Silvia, darling, the most triumphant recall of a delighted audience is not worth one of those sweet, dear smiles.

LA SILVIA. You are right! You are right!

MRS. SHERWOOD. I pass my life in adoration of my little idols at home; and, what's more, I positively adore my husband, as though my love were not a duty.

LA SILVIA. You are a happy woman.   [*Wipes her tears.*

Warner reads La Silvia a lecture on the proper duties of a wife, concluding, 'I only show how, in forfeiting your place at the domestic hearth, you forfeited the right to stand above the obloquy of the world—the right to claim the trust of those most near and dear.' She agrees vehemently with his many strictures, admits her terrible mistake, abases herself profoundly, and then is rapturously reconciled to husband and son as '*music tremolo*' plays in the orchestra. Her triumphant last words to Warner and the audience are:

> 'Tis mine again, the treasure flung aside,
> Domestic love, true woman's dearest pride.

With the emphasis on commercial and domestic reality and the concern in much drama to depict the *minutiae* of everyday existence, legitimate tragedy was doomed. Effectively, it had been dead for years before 1850; the verse 'drama', a compromise between tragedy and melodrama and an attempt of the old literary drama to keep alive—best represented by plays like *The Lady of Lyons* and *Richelieu*—languished badly after mid century. Yet verse plays were still written, and dramatists still imagined they could revive the classical forms. After twenty-five years of churning out prose dramas, comedies, and farces, Tom Taylor turned to historical verse drama and even a legitimate tragedy, *Joan of Arc* (1871). Poets still tried their luck with the stage. Tennyson, after the poor reception of *Queen Mary* (1876) and *The Promise of May* (1883), had notable successes with Irving's production of *The Cup* (1881) and, posthumously, with the tragedy *Becket* (1893)—but in a version ruthlessly cut and arranged for the stage by Irving. *Queen Mary* reveals the legitimate dramatist's familiar obsession with history; it is heavy with historical reference, as is the unacted *Harold*, published in 1877. Early in the next century came Stephen Phillips, with *Herod* (1901), *Paolo and Francesca* (1902), and other pseudo-Elizabethan verse tragedies, but Phillips's plays no more led to a genuine revival of this type of drama than did W. G. Wills's workmanlike and highly popular verse dramas for Irving, *Charles the First* (1872), *Eugene Aram* (1873), and *Faust* (1885). It is significant that much of the success of verse drama in the second half of the nineteenth century—and its output was very small in comparison with the enormous number of prose plays—is associated with the acting of Irving and his style of romantic-realist production. Without aids as eminent as these, the modern poetic drama would have disappeared, since the taste for it was virtually extinct.

Thus the legitimate drama, prosified, with a great deal of melodramatic incident and a happy ending, thrived in its altered form—or one could regard the matter in another light and say that the old melodrama, raised somewhat in respectability and dignity, but almost as energetic and sensational, was now enthroned in place of the legitimate. Whatever the case, the three- or four-act domestic prose 'drama' commonly in a contemporary setting, inheriting character stereotypes, physical excitement, moral outlook, comic relief, and musical accompaniment from its melodramatic progenitors, but tending to greater subtlety in character portrayal, greater restraint and naturalness in dialogue, and greater skill in construction, became the primary dramatic mode until its further refinement in the 1880s and 1890s.

Adaptation from the novel and from French plays continued busily. Whereas earlier the most popular novelists for the stage were Ann Radcliffe, Scott, Fenimore Cooper, and Bulwer-Lytton, after the accession of Victoria there were numerous dramatizations of Dickens (a most suitable writer for the prevailing domestic-realist taste in the theatre) and many of Ainsworth, Reade, Collins, Mary Elizabeth Braddon, Ouida, and Mrs. Henry Wood. The lack of legal protection against unauthorized stage adaptation until later in the century made popular fiction writers an easy source of plots and income for the fast-working adapter. So innumerable were plagiarisms and borrowings from the French that some critics felt that native English drama was doomed to extinction. French authors were unprotected by law against English plagiarism until the International Copyright Convention in 1886, and authors and managers made regular prospecting trips to Paris. During the process of translation to the English stage, the French originals lost much of their Gallic flavour; nevertheless in 1854 W. B. Donne complained that 'in most cases of the announcement of a new and successful piece, its French parentage is openly avowed, and credit taken for the skill displayed in its adaptation to a British audience. . . . The popular drama of the day is accordingly in no intelligible sense of the term national, but, like so much of our costume, a Parisian exotic.'[1] Although from the late 1820s Scribe's plays followed Pixéré-court's on to the English stage, and wholesale borrowing from French originals occurred many years before 1850, the period from 1850 to 1880 saw this adaptation at its height. Except during the 1850s, English dramatists were little interested in Hugo and the French romantic drama. They preferred to learn the technical proficiency of Scribe's powers of manipulation, invention, and economical construction, qualities that, though mechanical, were greatly to benefit English drama, which stood in need of much improvement in this area.

Since the Victorian 'drama' is to a considerable extent melo-dramatic, it becomes no longer profitable to conduct a separate examination of the melodramatic form. Before 1850 the two- or three-act melodrama for the minor theatres—Gothic, nautical, or domestic in emphasis—could be studied apart from the legitimate five-act tragedy and the poetic play. After 1850 the West End theatres developed the kind of drama described above, and such distinctions are meaningless (all the plays in this volume opened at West End theatres). At the minor theatres the older melodramas continued to flourish, although the Gothic slowly disappeared and the nautical ran well behind the domestic in popularity. Melodramas such as *The Poor Needlewoman of London* (1858) at the Marylebone, *Love and Duty, or My Mother, My Wife, and My Child* (1850) and *The Old Mill Stream* (1875) at the Britannia are typical of neighbourhood working-class entertainment in the second half of the century. H. J. Byron, the author of many popular bur-lesques of melodramas,[2] also wrote strong dramas, often for the provinces, like *The Lancashire Lass, or Tempted, Tried, and True* (1867). In this involved play the villain Robert Redburn

[1] *The Quarterly Review*, xcv (June 1854), 75–6.

[2] The gradual decline of melodrama can be at least partly attributed to destruc-tive burlesque, itself a sign of the growing sophistication of the fashionable and intellectual part of the public, who became increasingly intolerant of the old melo-dramatic verities. However, melodrama survived, elderly but active (notably in the provinces) until well after the First War. The combination of the war, Freudian psychology, the cinema, modern sophistication, and the interior, fragmented, amoral direction of twentieth-century art, finished it off in the theatre—but not in the cinema and on television.

fails in three plots out of four (a poor average, even for a villain): on the virtuous farm girl, Ruth Kirby, on the heiress Fanny Danville, and on the life of Ruth's eventual husband, Ned Clayton. Here we are on familiar territory. The characters are described in the cast list according to conventional stock company lines of business: Johnson (Character Lead), Spotty (1st Low Comedy), Jellick (1st Old Man), Sergeant Donovan (Irishman), Phil Andrews (Utility), Fanny Danville (Walking Lady), etc. Indeed, the survival of the character stereotypes of melodrama was closely related to the usual specializations within the old stock company, whose disappearance was a factor contributing to melodrama's decay. *The Lancashire Lass* has many music cues to bring characters on and off and to stress emotional situations. Costume and make-up indicate moral position and behaviour pattern: for instance, in the Prologue Redburn has a moustache, a soft black felt hat, and smokes a cigar; in Act I he wears a black frock-coat, a flower in the button-hole, and carries a cane—all traditional marks of a villain. The villainess (a notable aspect of melodrama after 1850) has black hair and eyebrows, a dark complexion, and appears at first *'with showy ribbons'* and ear-rings. At the mention of Ned Clayton, whom she hates for rejecting her, she indulges in *'business, she twitches her fingers and bites her lips'*. Later, on the point of dying of sin, humbled and repentant, she totters in to *'music, piano', 'her hair untidy, her dress draggled, her appearance emaciated, that of an outcast in the lowest depths of misery'*. The dialogue is also generations old: Ruth Kirby, engaged in the heroine's customary pastime of denouncing the villain, tells Redburn, 'Those who pursue the dishonorable path you have trodden sooner or later must arrive at the goal of disgrace and shame.'

One must remember, then, that at the same time the drama was refining itself and heading away from melodrama toward a late-century sophistication and a greater complexity, the theatre continued to find room for the traditionally .simple, unrestrained, extreme forms of melodramatic expression. In the same year, 1893, that *The Second Mrs. Tanqueray* opened at the St. James's, the Burmese War was fought at Drury Lane in Harris and Pettit's *A Life of Pleasure*; in 1896 Jones's *Michael and His Lost Angel* failed at the Lyceum while *The Sign of the*

Cross began a triumphant career at the Lyric and an overblown nautical melodrama, *True Blue*, by Leonard Outram and Stuart Gordon, appeared at the Olympic. In 1898 *Mrs. Warren's Profession* was first published and Walter Melville's sensational *The Great World of London* thrilled audiences at the Standard. While the more intellectual playgoers and critics responded to the new seriousness of Ibsen, Jones, and Pinero, and followed the critical lead of William Archer, the great mass of spectators comfortably enjoyed the light entertainment, romance, spectacle, and excitement provided for them in conventional fare. They did not care for thought in the theatre, and never heeded despondent comments on their taste such as 'The majority of playgoers are neither very intelligent nor more than half-educated. Horseplay is more to their taste than wit; claptrap and strained sentiment preferable to anything like subtlety or study of character.'¹ They were content to let Clement Scott be their spokesman, and his attitude toward a 'distasteful' society play, *Ariane* (1888), by Mrs. Campbell Praed, foreshadowed his violent reaction to Ibsen and explained why melodrama remained popular for so long:

> The dramatist who trumpets forth the bad, and conceals the good, is unworthy of his calling. The play that belittles and degrades the manhood, and the womanhood, of those who watch it is unworthy of public recognition. . . . There is no pleasure in revelling in what is unwholesome and disagreeable. The playhouse is not a charnel house; the drama is not a dissecting knife. When I am asked 'why we go to the play', I should answer thus: Not to enjoy the contemplation of the baseness, and brutality, of life; not to return to our daily work more oppressed, more discontented, more dissatisfied, more heartless, but to believe in hope, in faith, in purity, in honour, in nobility of aim and steadfastness of purpose. We must enforce the good, without showing the bad.²

There is no doubt, however, that minority tastes were becoming more influential in the theatre. *The Theatre's* judgement of the 'majority of playgoers' was correct, and this majority remained a powerful conservative force in public taste. Nevertheless, in spite of seeming set-backs and retrogressions, rapid changes were taking place. In 1884 Jones startled

¹ 'The Dearth of Dramatists', *The Theatre* (April 1897), p. 208.
² 'Why Do We Go to the Play?', *The Theatre* (March 1888), pp. 123–4.

audiences with an unflattering picture of Dissenting hypocrisy in *Saints and Sinners*, even though he accepted a happy ending from Scott, as Pinero did from the cautious John Hare in *The Profligate* (1889), in which he attacked the social double standard and condemned the male philandering conveniently accepted by society. *The Profligate* has neither hero nor villain in the old sense; the drama was shedding its old character stereotypes as it evolved. During the 1880s and early 1890s Jones was giving lectures and writing articles on behalf of the serious drama, which he published in 1895 under the significant title of *The Renascence of the English Drama*. In 1882 Archer produced an astute work of criticism, *English Dramatists of To-Day*, which respectfully but firmly rejected the drama of the past in the persons of Boucicault, Tom Taylor, Robertson, and others, and hailed the coming drama of Jones and Pinero. Indeed, theatrical criticism, which now attached more importance to the play than the performer, was improving greatly in quantity, quality, and influence. Editors regarded it as an important part of their publications, and the space allotted to it was considerably larger than that today. In the 1890s, a period of critical struggle unmatched in bitterness and acrimony to this day, battle-lines were drawn up over Ibsen, the Independent Theatre, the censorship, and managerial policies, on which the firing was heavy and furious. A decade that saw Archer, Shaw, Scott, Max Beerbohm, A. B. Walkley, Justin McCarthy, J. T. Grein, and C. E. Montague writing on the stage could well pride itself on its dramatic criticism.

By 1890 Archer was publishing his translations of Ibsen, Edmund Gosse had written articles on him (as early as 1872), Shaw had lectured on him to the Fabian Society, and the insular English stage at last became aware of Continental playwrights other than the French, and of the sort of radical, experimental theatre that had developed in Europe. Adaptation from the French, though continuing all through the 1890s, was far less than before, and original English plays outnumbered French adaptations; Archer estimated that from 1893 to 1898 these latter formed less than one-fifth of West End output.[1] Nevertheless, authors like Pinero and Jones had learned valuable lessons in technique from *la pièce bien faite* of Sardou, the

[1] *The World*, 5 February 1898.

popular successor to Scribe in the English theatre from the seventies to the nineties, and turned this French expertise to good account in their own work. Now, however, Ibsen and not Sardou was the centre of attention. In the ten years from 1889 London saw *The Doll's House, Ghosts, Hedda Gabler, Rosmersholm, The Master Builder, John Gabriel Borkman, The Enemy of the People, Little Eyolf, The Wild Duck,* and *The Lady from the Sea*; in the climactic year of 1893 there were six Ibsen productions.[1] Most of them ran for several performances only; they were seen by comparatively few people, and critical hostility was immense. Irving was quite right when in 1895 he told a newspaper reporter in Boston that he saw no signs of a general response in England to this kind of drama; 'the London public won't go to see the Ibsen plays, except, of course, at an occasional performance. The public still loves the romance of life.'[2] But after their exposure to Ibsen, critics and playwrights and the intellectual section of the public could never again think in the old ways. Pinero, summing up the situation, wrote that 'during recent years the temper of the times has been changing; it is now a period of analysis, of general, restless inquiry . . . it naturally permits to our writers of plays a wider scope in the selection of the subject, and calls for an accompanying effort of thought, a large freedom of utterance'.[3] The Independent Theatre, founded in 1891, took up the cause of a theatre for the mind; its fifth production was *Widowers' Houses* in 1892. Its successor, the Stage Society, was founded in 1899, and these organizations were virtually the only channels through which intellectual European drama and serious work by unknown English authors could reach the public.

In the 1890s, therefore, the general mood of the theatre was one of ferment, hopeful prophecy, and—despite an unshakeable band of pessimists—a spirit of self-congratulation on things well done that had been absent from theatrical comment for generations. Looking back from the lofty eminence of 1894 to an article in *The Theatre* on the state of the stage in 1878, a writer

---

[1] In 1895 the Ducal company of Saxe-Coburg-Gotha performed Sudermann's *Heimat, Die Ehre,* and *Der Vogelhändler* in London. *Heimat,* translated by Louis Parker as *Magda,* was done in 1896. Quite a different play, Maeterlinck's *Pelléas et Mélisande,* was given by the Théâtre de l'Œuvre; in 1898 there was an English version.   [2] *The Theatre* (November 1895), p. 302.
[3] 'The Modern British Drama', *The Theatre* (June 1895), p. 348.

for the same periodical noted that those sixteen years had seen the managements of Irving, Tree, Hare, and Alexander, the work of Gilbert and Sullivan at the Savoy, the appearance of Jones, Pinero, Wilde, and Shaw, the eruption of Ibsen, and the Independent Theatre. He concluded:

> Had anybody prophesied sixteen years ago that Paula Tanqueray would be licensed by the Lord Chamberlain, that her tragic story would be hailed as the highest achievement of the modern English dramatist, that it would be the subject of sermons, and accepted by Mrs. Grundy as a valuable object lesson in actual life, the echoes of August, 1878, might come to us with a burden of playful derision.[1]

Sixteen years ago, too, an article in the next issue pointed out, 'there were three or four theatres at which plays were put beautifully on the stage. Now there is not an established management in the west-end of London which does not mount every play adequately; and the influence of the west-end is felt both in the cheaper London houses and throughout the provinces.'[2]

By contemporary European standards the English drama was still, despite the progress made, cautious and timorous in the treatment of new themes. Marital and sexual problems were handled hesitantly, and serious social issues appeared in few plays. The most radical English dramatist, Shaw, was unable to obtain a proper public hearing until the Stage Society productions of 1899 to 1905 and the Vedrenne–Barker seasons at the Court from 1904 to 1907. Oscar Wilde, for all his wit, polish, and social elegance, disdained new subject matter entirely and employed ancient, creaking melodramatic machinery in his three dramas, *Lady Windermere's Fan* (1892), *A Woman of No Importance* (1893), and *An Ideal Husband* (1895). Jones, whose conservative dramatic practice sometimes contrasted oddly with advanced opinions in his public pronouncements and critical writing, became a dogmatic upholder of accepted social conventions and 'the rules', and a violent opponent of Ibsen and realistic 'unpleasantness'. The more daring Pinero temporized with new trends, and, although refusing to save Paula Tanqueray's life, weakly offered Agnes

[1] 'Our Stage To-Day', *The Theatre* (September 1894), p. 90.
[2] 'Stage Art To-Day', *The Theatre* (October 1894), p. 155.

Ebbsmith pastoral Christian redemption and, except for his bitter comedy-drama *The Benefit of the Doubt* (1895), waited until the next decade before doing serious work again.

Other plays of the nineties display the same spirit of English compromise between new ideas and serious treatment on the one hand, and older material and attitudes on the other. They are frequently trapped between an attempt to implement the new dramatic rigorism and a wriggling out of the consequences of its consistent application, a position weakened still further by the resort to familiar melodramatic devices. The heroine of Haddon Chambers's *John-a-Dreams* (1894), Kate Cloud, the daughter of a prostitute and herself driven by necessity to prostitution in former days, reveals this dreadful past to the poet Harold Wynn and his horrified clergyman father. However, both accept the situation and a happy match seems ensured. Yet among these real characters and a problem of genuine dramatic interest, Chambers introduces a conventional villain, Sir Hubert, a romantic scene on a moonlit yacht, and a conclusion in which the desperate Sir Hubert drugs Wynn and falsely persuades Kate that Wynn has renounced her. Sir Hubert then takes her to his yacht, but as it is about to sail Wynn and his father arrive, the situation is explained, and Sir Hubert rows off desperately to an open and stormy sea. In Constance Fletcher's *Mrs. Lessingham* (1894), Walter Forbes nobly marries Mrs. Lessingham, his mistress of five years ago, when she returns to him after her nasty husband dies, although he is engaged to and deeply loves Lady Anne Beaton. Equally nobly, Lady Anne gives Forbes up and politely makes way for Mrs. Lessingham. In spite of the romantic posturing and impossibly honourable positions taken up by the characters, there is some dramatic power in Forbes's suffering after a year of this marriage and Mrs. Lessingham's despair when she knows of it. Then she drinks poison—a popular article of female toiletry on the stage of the eighties and nineties—and dies, and Lady Anne gives her hand, not to Forbes, but to his loyal friend. The author could find no better means to cause Mrs. Lessingham's agony of spirit and suicide than by her accidentally overhearing Forbes speak of his misery and his undying love for Lady Anne. Better than either of these plays is H. V. Esmond's *The Divided Way* (1895), in which Gaunt Humeden, returned from Africa after many years, finds that the woman he loved, Lois, has, believing him dead, married his half-brother Jack. After this conventional start, Humeden and Lois find they still love each other; Humeden decides to leave for Egypt to save the honour of all concerned, and Lois comes to his house determined to accompany him. But he will not take her; she is afraid to participate in a suicide pact, and when Jack arrives to bring her home, she drinks poison and walks out into the night. Like Esmond in this play, no dramatist had yet had the courage to let two people like this work out their destinies together, unpunished by the last act. Poison was not a happy ending, but too often an easy and satisfactorily sensational one.

After *The Second Mrs. Tanqueray* and the Ibsen *annus mirabilis* of 1893, the cause of serious drama languished for several years. Managers became wary of the problem-play, and the great successes were adaptations of George du Maurier, Stanley Weyman, and Anthony Hope. The romantic melodrama of Edward Rose's versions of *The Prisoner of Zenda* and *Under the Red Robe*, both produced in 1896, prompted Sydney Grundy to the old complaint that only a small minority would take drama seriously and that 'the sober-minded, thoughtful mass of the English public are not play-goers'.[1] Robert Buchanan lamented that 'the hope of a national drama dealing with the great issues of modern life, has been adjourned *sine die*. . . . *Trilby* frolics barefooted over the grave of *Hedda Gabler*, and the spectre of Dumas the elder strides jackbooted past the urn of our well-cremated Mrs. Tanqueray.'[2]

However, the adjournment was only temporary, and the first decade of the next century saw more and better work done. By 1900, then, the English drama and theatre had crossed the threshold into the modern era and achieved a level of technical competence, subtlety of treatment, and mastery of stage production, that crowned a century of development. Nothing can be more mistaken than to imagine that the modern English theatre began about 1880 or 1890, or even 1865 with Robertson and the Bancrofts. The first date represents a culmination, not a beginning; the drama and theatre of the last two decades of the century can be fully appreciated only in

---

[1] Introduction to William Archer, *The Theatrical 'World' for 1897* (1898), xvi.
[2] 'A Word on the Defunct Drama', *The Theatre* (October 1896), p. 208.

relation to what had gone before. *The Second Mrs. Tanqueray* and Jones's *Mrs. Danes' Defence* are ages removed from *The Miller and His Men* and *Virginius*, but the gap of eighty years between them is bridged by dramatists and plays whose techniques can be related forwards as well as backwards. Looking at it another way, Jones, Pinero, Wilde, and Shaw would not have written in the way they did without the work of Boucicault, Tom Taylor, and others before them, and the plays of Boucicault and Taylor are an outgrowth of domestic melodrama and early nineteenth-century audiences' love of the sensational. English tragedy and melodrama began the century full of rhetoric and poeticity on the one hand, and violence and a healthy vulgarity on the other; they left it, transmuted into virtually one form, rather more quietly, tastefully, and prosaically, with a healthy middle-class strength. The new drama, however, is recognizably the descendant of the old.

Engaged. The end of Act I, and other scenes.

III. COMEDIES

In 1821, a critic reviewing *The School for Scandal* at Drury Lane was moved to reflect, not only upon the performance itself, but also upon the comedy of Sheridan and the Restoration, and its place upon the modern stage:

It is the bustle and stage incident alone of these pieces which bear them up in the present day, aided possibly by a reading interest in a small portion of the audience. . . . We suspect, indeed, that the composition of a modern audience differs essentially from that of one of half a century ago. At the latter period, the prosperity of a theatre depended mainly on people of rank, and a critical Pit. . . . All this is swept away by the enlargement of theatres, and the immense alteration produced by the commercial intoxication of the last thirty years— nine-tenths of an audience will not come to listen to what is chiefly interesting to the other tenth. This simple fact alone will account for the non-attraction of some of our very best comedies . . . they are not sufficiently *frappant* for the multitude, upon whom their wit, humour, and antithesis descend like lightning upon an iceberg.[1]

Complaints about the taste of audiences and the 'decline' of comedy are legion among critics in the first half of the nineteenth century; this reviewer's remarks can serve as a starting-point for an introduction to a selection of nineteenth-century comedies.

Sentiment, morality, and the coexistence of the comic with the serious and pathetic, all significant aspects of eighteenth-century comedy, survive and are intensified in early nineteenth-century comedy, but the sense in the former of refinement, grace, and social elegance is weakened to the point of vanishing. Virtually gone also is any strong feeling of social norms and proprieties. The relatively stable social order and often narrow social focus of comedy disappeared in a theatre that no longer expressed, either in its drama or in the character of its audience, the superiority, disciplined restraint, and social control of the fashionable aristocracy and the educated middle class. Social and political change, the enlarging of the patent theatres, the

[1] The review, in an unidentified newspaper clipping, is signed 'G.'

broadening and inevitable coarsening of audience tastes—all this brought with it a demand for a new kind of comedy, incorporating the most favoured elements of the old but discarding much in order to make room for what appealed to contemporary taste. Yet one element of eighteenth-century comedy remained stable all through the nineteenth century. Despite the changing composition of audiences and fluctuations in taste, comedy was centred in the middle class: its social settings and domestic concerns were those of the middle class, its characters and viewpoints predominantly middle-class characters and middle-class viewpoints. This is not true of melodrama, farce, and pantomime, and a study of the repertory of East End theatres after 1843 (the date when 'legitimate' comedy could legally be played outside the major theatres) shows that three- or five-act comedy played an infinitesimal part; its world was irrelevant to the lower-class audiences of these theatres.

Writers early in the century noticed aspects of comedy that they found disagreeable. Elizabeth Inchbald was more restrained than most: admitting that her *To Marry or Not to Marry* (1805) was too refined for the new taste, she remarked:

The stage delights the eye far oftener than the ear. Various personages of the drama, however disunited, amuse the looker-on; whilst one little compact family presents a sameness to the view, like unity of place; and wearies the sight of a British auditor fully as much. Incidents, too, must be numerous, however unconnected, to please a London audience: they seem, of late, to expect a certain number, whether good or bad. Quality they are judges of—but quantity they *must have*.[1]

Leigh Hunt, one of the most determined foes of the new comedy, accused dramatists of 'an inveterate love of punning', 'a deformed alteration of common character and incidents', and 'a dialogue either extremely flowery or extremely familiar'.[2] He declared that it was impossible for the town to relish delicacy and graceful sentiment while indulging their current taste for buffoonery, since 'we have been like those unfortunate youths, who having got among frivolous acquaintances, place all their enjoyment and idea of social wit in horse-laughter and a certain

---

[1] 'Remarks' on *To Marry or Not to Marry*, in *The British Theatre*, ed. Elizabeth Inchbald (1808), xxiii.
[2] *Critical Essays on the Performers of the London Theatres* (1807), p. 52.

noisy nonsense, removed from all that is elegant, rational, and respectable.'[1] A German visitor lamented that 'most English comedies, although bustling, witty, and humorous, do not possess that refinement and delicacy of the best French comedies',[2] and grew indignant about English dramatists 'who disarm the rage of the critics by entering the lists with Joe Miller. Wit never was more shamelessly prostituted or more casually maltreated than by these unlucky bon-mot hunters. Indeed, it appears most extraordinary how these buffooneries are permitted to disgrace a stage where the majesty of Shakespeare commands veneration.'[3]

The drama of the first half of the nineteenth century was the favourite game of angry and contemptuous critics, who flushed comedy, tragedy, spectacle, and melodrama alike from the dark woods of 'decline' and 'illegitimacy', and pursued them energetically in repeated but vain attempts to hunt the quarry to a death that would rid the theatrical land of impure and noisome beasts and restore it to the exiled monarch of legitimacy and the rule of taste. It is more helpful for us to accept that drama on its own terms, illustrate its constituent elements, and with hindsight denied to the early nineteenth-century critic relate it to the drama that was to follow.

An initial impression of the comedy of the period 1790–1820, the comedy written by Colman, Frederic Reynolds, Thomas Dibdin, Andrew Cherry, Thomas Holcroft, Thomas Morton (its chief authors), and others, is of a lack of aim and a deficiency of form, of an uncertainty of comic purpose, of a bustling attempt to please everybody by any available means. A closer look, however, reveals a pattern of writing and subject-matter which was surprisingly repetitive and homogeneous over the short time when this kind of comedy was in full flower. It was bourgeois and anti-aristocratic, strongly sentimental and heavily moralistic. It endlessly proclaimed the beauty of virtue.

---

[1] *The Examiner*, 21 January 1810.

[2] C. A. G. Goede, *The Stranger in England* (1807), ii. 220.

[3] Ibid., ii. 198. Half a century later George Vandenhoff was complaining about comedy in almost the same terms as these earlier critics: 'Vulgar familiarity passes for easy elegance; strut and swagger for dignity and grace. Buffoonery is more welcome to the general audience than humour; practical jokes than the most sparkling wit; and everything is sacrificed to the bringing down a round of applause, or the raising a boisterous laugh.' (*Dramatic Reminiscences* (1860), p. 310.)

It idealized the simple, the rustic, and the domestic. It was strongly patriotic, including in praise of native land the glories of commerce, agriculture, the soldier and sailor. Although it indulged extensively in heavy drama, its villains were remarkably weak and susceptible to reform. Oddly coexisting with intensely melodramatic elements were equally strong components of low comedy and eccentric characterization that provided most of its humour. The best of it dashed breathlessly towards a fifth act, unhampered by all this lumber of content and untroubled by any thought of a well-made plot, in a style that did not so much communicate speeches as hurl great chunks of rhetoric, melodrama, farce, and pseudo-wit at audiences which responded with delight because of the brilliance of actors who had thoroughly mastered seemingly impossible material. Such a comedy defies definition: calling it a middle-class marriage between farce and melodrama would be near enough for our purposes.

Indeed, one of the most striking features of this comedy is the mixture of the pathetic and potentially tragic with the comic and farcical; frequently the two elements are quite unrelated. A pattern of this type is, of course, nearly as old as English drama. Comic elements appear in otherwise serious miracle and morality plays: tragi-comedy established itself early on the stage, and Shakespearean tragedy is not without ingredients of low comedy. Comedy itself could contain elements of tragedy and pathos. To go back no further than the eighteenth century, the immediate ancestor of the serio-comic drama now under consideration is the sentimental comedy of Cibber, Steele, Kelly, and Cumberland (an author still writing in the first decade of the nineteenth century). The reviewer of *The School for Scandal* quoted above said that 'the truth cannot be concealed—we have become a melodramatic people'. Melodrama alternates the violent and pathetic with the absurdly farcical with no consciousness of incongruity; such a pattern was essential to the melodramatic form.

The most melodramatic comic dramatist writing around the turn of the century was Thomas Morton. In *Speed the Plough* (1800) the fearful secret of Sir Philip Blandford is revealed—years ago he found the woman he was to marry embracing his own brother. Stabbing him to the heart, he fled the country and gambled away his estates, which fell into the hands of the mysterious Morrington, who did not seek to possess them. He lives broodingly in a Gothic castle with a secret chamber in which is hidden the bloody knife used in the stabbing. As it turns out, Morrington is Sir Philip's perfectly recovered brother, protectively watching over him and the estate. Both men suffer acutely from bad consciences. The virtuous young hero, Henry, is the offspring of Morrington's illicit love. The play ends emotionally, to say the least:

MORRINGTON. Kneel with me, my boy, lift up thy innocent hands with those of thy guilty father, and beg for mercy from that injured saint. [HENRY *kneels with him.*]

SIR PHILIP. O God! How infinite are thy mercies! Henry, forgive me —Emma, plead for me. There! There! [*Joining their hands.*]

HENRY. But, my father—

SIR PHILIP. [*Approaching.*] Charles!

MORRINGTON. Philip!

SIR PHILIP. Brother, I forgive thee.

MORRINGTON. Then let me die—blest, most blest!

SIR PHILIP. No, no! [*Striking his breast.*] Here—I want thee here. Raise him to my heart. [*They raise* MORRINGTON. *In the effort to embrace he falls into their arms exhausted.*] Again! [*They sink into each other's arms.*]

HANDY JUNIOR. [*Comes forward.*] If forgiveness be an attribute which ennobles our nature, may we not hope to find pardon for our errors—*here*? [*The Curtain falls.*]

Similarly, in Morton's *The School for Reform* (1805), Lord Avondale, about to marry Julia, is confronted by a wife whom he abandoned twenty years ago to further his career as a diplomat. Their son Frederick, who loves Julia, discovers his parents, and his own identity is revealed by a mark on his neck, put there by the Yorkshire countryman Tyke, in whose care Frederick was placed when an infant. Towards the end of the play Avondale, disguised in mask and cloak, seizes evidence of his past and flees; in order to save him Frederick assumes his disguise, is taken for the mysterious robber, and sent to prison, where Tyke recognizes him from the mark on his neck. All are reconciled in the happy ending. Tyke himself is a tragi-comic figure with a criminal past who reforms through a chance encounter with his old father. The stage directions for Tyke indicate the intensely emotional nature of his part. He *'speaks with difficulty and sighs heavily'*, *'looks with a vacant stare of horror'*, *'tears his hair in agony'*, *'groaning, strikes his Breast'*, *'laughs hysterically'*, and, recognizing his father, *'by Degrees he tremblingly falls on his Knees, and clasps his Hands in energetic Devotion'*.

Obviously influenced by the Gothic novel and Gothic tragedy, French and German sentimental drama, melodrama, and plays like Colman's *The Iron Chest* (1796), *Speed the Plough* and *The School of Reform* would hardly seem to qualify as comedies. Yet the first two acts of *Speed the Plough* are mainly humorous, with excellent comic characterizations in Ashfield, a Hampshire farmer, Sir Abel Handy, whose inventions are always going wrong, and his son Bob, who fancies he can do things better than anybody else and fails miserably. Five characters out of twelve are comic. In *The School of Reform* the pure comedy devolves upon Ferment, furious because his wife will not talk to him, and his silent spouse. In both plays, as in almost all comedy of this kind, there is little attempt to integrate the comic with the serious plot. The two blithely coexist, as they do in melodrama.

The comedy is stronger in Reynolds than in Morton, although the mixture is much as before. In *Life* (1800) the penurious Marchmont, living humbly with his adoring daughter Rosa and persecuted for non-payment of rent by the evil Craftly, finds—in a scene of wild emotional abandon—the mysterious Mrs. Belford to be the wife whom he left and believed dead years before. The wealthy Primitive, who deserted a daughter as Marchmont deserted a wife, discovers her in the person of the same Mrs. Belford. If Marchmont is subjected to the half-hearted villainy of Craftly, Mrs. Belford endures an abduction attempt from Clifford, who pursues her feebly throughout the play. Together with these characters are the stupid Lackbrain, Primitive's adopted son, and Sir Harry Torpid, a jaded elegant consumed with boredom unless agitated by events that create in him intense feeling and the desire to dash about helping the suffering virtuous. Thus melodramatic plot lines and melodramatic emotions are mingled with feverish comedy and a great deal of sentiment and goodheartedness. Like all the good characters in Morton's plays and their near relations in a dozen other Reynolds comedies, Primitive, Rosa, Marchmont, Mrs. Belford, and Sir Harry Torpid trail clouds of virtue behind them and exude endless worthy sentiments, typical of which is Sir Harry's 'Let a man make virtue his pursuit, and he'll find life a very pleasant spree, I'll promise him.' 'None but madmen would forsake that peace which virtue yields—preserve it—cling to it. Fortified with that, you boast a bulwark may defy the world' is one sentiment of many like it from Reynolds's *The Delinquent* (1805). Here the mysterious Delinquent (Sir Arthur Courcy, as he really is) is in the power of the villain Sir Edward Specious and reluctantly aids him in a plot to abduct the beautiful Olivia. It transpires that not only is the Delinquent Olivia's father, but also the husband of Olivia's governess, Mrs. Aubrey, who long ago had so plunged him into debt with her extravagances that he was forced to flee his creditors into exile; however, she is atoning by tenderly watching over her daughter Olivia, who does not know her real identity.[1] In the end Sir Arthur forgives his wife and Sir Edward relents, declaring, 'To persist in plunging in despair parent and child, long parted and thus found, demands that daring and ferocious spirit which still, thank heaven, your coward master needs'—a speech which alone demonstrates that *The Delinquent* is not true melodrama, since it would make any genuine melodramatic villain turn wrathfully in his grave.[2] Alongside this incredible and casually motivated plot—Reynolds took less trouble with his plots than his contemporaries, who themselves took very little—is a comic plot in which the dashing rake young Doric makes up to his rich uncle and falls in love with Olivia. There is also the hypocritical

---

[1] It can easily be seen how much Reynolds owed to his borrowings: not only from an enormously popular play like Kotzebue's *The Stranger* (1798), with Kemble in a part much like the Delinquent (which he also played), and from other dramatists such as Morton (*Life* and *The Delinquent* strongly resemble *Speed the Plough* and *The School of Reform*), but also from himself.

[2] Sir Edward Specious in this play, and Craftly and Clifford in *Life*, are examples of the debilitated villains, frequently aristocrats, common to this school of comedy. Others are Malcour in Reynolds's *Folly As It Flies*, Sir Charles Cropland in Colman's *The Poor Gentleman*, and Squire Chevy Chase in Thomas Dibdin's *The School for Prejudice*. These three also make ineffective attempts upon a woman's virtue and are easily foiled. True villainy could not exist in the excessive benevolence and sentimentalism of these plays; the melodrama in them is therefore not nearly as dark as in real melodrama.

Miss Stoic, who pretends to love country seclusion, and the blustery, good-hearted Major Tornado, Olivia's guardian.[1]

No matter, then, how strong were the serious parts of their plays, authors were careful to justify the title of comedy by a generous proportion of comic material. To create humour, they relied—apart from verbal wit—upon eccentricity and low comedy in which Irishmen and countrymen abound. Major Tornado, Sir Abel Handy in *Speed the Plough*, Sir Harry Torpid in *Life*, Sir Solomon Cynic in Reynolds's *The Will* (1797), Colman's energetic philanthropists Sir Robert Bramble in *The Poor Gentleman* (1801), and Torrent in *Who Wants a Guinea?* (1805), are all eccentrics and 'humours' characters of one kind or another. The list of low comedy characters is longer, and since they are often the heart of a dramatist's comic appeal they spend a great deal of time on stage. Colman is especially rich in them: Stephen Harrowby in *The Poor Gentleman*, a farmer's son obsessed with soldiering; Dennis Brulgruddery and Dan in *John Bull*; and the Yorkshire servants Solomon Gundy and Andrew Bang in *Who Wants a Guinea?* Selfish, shrewd, stupid, silly, sentimental, drunken, virtuous, and loyal, they sometimes serve higher purposes than low comedy, and bear a burden of morality and sentiment as well. Sharing characteristics of both eccentric humour and low comedy are such imaginative creations as the pedantic, money-hunting tutor Pangloss in Colman's *The Heir-at-Law* (1797) and the apothecary Ollapod in *The Poor Gentleman*, whose vocabulary is a strange blend of medicine and hunting.

These comic ingredients were much in demand, and playwrights ignored them at their peril. Reflecting on the failure of her *To Marry or Not to Marry*, an elegant but rather grave comedy, Elizabeth Inchbald said that 'it appears as if the writer of this comedy had said, previous to the commencement of the task, "I will shun the faults imputed by the critics to modern dramatists; I will avoid farcical incidents, broad jests, the introduction of broken English, whether Hibernian or provincial".' The result, she confessed, was unsatisfactory. 'In the dearth of

---

[1] Tornado comes from India, Primitive in *Life* from the West Indies. In comedy of this period, and in earlier and later comedy as well, these geographical areas were guarantees of a good, albeit careless heart, an abrupt though kindly manner, an innate sense of justice and fair play, and a disposition to relieve distress.

wit, an audience will gladly accept of humour; but the author who shall dare to exclude from his comedy the last, without being able to furnish the first, assuredly must incur the rigorous, though just sentence of dulness.'[1] To be pleasantly amused was not enough for an English audience; it wanted to laugh, and laugh loudly, as well as shed tears at the pathetic parts. Of the success of Colman's *John Bull* (1803) and the hostility of the critics to comedy, Mrs. Inchbald noted:

The introduction of farces into the entertainments of the theatre has been one cause of destroying that legitimate comedy which such critics require. The eye, which has been accustomed to delight in paintings of caricature, regards a picture from real life as an insipid work. The extravagance of farce has given to the town a taste for the pleasant convulsion of hearty laughter, and smiles are contemned as the token of insipid amusement.[2]

The pathetic, the sensational, the eccentric, and the farcical were not the only essentials of turn-of-the-century comedy. The strong expression of sentiments on all possible occasions—again a characteristic of melodrama—together with the impregnable virtue of nearly every major character, raised comedy to ethical heights it never reached even in its most fervently righteous moments later in the century. More interesting than the energetic pronouncements of a general morality is the subject-matter of particular sentiments, or 'claptraps', as objecting critics called them.[3] In Reynolds's *Folly As It Flies* (1801) the repentant Lady Melmoth, who has ruined her kindly husband with her thoughtless extravagance, addressing herself to the ladies in the boxes ('ye votaries of dissipation'), declares, 'I know, I'm sure, that in the splendid equipage and dazzling dress ye never taste one moment of substantial joy. Then seek it in your husbands' and your children's hearts—make home a shelter 'gainst the storm; and, let it roar around, still shall you find domestic life the scene of peace!' Here sounded one of the major themes of the nineteenth century, not in comedy alone but in all forms of drama, as well as in the novel. 'Domestic life the scene

---

[1] 'Remarks' on *To Marry or Not to Marry*.
[2] 'Remarks' on *John Bull* in *The British Theatre*, xxi.
[3] 'The moral point is everything', Charles Lamb remarked wearily of the comedy of his time. (*The Dramatic Essays of Charles Lamb*, ed. Brander Matthews (1891), p. 149.)

of peace' was an ideal that burned brightly on the stage throughout the century. Reynolds, Colman, Morton, and their colleagues depicted relationships between father and son, father and daughter, and husband and wife, with intense feeling. Old Dornton in Holcroft's *The Road to Ruin* (1792) dotes passionately on his profligate son Harry, and with equal passion tries to repress this love and drive him from home for his follies. But he cannot bring himself to do it, and there is a final reconciliation. The scenes between father and son, powerfully written, are the emotional core of the play. Father–daughter relationships aroused the maximum domestic emotion: the brooding protectiveness of Worthington for Emily in *The Poor Gentleman*, the outbursts of emotion when long-lost daughters are restored to their fathers in *Who Wants a Guinea?*, *The Will*, *Life*, *The Delinquent*, and *To Marry or Not to Marry*. The reconciliation of erring wives with now forgiving husbands is important in many comedies written after *The Stranger* and the reunion in that play of the repentant Mrs. Haller with the proud and mysterious Stranger.

Together with the idealization of domestic bonds went the accessory though subordinate idealization of various aspects of English life and character, the virtues of a simple country existence, the pursuit of agriculture, and the ownership of land. John Grouse, the Yorkshire gamekeeper in Thomas Dibdin's *The School for Prejudice* (1801), foils villainy and fulfils a moral function that sometimes belonged to low-comedy countrymen.[1] Sir Charles Cropland in *The Poor Gentleman*, a town man at heart, is morally corrupt and contaminates the wholesome Kentish countryside. His steward reminds him of his duty 'to support the dignity of an English landholder, for the honour of old England; to promote the welfare of his honest tenants; and to succour the industrious poor, who naturally look up to him for assistance'. (As in melodrama, the moral tone is hostile to the aristocrat—but not to the landowner, generally a figure of opprobrium in melodrama.) Looking forward to an idyllic

---

[1] The hero is named Frank Liberal, and behaves accordingly. Virtue is so extensive that it possesses the Jewish money-lender Ephraim, idealized after the manner of the do-gooding Sheva in Richard Cumberland's *The Jew* (1794). Ephraim restores £10,000 he finds in the lining of an old coat to its owner, saying, 'Ten thousand pounds is no more recompence for de loss of a good conscience than if it was a dwopenny bank-note.'

retirement in the country with his adopted son Lackbrain, Primitive in *Life* declares enthusiastically that 'the English cottage is, and ever will be, the seat of peace, industry, and virtue'. He is disappointed, not by the cottage, but by the hypocrisy of Lackbrain and his wife, who only pretend to love the country in order to secure Primitive's wealth, and actually lead a fashionably dissipated life. The simple rustics of *The Heir-at-Law*, Cicely and Zekiel Homespun, come to London in search of Cicely's sweetheart Dick Dowlas, who incidentally describes an English farmer as 'one who supports his family, and serves his country, by his own industry. In this land of commerce . . . such a character will be always respectable.' Dick tries to desert Cicely because he is now heir to a title and wishes to become a man of fashion, but conscience and love prove too much for him. The Homespuns, honest, affectionate, and worthy, are clearly the main repository of the play's virtues. Farmer Ashfield in *Speed the Plough* and Farmer Harrowby in *The Poor Gentleman*, characters partly sentimental and partly comic, upright and true men both, are idealized as the very soil of England.

The soldier, the sailor, and the man of commerce take their place beside the countryman and the farmer in comedy's hierarchy of values. Highly patriotic sentiments are frequently expressed, such as 'I wish I may be shot if I can give harsh treatment to an honest man in misfortune, under my thatch, who have wasted his strength and his youth in guarding the land which do give us English farmers a livelihood' and 'A gallant soldier's memory will flourish, though humble turf be osier-bound upon his grave. The tears of his country will moisten it, and vigorous laurel sprout among the cypress that shadows its remains.' A low-comedy servant who prides himself on his excruciating French refuses to take a farthing from a distressed English sailor, and is told, 'Whatever your proficiency may be in French, such language is pure English, and that of the best subjects in the British dominions.' The man of business is likewise elevated. Old Dornton in *The Road to Ruin* is a City merchant to be admired for his moral and financial integrity as well as his love for his son. In *The Heir-at-Law* Daniel Dowlas, a simple chandler, succeeds to the title and fortune of Lord Duberly and tries to improve his language and manners to fit his new position. However, he feels uncomfortable, cannot leave the chandler behind him, and for his attempt is satirically rebuked. In the play's value system, being an honest chandler is better than being a peer. The real heir turns up alive to claim the title, and Dowlas resumes his proper social and moral station. The social responsibility of the landowner and merchant is repeatedly emphasized. Endeavouring to persuade the miserly Hogmore to aid the victims of a village fire, Heartly in *Who Wants a Guinea?* tells him, 'The wealthy of this land forbid the drops of disappointment to fall from labour's eye and rust the ploughshare. Industry is the source of our country's riches; and English policy would teach opulence to dry the peasant's tear, if English justice and generosity did not continually prevent its flowing.' The philanthropist (a not uncommon figure in contemporary comedy) of the same play asks his friend to 'look at the commercial names that swell every list of national subscriptions, and then tell me whether men of the highest rank do not acknowledge, with pleasure, the merchant's kindred ardour in the country's welfare'.

The comedy of the late eighteenth and early nineteenth century is interesting and important, not only in its own right as the most flourishing 'legitimate' drama of its age, but also for what it led to, since it established a comic pattern that with some modification became in its essentials the comedy of the Victorians. To the idealizing of domestic ties the Victorians added what was peculiarly their own, a strong feeling for home and hearth. Marriage and domestic life, though no less sacred, were treated more prosaically and with more realistic detail. Eccentric character and low comedy remained major sources of humour for the early and mid Victorians, and most comedy still contained, in varying degrees of emphasis, pathetic and potentially tragic elements, melodramatic plots, and character types. Morality, sentiment, and the glories of virtue were adapted, as dramatic material, to differing social contexts and expressed with somewhat less *braggadocio*. The process of refinement and domestic realism that gradually occurred in comedy as in other forms of nineteenth-century theatre cannot disguise the fact that the Victorian playwright's basic material and his moral attitudes were in substantial part an inheritance from an earlier comedy and not his own invention.

For this reason alone the plays of Colman, Reynolds, Morton, and Holcroft are significant, and there are further grounds for rebutting the oft-repeated charge, made by contemporaries and later generations of critics, that their theatre was irrelevant to the world they lived in. Perhaps Dutton Cook stated the case most succinctly: these comedies 'belong exclusively to the playhouse and the players. They reflect real life and manners in no way; as pictures of the period in which they were written they have no kind of value. They are mere theatrical contrivances for the display of the actors' peculiarities for winning laughter at any price from the audiences, and dismissing them amused with the slightest possible tax upon their reflective powers.'[1] This statement is true in so far as it pertains to the abilities of the actors. But putting aside the question of the dramatists' intentions, which were certainly not to paint a faithful picture of the period, there is no doubt that the restlessness, the bustle, the structural carelessness, the sentimental liberalism, the idealization of the simple country life, the simplistic morality, and the heavy drama of the comedies pleased the taste of a public unlikely to favour a theatre that had nothing to do with the age in which it lived. In fact, these characteristics admirably reflect, in a manner that had to be non-political and socially harmless in order to satisfy the Examiner of Plays, the general sense of being unsettled, of restlessness and social unease after the French Revolution, the breakdown of traditional standards of gentility and graceful living, the fashionable liberal sentimentalism, the upthrust into a less stable society of a vulgar and poorly-educated class of people with flamboyant artistic tastes, and the developing moral sense that was to culminate in a Victorian ethic. Through the general rather than the particular the comedy of the age mirrored significant aspects of the times. When one realizes in how many ways another contemporary dramatic form, the melodrama, was socially and philosophically relevant to the age that gave it birth, the accusation that the

[1] *Nights at the Play* (1883), pp. 13–14. These comments come from a review of a revival of Morton's *The Way to Get Married* (1796) at the Olympic in 1867. Cook complained that 'everything is sacrificed to farcical incident and extravagance of character . . . the whole comedy hangs loosely together' (p. 14). The play had been cut, especially in its serious parts, and Cook thought that no modern audience would tolerate the original in its entirety.

comedy of the early nineteenth century—or of any other period in the century, for that matter—was completely isolated from contemporary life and thought simply cannot be sustained.

After 1810 there was a decline in the vigour and humour of a comedy that had been pre-eminent for twenty years. Colman's last comedy was performed in 1805; Holcroft's in 1806; Reynolds's in 1808; after 1807 Morton wrote only three comedies in twenty-three remaining years of playwriting. Both Colman and Reynolds took up other dramatic forms, perhaps realizing that the five-act comedy with pretensions to legitimacy belonged to the past. Imitators were numerous and even more objectionable to critics than their masters, and no single playwright or group of dramatists was acknowledged as being at the head of comic writing. Although there were many excellent comic actors on the stage, by the 1820s the older generation that performed so brilliantly in Colman and Reynolds and Morton was passing away. Mrs. Mattocks retired in 1808; Lewis in 1809; Bannister in 1815; Johnstone in 1820; Emery died in 1822; Munden retired in 1824; Mrs. Davenport and Fawcett in 1830. The actual quantity of comedies performed appears smaller after 1810; success was doubtful in that area, and dramatists turned more and more to melodrama, spectacle, musical comedy, and farce. The growing number of minor theatres, confined by law to playing the 'illegitimate', increased their output, and the patent theatres, caught between the responsibility of presenting the traditional, legitimate drama and the dire financial necessity of cashing in on the popularity of the illegitimate, compromised by devising playbills made up of both.

Thus an increase in low comedy and farcical comedy, and the heightening of a strong tendency to vulgarity found in the earlier comedy, is not surprising. As the attendance of the fashionable classes at the theatre declined and managers began to cut prices to attract less select audiences, this trend accelerated. In William Moncrieff's *Wanted a Wife* (1819),[1] for instance, most of the humour arises from low-comedy characters and farcical plotting. Separately but simultaneously advertising in the Echo Office for a wife and a domestic place, Arthur Wildfire and his servant Frank are taken up by a young lady and her middle-

---

[1] Moncrieff complained in the preface to the printed play that Drury Lane was two-thirds empty on opening night.

aged aunt. The young lady believes that Wildfire is the servant she advertised for, whereas he believes that she answered his advertisement for a wife; the aunt understands that Frank, who thinks he has found a place as her servant, is actually replying to her advertisement for a husband. The quadruple misunderstanding lasts, quite incredibly, until the end of the play. The amusement here is provided by the farcical complications; additionally there is the low comedy of the proprietor of the Echo Office, an Irishman, M'Shift, and his Yorkshire servant, Jolt, parts played by Johnstone and Emery respectively. The fullblown sentiment has disappeared, and with it any sense of elegance or refinement; the serious interest has been reduced to the unimportant and extraneous story of a young orphan seeking her father.

Since audience taste in humour was moving towards the obvious and the farcical—a movement apparent in turn-of-the-century comedy, where nevertheless an older though debased tradition of wit and foppery lingered by its side—the growing emphasis on farce in comedy is unremarkable. Clearly the comedies which succeeded did so mainly or entirely because of low-comedy interest and the excellence of low-comedy acting. Two such plays featured Liston in low-comedy roles. In Theodore Hook's *Exchange No Robbery* (1820), the landlord of the Pig and Windmill tries to pass off his lubberly potboy son, Sam Swipes (played by Liston), as the rightful husband-to-be of a refined and wealthy heroine. The play centres on Sam Swipes's behaviour in this ridiculous situation. Several scenes are set in the Pig and Windmill, and Liston's performance—Sam became one of his best-known parts—must have been virtually the only source of humour in an otherwise weak comedy. Clumsy, vulgar, carousing in the servants' hall, and roaring out praises of his beloved kitchen-maid Polly, Sam of course looks quite ludicrous 'in the extreme of fashionable dress, except the head, which remains in the original plebeian style'. In *Paul Pry* (1825), by John Poole, the social setting is more elegant, but it is typical of the comic dramatist's indifferent plotting and inability to express a variety of humour that the main interest of the play attaches to an incidental character who only becomes involved in the plot at the very end. Paul Pry, a thick-skinned vulgarian played by Liston (probably his most famous part), insatiably curious about private family matters, questioning, spying, infuriating everybody by intruding when quite un-wanted,. wanders around the fringes of a plot that is otherwise serious though relatively unemotional. Pry is threatened with violence when caught peeping through the keyhole of a garden door; he is also chased by dogs and gets his clothes torn when taken for a thief.

This kind of comedy possesses the same eccentricity of behaviour and helter-skelter extravagance as that of the previous generation, with the developments noted above. In 1844 Catherine Gore commented on her own comedy, *Quid Pro Quo*, which won the prize of £500 in a competition to determine the best comedy submitted to a panel of judges, and was performed at the Haymarket:

A general feeling of disappointment has arisen from the mistaken idea that the prize purported to produce what is termed a high-life comedy; a style of piece which the experience of the past twenty years proves to be wholly ineffective on the modern stage. No such object was suggested by the manager; and a bustling play of the Farquhar, or George Colman school, appeared far more available to the resources of the theatre, and the taste of the play-going public. Were the boxes often filled as I had the gratification of seeing them for the first representation of 'QUID PRO QUO', with those aristocratic and literary classes of the community who have absolutely withdrawn their patronage from the English stage, for *their* more refined pleasure, a new order of dramatic authors would be encouraged to write, and of performers to study. But no one familiar with the nightly aspect of our theatres will deny that they are supported by a class requiring a very different species of entertainment, for whose diversion, exaggeration in writing and acting is as essential, as daubing to the art of the scene-painter. Now that professional distinctions are extinct, and that the fusion of the educated classes has smoothed the surface of society to a rail-road level, a mere Daguerreotypic picture of the manners of the day would afford little satisfaction to the disproportion and caricature *established into the custom of the stage* by the exigencies of our colossal patent theatres.[1]

---

[1] Preface to *Quid Pro Quo*. From the 1840s there were many suggestions that the new conformity in manners and dress deprived dramatists of important comic material. As late as the 1880s Joseph Knight said, 'With the abolition of distinctions of costume, the chances of eccentric comedy were seriously impaired. Bob Acres or Tony Lumpkin would now be found in the stalls of a theatre in no wise distinguishable from the rest of the audience, and Dr. Pangloss, should he return, would discard wig, cocked hat, and cane, and appear in a black coat and waistcoat and subfusk continuations.' (*The Theatre*, September 1881, p. 171.)

Quid Pro Quo is socially a cut above comedies like *Wanted a Wife* and *Paul Pry*, and more a comedy of high life than 'a bustling play . . . of the George Colman school', despite Mrs. Gore's professed intention to write in 'a broader style as a dramatist, than as a novelist', a style that would be 'likely to provoke the greatest mirth of the greatest number'.[1] The relative refinement of *Quid Pro Quo* showed that some attempt was still being made to provide comic entertainment for the fashionable and educated classes of society.

There are other evidences of this attempt, and nothing could be more wrong than to believe that from about 1810 to Victoria's accession theatre audiences were a boorish rabble hungering only for farce, sensation, and jolly pantomime. A considerable audience—though not considerable enough for the financial comfort of most managers—was still interested in the legitimate drama and a theatre of taste. Not legitimate drama, because it was illegal to perform it in the minor theatres before 1843, but tasteful and elegant even in their illegitimacy, are the musical extravaganzas, burlesques, and burlettas performed under Madame Vestris's management of the Olympic from 1831 to 1839. A part of the Olympic's repertory consisted of short comedies, often in two acts, containing songs and written after French models by authors such as J. R. Planché, Charles Dance, and T. H. Bayly. The tone of these *petites comédies* can be restrained and even refined; some of them are notably free from the heavy emphasis on farcical situations, low comedy, and vulgar characterization common enough in comedies at other theatres. For instance, in Dance's *The Beulah Spa* (1833), Caroline Grantley wishes to push the hesitant Beauchamp into proposing to her. She disguises herself, first as a minstrel to sing him a love song, and then as a gypsy to tell his fortune. Finally she reveals herself and he does propose. The plot is simple and the general tone fairly elevated. Even simpler is the same author's *A Dream of the Future* (1837). Captain Lovelock and Dr. Mildmay arrive at the home of Mr. Harbottle to take his nieces, Georgina and Honoria, to a ball and to propose marriage. Honoria refuses the timid Mildmay and Georgina accepts the dashing Lovelock. After the ball, Honoria has a dream that she relates to her sister in song: forty years have

[1] Preface to *Quid Pro Quo*.

passed, and she is a dissatisfied old maid, mocked by a contemptuous and successful Mildmay and the unwilling observer of the philandering Lovelock's scurvy treatment of his wife Georgina. The relation of the dream has a salutary effect: when the men arrive Honoria accepts Mildmay and Georgina rejects Lovelock, who then reveals himself as the fortune-hunting scoundrel he really is. All this is rather delicately and quietly expressed; broad humour is confined to Harbottle's penchant for wine and the low comedy of an Irish servant with a muddled vocabulary. The parts of Caroline Grantley and Honoria in these two pieces were played by Vestris: sentimental, witty, and refined, her heroines set the mark of elegance and taste upon a comic style that at its best possessed considerable charm and grace, and whose plots were usually economical and deftly managed. The characteristics of charm, delicacy, a tender sentimentalism, and a restraint of expression often found in these *petites comédies* but hardly anywhere else in contemporary comedy, had to wait thirty years for further development, when they became key elements of Robertsonian comedy.

A direct attempt to perpetuate the most traditional kind of legitimate comedy and to appeal to a higher level of public taste than that catered for by the ordinary run of comic entertainment was the writing of poetic comedies after the manner of the Elizabethans. This was part of a larger effort to deflect the whole course of the drama from the channels in which it was inevitably running and to recapture the vanished glories of an Elizabethan drama that had received the accolade of 'literature'. The main impetus of this movement was tragic, but comedies were also written; the most admired poetic comedies in their time were by John Tobin and Sheridan Knowles. Tobin's *The Honey Moon* (1805: posthumously produced), a skilful and not unpleasing mixture in blank verse and prose of the plots of *The Taming of the Shrew*, *Twelfth Night*, and *Much Ado about Nothing*, with other matter, was praised by George Daniel in the preface to the Cumberland edition (1827) in terms which clearly convey the literary movement's lofty rationale and haughty contempt for the enemy:

He [Tobin] had drank deep at the pure fountain-head of English Poetry —the works of our ancient dramatists. From them he acquired a correctness of taste, a fertility of thought, and a harmony of language, that none of his contemporaries have attained. . . . Farcical plot and sprightly nonsense, oaths and obscenity, he left to those authors who, for many years, monopolized the stage to the total exclusion of superior talent; had he descended to compound such base materials, he might, like them, have inherited temporary popularity and lasting contempt; but he adopted a wiser and more independent course, sacrificing present advantage for the nobler award of posterity. . . . Thus has the author of the Honey Moon, by *one* happy effort of taste and genius, attained a rank in literature, which the vapid and multifarious productions of his contemporaries shall in vain aspire to.

In the 1830s the name of Knowles was joined with that of Tobin. By the time he came to write comedies, Knowles's considerable reputation had already been achieved by tragedies and dramas like *Virginius* (1820), *William Tell* (1825), and *The Hunchback* (1832). His three comedies are set vaguely in Elizabethan times, two of them in London, and are written in a sometimes tolerable blank verse and a painfully laboured imitation of Shakespearean prose. The plots are romantic, the characters mostly high-born, and the idealization of domestic relationships intense. In *The Beggar of Bethnal Green* (1834) Lord Wilford sees Bess, the daughter of the blind beggar Albert (actually a nobleman), in the street, falls in love with her, discovers her again as the barmaid of an inn, and marries her. The Queen acts as *dea ex machina*, and Albert is restored to high estate. In a comic sub-plot the swollen-headed son of Old Small dresses as a lord and marries a chambermaid in the belief that she is a lady. The plot of *The Love-Chase* (1837) has echoes of *Much Ado about Nothing*: the reluctant Wildrake falls in love with the quarrelsome, witty, jealous Constance, and Waller pursues his love for Lydia, maid to the Widow Green, under the guise of wooing the complaisant Widow. Widow Green is in turn pursued by old Sir William Fondlove, who mistakenly believes that she dotes passionately upon him. Constance at last sees that Wildrake loves her; Wildrake's friend Trueworth discovers that Lydia is really his sister and therefore a lady;[1] Widow Green accepts Sir William because nobody else will

---

[1] Like Bess in *The Beggar of Bethnal Green* and Virginia in *Virginius*, Lydia is another of Knowles's impossibly sweet, ethereal, and morally perfect heroines, all of them intended as ideal types of young womanhood.

have her. *The Love-Chase* is Knowles's best comedy, and the most popular one in his day. It is certainly superior to *Old Maids* (1841), written for Vestris and Mathews at Covent Garden, in which Thomas Blount rises from journeyman jeweller in his father's shop to Colonel in the army and wins the heart of Lady Blanche. At the same time Sir Philip Brilliant, a fop with a good heart, falls in love with Blanche's friend Lady Anne, and becomes as a result a quieter, worthier man.

The plots of Knowles's comedies indicate his devotion to his sources and his approach to comic material. Yet he catches only something of the outward manner of Elizabethan comedy; the imitation of externals is clever, but there is little life or vitality within—the usual fault of the legitimate school. Knowles's verse and prose can be prolix and clumsy, and the comedies are without the vitality of the tragedies and dramas, which at least contain a degree of vigorous action and a tragic passion of sorts. As with the tragedies and dramas, however, Knowles was fortunate to find his comedies acted by the best players of the day, performers of the quality of Vestris, Mathews, Harley, Webster, Mrs. Nisbet, and Mrs. Glover. As in the tragedies and dramas too, Knowles's essentially domestic spirit is all-embracing. Parental love and the family relationship are at the emotional heart of *The Beggar of Bethnal Green*, for example, as they are in *Virginius* and *William Tell*. Bess loves Lord Wilford as soon as she lays eyes upon him because he resembles the miniature of her father. Albert's grief when his daughter is taken from him is intense; similarly, Old Small bewails the loss of his son:

> Sir, you see
> A poor old man that has an only son,
> Whom he, in evil hour, let go from him,
> Thinking that he could live without him, till
> The task he tried, but found too hard a one . . .
> Yet was my fault my love—
> My too fond love! So fond it could not see
> How duty could be harsh and yet be kind.

Knowles's preference for centring his plots upon the relationship between parent and child is more evident in the tragedies and dramas than the comedies, although it is obvious in *The*

Beggar of Bethnal Green. In his plays generally this theme is more prominent than in the comedies of Colman, Reynolds, Morton, and Holcroft. No matter how hard he tried to be Elizabethan and legitimate, in treating this subject at least Knowles could not avoid contemporaneity.

Since poetic comedy with Elizabethan settings was not attuned to an age much more interested in prosified images of daily life, it dwindled away.[1] Between 1810 and 1840 there was a curious thematic hiatus in comedy. Many years after 1810 were spent imitating Colman and Reynolds and their like, and a desire to say something about the modern world did not reach comedy for some time. In the 1830s Knowles's domestic themes were truly modern, but his style and setting were not; on another level the domesticity of Buckstone's three-act farces in the same decade is again contemporary. With the 1840s a change came over comedy. Not only was it becoming gradually more domestic and realistic, though still with a strong admixture of rhetoric which it never wholly lost, but also thematically more significant. In sum, comedy was modernizing itself. In 1844 the prologue to *Quid Pro Quo* declared:

> 'Tis time to turn some newer page, and show
> Life as it is, and manners as they go . . .
> Tonight our cost and care
> Would picture—English manners as they are.

Mrs. Gore's play hardly fulfils this intention, but within the framework of ideals and fantasy in which they all operated, the comic dramatists of the 1840s and of succeeding decades did indeed treat of subject-matter relevant to modern life.

The major themes explored in comedy over the next thirty years were those of wealth and social ambition; the virtues of rustic and domestic simplicity; the artificiality and moral inferiority of Society; the idealization of womanhood, the marriage bond, and domestic harmony; and the assertion of the rightful authority of husband over wife. Such themes readily

---

[1] One of the better poetic comedies of the second half of the century is Westland Marston's *Donna Diana* (1863). Written in blank verse and set in Barcelona, the play is gracious, elegant, and correct, yet essentially lifeless. The verse, though rather flat, is simpler than Knowles's, and free of his laboured conceits and tortured syntax.

interconnect, frequently two or three in the same play. Thus discussion of each one separately is somewhat artificial and a little difficult, especially since Victorian playwrights did not as a rule think out their ideas clearly and develop them carefully. George Henry Lewes, in urging English dramatists to follow French models of construction and character representation, complained of English comedy that 'any materials, however carelessly gathered, are thought good enough, so that the "jokes" be abundant. Constructing a story as the development of some idea—grouping around that the characters which will most clearly set it forth—and subordinating the *writer* to the *dramatist*—these are processes which, however necessary, our dramatists disdain or overlook.'[1] The method might have been sloppy and sometimes little different from the method of fifty years before, but the ideas were certainly there, no matter how awkwardly worked out.

Bulwer-Lytton's *Money* (1840) is a satirical examination of the importance of wealth, or the lack of it, in determining conduct and attitudes. The author may have known Douglas Jerrold's *The Golden Calf* (1832), a remarkably cogent and disciplined attack upon the corrupting power of wealth. A mysterious *deus ex machina*, Chrystal, forces the dissipated, ruined Mountney to see the folly of his ways and return to his father's honourable (but unspecified) trade, which the snobbish profligate had previously scorned. In one ironic scene, Chrystal invites Mountney's elegant and heartless 'friends', who think Chrystal enormously rich, to dinner in Theobald's Road at the unfashionable hour of one, makes them lay the table, tend to the fire, and cook the mutton chops, all the time relishing their discomfiture. He waxes eloquent on the play's main theme:

When 'tis not asked, 'What can a man do?' but 'What seems he to possess?' not 'What does he know?' but 'Where does he live?' and when this passion for appearance stays not with some hundred gilded nondescripts, but like one general social blight is at this moment found in every rank, in every walk—for a verity, we may not call the present age the age of gold or of silver; but, of all ages else, the AGE OF OUTSIDES!

So consistently ironic, bitter, and savage is the tone of *The Golden Calf* that, although called a comedy, it is more of a

[1] *The Leader*, 17 May 1851.

drama, a fact that again draws attention to the problem in this period of dramatic definitions and to the comfortable coexistence, in comedy after comedy, of the serious and the comic, the melodramatic and the farcical, the punning joke and the tender sentiment.

Jerrold continued his attack in *Bubbles of the Day* (1842), set specifically in '*London in 1842*'. The subjects of his wrath here are the aristocratic fool in Parliament, Lord Skindeep; the business adventurer ('the bandit of society—the brigand of a city') Smoke; the money-lender Shark; and the fawning hanger-on, Sir Phoenix Clearcake. The first act is promising, but thereafter Jerrold turns away from the themes he began with to trivial love and plot entanglements, although these are centred around money and property. A thematically significant first act that dribbles away into trivia occurs commonly in Victorian comedy, and in Jerrold more than once. His writing for the minor theatres (including *Black-Eyed Susan*, *Thomas à Becket*, and *The Golden Calf*) is more interesting, vital, and consequential than his later 'legitimate' work for more important theatres, represented by indifferent comedies like *Bubbles of the Day*, *Time Works Wonders* (1845), and *St. Cupid* (1853).

Dramatic satire upon wealth was hardly peculiar to the Victorians, and Jerrold's obvious anger in *The Golden Calf* is rather generalized. More particular in the sense of an immediate social context is the satire in Dion Boucicault's *The School for Scheming* (1847). Here all the plot lines develop the central idea of what people will do to attain position and fortune and whom they will sacrifice in order to achieve them. The aristocratic Claude Plantagenet schemes to escape his debts by marrying the seemingly wealthy Mrs. Fox-French, the headmistress of a finishing school that teaches girls the social arts necessary to ensnare rich and titled husbands, and she marries him for the same reasons. Each is actually ruined and trying to cheat the other; the mutual deception is revealed in an excellent and bitter scene conducted while the bailiffs wait offstage. Plantagenet's daughter Helen, dazzled by wealth and the prospect of a title, and callously manipulated by her father, rejects the man she really loves but in her turn is rejected by the aristocrats she pursues. Like Evelyn in *Money* and Chrystal in *The Golden Calf*, the mysterious Sykes, who finally reveals himself as the father of Helen's unsuccessful suitor, acts as chorus and comments savagely on the ways of the world.[1] The most interesting character in the play is the low-comedy Perkins, who assumes the name of The Macdunnum. He schemes feverishly to be a wealthy capitalist, floats companies, raises stock, apes the aristocracy, is exposed and ruined. 'Commerce' and 'progress' are the keynotes of this part of the play. The Macdunnum has an exchange on these topics with the girl who loves him but whom he discards after obtaining temporary wealth.

MACDUNNUM. This is the age of iron and locomotion.
SALLY. Say rather the age of paper and arrest.
MACDUNNUM. When England's aristocracy are ennobling her enterprise, making speculation fashionable.
SALLY. And England's merchants enriching her Gazette, making bankruptcy respectable.
MACDUNNUM. Oh, Sally! What a definition of our commercial progress!

Early in the play, The Macdunnum, bewildered by the web of pretence and speculation thickening around him, doubts the reality of existence:

There's no reality anywhere—the very age is electro-plated—figures on the top—humbug underneath. . . . It is the same everywhere—all unreal. Facts exist no more—they have dwindled into names—things have shrunk into words—words into air—cash into figures—reputation into nothing. This is the reign of NOTHING: to possess it is the surest foundation of fortune in every walk of life. Examine the pocket of the capitalist—*nothing*! Penetrate the skull of the politician—*nothing*! Value the credit of a free and enlightened state—*nothing*, or your own—*nothing*! Thus ridiculed, despised, calumniated, *nothing* is the philosopher's stone of our age; it turns all it touches into gold—to fame—to beauty—and all the other cardinal virtues. Scepticism is our faith, and this is our creed—trust a stranger never; your friend when you cannot help it, and yourself as little as possible. Even seeing is no longer believing.

Were it not for its fifth act, *The School for Scheming* would be one of the century's best comedies, but it collapses in a welter of improbable reconciliations and reunions, sudden financial windfalls, and platitudinous sentimentalizing. Boucicault was

---

[1] The drama of the day had a fondness for the protective fairy godfather, like Chrystal and Sykes, who makes everything come right in the end.

either unable or unwilling (given the demands of the conventional happy ending) to work out his plot in terms of the irony and satirical strength of the first four acts.

Despite these flaws, *The School for Scheming* is a significant comedy, and indeed Boucicault's only one. *Alma Mater* (1842) and *Old Heads and Young Hearts* (1844) have nothing to say. The former belongs to that class of nineteenth-century comedy eschewing any serious matter, and presents an Oxford in which drinking, racing, and love-making are the only approved occupations of university students. The play is full of faded character types of an older comedy and is extremely trivial in plot. The love entanglements of *Old Heads and Young Hearts* are complicated to the point of incoherence. Here again are the familiar marks of Boucicault's determined attempts to write legitimate comedies: bustling plot activity of little consequence, excessive dependence on eccentric characterization, forced plays of wit, and a generous sprinkling of strained metaphors and similes. His best-known comedy, *London Assurance* (1841), looks back rather than forward, and has nothing in it of the new age except surface manners and dress. The general rattle and bustle, the gulled fop who ends as a moralist, the laboured rhetoric, the fundamental decency, goodness, and kindness of its principal characters—these qualities place *London Assurance* at the end of the eighteenth century rather than in the middle of the nineteenth. In any case, Boucicault's métier was not comedy but romantic drama and Irish melodrama with strong comic elements, and he did not find it until the 1850s and 1860s.

The materialism of the age, its social ambition and self-seeking drive towards status, wealth, and privilege, are topics not really explored in pre-Victorian comedy. The Victorians explored them at some length, and they also brought to comedy a strong sense of class and a militancy about class that was not there before. *Money* and Tom Taylor's *New Men and Old Acres* (1869) dramatize such subject-matter, which also occurs in many plays of about this period. The ridiculousness of Daniel Dowlas, chandler, trying to be Lord Duberly, and the folly of his son's imitation of a man of fashion are ridiculed in Colman's *The Heir-at-Law*; in Knowles's *The Beggar of Bethnal Green* and *Old Maids* social-climbing sons are rewarded for their efforts by being duped into marrying servants. However, an acute class-consciousness, the theme of social ambition in a clearly defined class situation, and hostility to members of a lower order pressing upwards by means deemed vulgar, became common only in Victorian comedy.

In *Quid Pro Quo* a retired stationer, foolishly enamoured of the aristocracy, aspires to a seat in Parliament and a baronetcy; the Earl whom he so greatly admires dreams of a Garter and hypocritically spouts radical sentiments in support of his election interest. Both characters are satirically conceived, but the weight of condemnation falls more heavily on the former. The characters of Jerrold's *Retired from Business* (1851), set in the village of Pumpkinfield, include the Pennyweight family. Mrs. Pennyweight, the wife of a prosperous retired greengrocer who can see nothing wrong with his former trade, re-names the family Fitzpennyweight and changes the name of Candlemas Cottage to Torchlight Lodge, redecorating in the gaudiest *nouveau-riche* taste to the amazement of her husband. At all costs, she tells him, the secret of his trade must be kept from the village, for it is a terrible thing to have been a grocer. The neighbours begin to call, and Mrs. Fitzpennyweight, aided by Puffins, a snobbish retired Russia merchant, sorts out those who are socially acceptable from those who are not:

PUFFINS. To be plain. In Pumpkinfield, the gentry of previous whole-sale life do not associate with individuals of former retail existence. The counting-house knows not the shop. The wholesale merchant never crosses the till. . . . Thus, in Pumpkinfield, there is what we call the billers and the tillers; or, in a fuller word, the billocracy and the tillocracy. . .

PENNYWEIGHT. And wholesales don't mix with retails? I think I see. Raw wool doesn't speak to halfpenny ball of worsted—tallow in the cask looks down upon sixes to the pound, and pig iron turns up its nose at twopenny nails.

Both Puffins and his friend Creepmouse, a retired army tailor, try with disastrous results to save their children for marriages with rank, and they look down contemptuously upon neighbours like the good-hearted Jubilee, a retired pawnbroker. The Puffins doctrine is exploded, but unfortunately the social promise of Act I evaporates in later acts. Instead of developing the interesting ideas he begins with, Jerrold abandons them to concentrate upon a series of love affairs among the younger generation of Pumpkinfield; thus the play peters out disappointingly, with love conveniently solving class problems.

Pennyweight's clash with his wife points to another major theme of mid-century comedy: the domestic ideal and the proper relationship between wife and husband. The text for this dramatic sermon could be taken fron the pious utterance of a character in Edmund Falconer's *Extremes* (1858): 'Marriage is at once the most solemn and the most beautiful mystery of this life; and as among nations a reverence for its sacredness, as an indissoluble, an intransgressible bond between two beings, and *only* two, is the highest test of civilization, so the nobler the estimate individual man or woman forms of its obligations, the higher must each be lifted in the scale of humanity.' 'Do you not believe me?' he asks, and the woman replies, 'I do, I do, with all my heart and soul.' On both the comic and serious levels Victorian comedy worked out the secular implications of this speech, dwelling especially upon the marital obligations of the wife as well as enumerating her ideal attributes. *Masks and Faces* (1852), by Tom Taylor and Charles Reade, shows two women in sharp contrast: the gay, careless, immoral, generous Peg Woffington and the simple, timid, domestic Mabel Vane, newly married to a man infatuated with Woffington. The underlying pattern of the play is melodramatic, with a comic man in the distressed poet and painter Triplet, a suffering heroine in Mabel Vane, and a villain in the aristocrat Sir Charles Pomander, who pursues her. Woffington is the female lead, and with her wit, charm, and bubbling personality she easily captures masculine attention. But there is no doubt that Mabel Vane is meant to be the true heroine and that the audience saw her as one. Woffington in fact regards Mabel as her personal ideal and renounces Mabel's husband, telling her, 'Angel of truth and goodness, you have conquered.'[1] Another ideal wife is Mrs. Fitzherbert in Taylor's *Victims* (1857)· devoted and hardworking, she earns just enough money by dressmaking to pay for the idle pleasures of a husband who aspires to literary fame, treats her indifferently, and even refuses to acknowledge her as

---

[1] The view of eighteenth-century actors taken by *Masks and Faces* is thoroughly sentimental: Cibber, Quin, and Mrs. Clive are basically decent and good-hearted, and Woffiington is a fairy princess who pours money and food into the household of the penurious Triplet.

his wife in case it should damage his literary reputation for bohemianism. She is clearly intended as a contrast to the affected Mrs. Merryweather, who keeps a salon and neglects her husband so badly that he cannot get a decent breakfast in his own house. The ideal woman of a later comedy by J. S. Coyne, *The Woman of the World* (1868), is not the ambitious, intellectual, and brilliant Mrs. Eddystone of the first act, but the tender, gentle Mrs. Eddystone of the last, who now occupies herself with charities and dotes over a cradle.[1] She then accepts the hero, and the implications are that she has not been enough of a true woman to be worthy of him before.

Conflicts that arise in marriage are nearly always resolved in favour of the husband. The amiable City merchant in *Victims*, Merryweather, with his decent middle-class values, is the norm and anchor of sanity in a crazy world of literary and intellectual affectation. At the end of the play his values are triumphant, the outside forces that create domestic discord are in retreat, and the wife comes to her senses. Coyne's *My Wife's Daughter* (1850) begins interestingly with the struggle of a gay man-about-town of twenty-eight, newly married to a widow of forty, to adjust himself to a quiet domestic existence; once again this promising theme is not sufficiently developed. The wife, over-fond, jealous, and short-tempered, eventually perceives her folly (all the fault is on her side) and begs her husband's pardon:

MRS. ORMONDE. For this I have been justly punished—for this behold me humble and penitent—[*About to kneel.*]

ORMONDE. Not there, dear Marion! But here in my bosom! [*Raises and embraces her.*] The storm raised by your jealous fears is past; the heavens smile again upon us.

MRS. ORMONDE. Oh, joy, joy! Dear Arthur, am I forgiven—my errors and your wrongs—forgiven?

ORMONDE. Aye, all forgiven, and forgotten, in this kiss. [*Kisses her.*]

One of the most triumphant assertions of a husband's superiority and authority comes in Taylor's *Still Waters Run*

---

[1] Running parallel to the sentimental idealism of the play is a good vein of comedy. The first act begins with a dramatist reading his latest work to a company that has fallen asleep on him, and in one purely farcical scene there is much hiding behind screens and in cupboards and smashing of china; three men successively conceal themselves in Mrs. Eddystone's bathroom, with resultant uproar.

Deep (1855), another of those Victorian plays that were entitled comedies but in which comic elements are subordinated to serious ones. The quiet Mildmay, a retired businessman, allows himself to be dominated by his wife and her aunt because he values domestic peace. They treat him with open contempt and admire the dashing Captain Hawksley, who has been the aunt's lover and now pursues Mildmay's wife. Mildmay proves himself when he confounds Hawksley's scheme to sell the family shares in a fraudulent company, forces Hawksley to return private letters with which he was blackmailing the aunt, outfaces him courageously when he demands a duel, and has him arrested for forgery. This demonstration of power in the world of men and business, together with the sudden assertion of Mildmay's domestic rights, ensures absolute submission on the part of his womenfolk. He tells the repentant aunt, 'You shall never find me wanting in duty and respect, but from this day forth, remember, there's only one master in this house, and his name is John Mildmay.' His wife receives similar treatment:

MILDMAY. Trust to me, henceforth, to make you what a wife should be. I should prefer to win you by a lover's tenderness, but if I cannot do that I know how to make a husband's rights respected.

MRS. MILDMAY. Oh, thank you, dearest, thank you—tell me of my faults—I will try to correct them. I will honour and obey you, as a wife should.

The advantages of the simple, domestically minded girl over the sophisticated (meaning unfeminine) woman as a marriage partner are considered unassailable in Victorian comedy, and a further advantage is obtained if the girl is from the country.[1] The contrast between rural virtue and aristocratic vice is familiar in melodrama, and the emotional intensity with which the village heroine is depicted is a consecration of ideal feminine virtues as well as a dream exercise in nostalgic recreation for urban audiences of rural origins. This contrast is incidental in many comedies of the Colman–Reynolds school, but Taylor's *An Unequal Match* (1857) is constructed around it. In Act I, set in a Yorkshire dale, Arncliffe confirms his proposal to Hester

---

[1] A rural setting is not essential for the expression of this theme. For instance, the superiority in simplicity and femininity of Mabel Vane over Peg Woffington, of Mrs. Fitzherbert over Mrs. Merryweather, and of the later Mrs. Eddystone over the earlier Mrs. Eddystone, is demonstrated in a London setting.

Glazebrook, daughter of a blacksmith, despite the news that he has inherited wealth and a baronetcy. In Act II the newly married couple are in Arncliffe's Hampshire home, and the baronet, all memories of his country idyll extinguished, despairs of his wife's unaffected simplicities and rural enthusiasms (she rises at five in the morning to help with the harvest). In a house full of sneering aristocratic guests he is further embarrassed by a visit from her father. Hester is contrasted with the elegant and sophisticated Mrs. Montressor, whom Arncliffe had courted before his marriage and now begins to admire again. He lectures his wife on proper social conduct:

ARNCLIFFE. You must learn to repress your feelings when they are out of keeping with the tone of society, to trifle where you wish to be serious, to smile when a frown would better express your real sentiments, to be tolerant of bores and civil to rivals, to accept light attentions lightly, to forget your early life and its associations; in a word, to fit yourself for the artificial world in which my position now places you.

HESTER. In short, to be no longer the Hester you loved in Glaizedale, but a different and—forgive me, Harry, if I say—not a better woman.

Shortly after delivering this homily, Arncliffe follows Mrs. Montressor to Ems; there he discovers that he abhors the fashionable tedium of spa life and yearns for his wife's sweet innocence and unspoilt simplicity, rejecting the cold artificiality he finds around him. Hester arrives in Ems, pretends to have reformed her character, and poses as a woman of the world— insincere, coquettish, artificial—the very person Arncliffe urged her to be in Act II. Horrified by this change, he learns his lesson and gets his values right by the time Hester undeceives him and the play ends.

Another comedy dealing with the same theme is Falconer's *Extremes*, a popular and successful piece in its day. Here the innate virtue of Frank Hawthorne, of humble Lancashire origins (a character full of lengthy moral precepts and ringing sentiments), together with the rustic simplicity and honesty—despite the comedy of their dress and dialect—of the Wildbriar family, are favourably contrasted with the affected and cynical behaviour of the members of Society present in the elegant country house that is the setting of the play. The heroine Lucy tries to discourage Frank by pretending to be frivolous and unkind, but fails to carry it through because frivolity and unkindness are not part of her real feminine self. At one point Frank, rebuking Jenny Wildbriar for insincere flirting, says, 'Cousin of mine, that is not the pulse of the honest unsophisticated heart of girlhood as it should beat in the breast of an English farmer's daughter.'

Contrasts between simplicity and artificiality are also found in *All That Glitters Is Not Gold* (1851), by John Maddison Morton and Thomas Morton Jr. The setting is the master's house and cotton-spinning factory in Bristol. The master, Joseph Plum, has two sons. Frederick, the younger, has been well educated and socially polished; a marriage is arranged with his like, Valeria. The elder son Stephen, blunt and workmanlike, sticks to the factory and loves Martha, one of the work-girls. The contrasts are between the virtuous, devoted Martha and the refined but morally weak Valeria on the one hand, and the gentlemanly but ineffectual Frederick and the rough, hard-working Stephen on the other. Plum is torn between the two worlds these characters represent. The comedy of the first act changes to pure melodrama in the second: by compromising herself Martha saves Valeria from seduction by an aristocratic villain and is involved in intensely emotional scenes in which she demonstrates heroic virtue. Superficial plot complications again obscure the original themes, which quite disappear from view.

The comedy in which there are strong dramatic elements is the predominant kind of nineteenth-century comedy. The intensity of these elements and the importance attached to them in the general context of plot structure, characterization, and thematic material, is a matter of degree and varies widely. A minority of comedies have nothing or very little that is serious about them, such as *Exchange No Robbery*, *The Beulah Spa*, and *London Assurance*. A nineteenth-century play can be termed a comedy, I believe, when the pathetic and potentially tragic, or melodramatic elements do not overwhelm the comic and are kept at least in equal balance with them. *John Bull* and *Money* are rightly 'comedies', then, but *Still Waters Run Deep* and *All That Glitters Is Not Gold* are not, at least not by this rule-of-thumb definition. These two and others like them have been discussed here because their authors or publishers called them comedies, and it is difficult to ignore contemporary terminology. Nineteenth-century dramatic nomenclature was, however, imprecise and constantly changing; the subject-matter of the 'melodrama', the 'drama', the 'comedy', and the 'farce' was extraordinarily eclectic; and to formulate *genre* definitions rather than describe and characterize dramatic trends is almost impossible.

Perhaps enough has already been said to demonstrate the emotional and situational range of nineteenth-century comedy, but one further example may illustrate this range and the problem of framing definitions. R. B. Peake's *The Title Deeds*, performed at the Adelphi in 1847, is called a comedy on the title-page of all editions. It is set in the London and Somerset of the present day. Morant, the senior partner of Fustic, Morant, and Fustic, on his way to the docks to redeem the failing fortunes of the firm in the West Indies, leaves a box containing bags of sovereigns and title deeds to a valuable West Indian estate in the hackney carriage of Humphrey Haywhisp. The Haywhisp family (father, young wife, children, old mother), struggling desperately against poverty, keep quiet about their find and buy a house in Somerset. The involved and incident-packed plot concerns four main actions: the Haywhisps' growing guilt about the money, the dissipation and gambling debts of sporting Philip Fustic (old Fustic's nephew), old Fustic's efforts to arrange a match for his two sons with the daughters of Mrs. Evergay (to whom he is markedly attentive), and the search for the important title deeds after Morant returns from the West Indies. All the characters rally round old Fustic when he is arrested for his nephew's debts; Haywhisp comes clean about the box containing the deeds, which is at last found in the ruins of Glastonbury Abbey where the demented old mother had secretly buried it by moonlight; Philip Fustic renounces his past life; and all ends happily. Three of the plot lines are strongly melodramatic, and the emotional potential of a bad conscience, guilt, remorse, bankruptcy, and ruin is fully exploited. On the other hand, Haywhisp's crony Peter Hush is a low-comedy part, and Haywhisp himself is involved in low-comedy scenes, including an extremely comic meal at an inn where a sporting gentleman, Turfy Goodwood (another low comedian), misunderstands the conversation of Haywhisp and

Hush at table and believes that they are desperate villains scheming to murder him. A second level of more delicate comedy exists in the interplay between old Fustic and Mrs. Evergay, and a third, rather more farcical, in the arrival of Fustic's sons from Jamaica, who, to the horror of the ladies, are coloured.

Thus *The Title Deeds* could either be termed a comedy with strong dramatic components or a drama with strong comic components; distinctions of *genre* are meaningless. One must also remember that the play was written for an Adelphi audience, whose tastes inclined more to farce and sensationalism than did the tastes of, for example, the Haymarket audience for whom Taylor wrote the relatively upper middle-class *An Unequal Match*. The part of Humphrey Haywhisp was played by O. Smith, a melodramatic actor of some repute, whereas Hush and Goodwood were performed by the Adelphi's great low comedians, Wright and Bedford. The size of a low-comedy part in the text—Goodwood's, for instance, is fairly small—was often no indication of its stage prominence in the hands of an accomplished comedian. Purely theatrical factors are therefore also essential in a careful determination of the character of a nineteenth-century comedy: we must take into account the theatre at which it was played, the audience of that theatre, and the actors in the piece. An examination of this kind will go far to explain the variety and breadth of comic material and style.

From the vantage point of the 1860s one could look back at the evolution of comedy and trace a continuous line of thematic and stylistic development stretching from Colman to Robertson; a similar line can be perceived in the development of theatre itself and in conventions of staging, acting, furnishing, costuming, and lighting. There is no need to stop at the 1860s; in 1900 the same observations could be made of a whole century's growth and change in both drama and theatre. Thus it is necessary to place the comedies of Tom Robertson in proper perspective, and briefly to consider the generally held view that in combination with the stagecraft that presented them these comedies were really the beginnings of the modern theatre, that Robertson himself was 'first in time among the dramatic writers of the present'.[1]

Essentially what Robertson did was to use the theme

[1] Allardyce Nicoll, *A History of English Drama*, 2nd edn. (1959), v. 131.

material and some aspects of his predecessors' dramatic technique, and employing them in a style distinctively his own gave unique satisfaction to a large middle-class audience whose theatrical taste he had correctly analysed. He was certainly fortunate to discover Marie Wilton and the Bancroft company, and they were fortunate to discover him. Although he was not paid munificently, he did better financially than any other dramatist of the sixties except Boucicault and possibly F. C. Burnand; in their turn the Bancrofts, after twenty years' management at the Prince of Wales's and the Haymarket, retired in 1885 with a net profit of £180,000.[1] A great deal of this amount was realized from the comedies of Robertson, and its size is hard proof of Robertson's popularity during these twenty years. In fact the Bancrofts gave nearly 3,000 performances of his plays, 800 of *School* alone;[2] an average of 150 performances a year for the period of their management.

In his first comedy—excluding *David Garrick* (1864), which is more drama than comedy—to achieve prominence, and the first to be staged by the Bancrofts, *Society* (1865), one notices the familiar preoccupations of Victorian dramatists. The poor but well-born Sidney Daryl is contrasted with the vulgar *nouveau-riche* Chodd Jr., who is trying to buy his way into Society. Despite the obviousness of the satire, the scenes involving the Chodds are excellently conceived. The younger Chodd tells Daryl how he intends to get on in the world:

CHODD JUNIOR. The present age is—as you are aware—a practical age. I come to the point—it's my way. Capital commands the world. The capitalist commands capital; therefore the capitalist commands the world.

SIDNEY. But you don't quite command the world, do you?

CHODD JUNIOR. Practically I do. I wish for the highest honours—I bring out my cheque-book. I want to go into the House of Commons —cheque-book. I want the best legal opinion in the House of Lords —cheque-book. The best house—cheque-book. The best friends, the best wife, the best-trained children—cheque-book, cheque-book, and cheque-book.

---

[1] Squire and Marie Bancroft, *The Bancrofts* (1909), p. 275.
[2] Squire and Marie Bancroft, *Mr. and Mrs. Bancroft On and Off the Stage*, 4th edn. (1888), ii. 409.

SIDNEY. You mean to say with money you can purchase anything?

CHODD JUNIOR. Exactly. This life is a matter of bargain.[1]

Daryl and Chodd Jr. are rivals for Maud Hetherington, whose aunt, the snobbish Lady Ptarmigant, tries to push her into a marriage with the moneyed Chodd. Finally Daryl defeats Chodd in an election campaign in the former's family seat, inherits a baronetcy and a fortune, and is accepted by Maud and Lady Ptarmigant. What is conventional in *Society* is the concern with money, the satirical treatment of the foolish aristocrat and the vulgar rich, the reliance on eccentric comedy (in the person of Lord Ptarmigant, who dozes in a chair where others trip over him), the heavy drama—Daryl's wild despair when Maud initially rejects him—and the clumsy plot, in which the author can think of no better reason for Maud to refuse Daryl than her believing that a little child for whom Daryl is caring is his illegitimate daughter. After the fashion of these plots she never questions him about the child; even more incredibly the little girl is actually the child of Lady Ptarmigant's dead son. One feels that Robertson hedges his bets: Daryl does not win Lady Ptarmigant's and Maud's consent because he is a good man and now clear of suspicion on the child's account, but largely because he has just inherited wealth and a baronetcy by the convenient last-minute death of his brother. Values based solely upon fortune, property, and birth are satirized, but at the end of the play it just so happens that Daryl possesses all three. What is new is the delicate restraint of a quiet, gentle, simple love scene—Robertson never wrote a better—between Maud and Daryl in a London square at twilight, the genuine humour of a scene in a bohemian literary club, and the economy of the dialogue in those portions of the play not given over to intense emotion (Robertson could pen as purple a passage of prose as anybody if he had occasion to). From the evidence of *Society*, Robertson's strength as a dramatist lay in satire, light and unforced comedy, the depiction of mild eccentricity, the small quiet moments of human contact, and the gentle sentimentalism of deepening love. In later plays these remained his strengths and were part of his distinctive contribution to comedy. In other

---

[1] Digby Grant's 'little cheque' speech concluding the first act of Albery's *Two Roses* is surely inspired by the words of Chodd Jr.

areas, where he exceeded the relatively narrow limits of his talents, he could be a very indifferent dramatist. Unfortunately, he too often strayed from what he could do best.

Robertson's next comedy, *Ours* (1866), has an even weaker plot than *Society*, and a quite incredible serious sub-plot in which a wife believes that her husband is giving money to a mistress whereas he has actually been protecting her cheque-forging brother, who never appears in the play, from the consequence of his crime. Robertson makes his first use of a love scene with two couples in which the dialogue is contrapuntal. All the characters turn up in the Crimea in the last act (Robertson was always a patriot), which develops around the domestic and comic use of food: the heroine makes a roly-poly pudding on stage while the mutton roasts, and we see in use or hear dis-cussed anchovies, bacon, marmalade, vegetables, sweets, game, flour, roasting, baking, boiling, and stewing. The play ends with the characters sitting down to eat what has been prepared. Thus the author ingeniously reduces the Crimean War to the proportions of a back parlour high tea; the domestication of the serious and dramatic could hardly go further.

Caste (1867) may also be analysed in terms of what preceded it; the merit of the play lies in the ability with which Robertson utilized familiar material and in the superiority of the result to so much comedy that attempted more or less the same kind of thing. The use of eccentricity and aberration is more apparent than in *Society* and *Ours*: Eccles, the Marquise, and to a lesser extent Hawtree provide this kind of humour. Amusement is again derived from the preparation and eating of food, and Sam and Polly indulge in much traditional and unrefined low-comedy business. Sam is also the man of commerce on the way up (though not, for the comfort of the Prince of Wales's audience, too far up), embodying as he does the ethic of hard work and 'go'; 'whatever's commercial is right', he says. In contrast the drunken Eccles—a splendid comic creation, perhaps the greatest in nineteenth-century drama—commands no respect because he does *not* work, and social agitation is ridiculous on his lips. The play is not in the least democratic and completely supports the *status quo*; the clash between classes is merely comic when the only militant representative of the lower orders is Eccles and the only standard-bearer of the aristocracy is the Marquise. From the moment that the relationship between George and Esther begins to operate on the emotional and pathetic level rather than the comic, and when it is isolated from the contrapuntal, undercutting comedy of Sam and Polly, Robertson in treating this relationship becomes almost indistinguishable from many a poorer playwright. It is worth noting that the heroine is the serious mother rather than the jolly actress full of life (the resemblance to *Masks and Faces* is close). Esther is the standard feminine ideal of nineteenth-century drama; she tells the Marquise, presumably in climactic order, 'I am a woman—I am a wife—a widow—a mother!'

After *Caste* Robertson's work deteriorated, and the narrowness of his achievement is more noticeable. *Play* (1868) is enfeebled by awkward misunderstandings and coincidental eavesdropping; away from an English domestic setting (the play is located in a German spa) Robertson seems uncomfortable, and unsure of himself in an attempt to be more romantic than usual. In obtaining strong curtains, a tradition Robertson found it hard to break away from, he repeatedly used tired, conventional stage business of a kind illustrated by the following example, where the deserted wife faints into the arms of the hero, thus precipitating a major misunderstanding with the heroine, Rosie:

Enter AMANDA *through arch, a smelling bottle in her hand, and almost falling.*

AMANDA. I understand all now! He loves another! I watched him; his looks, his manner, all confirm it! And she seems a mere child! Oh, why did I come hither?

[*Falls fainting on a stone seat.*

Enter PRICE, *by arch.*

PRICE. I left the lozenges somewhere here, and Rosie wants one. [*Sees* AMANDA.] Eh! What's this?

[AMANDA *reels backward and falls fainting into his arms.* MRS. KINPECK *sees all this from her perch, and gesticulates with her parasol to those above and below her.*

Enter FANQUEHERE, ROSIE, BROWNE, *and* TODDER, *from different points, to form picture.*

Eccentric comedy, in the persons of a peppery old gambler and a Prussian officer who can speak only one sentence of English, is much in evidence, and once again we find the vulgar and satirically treated *nouveau-riche* in Bodmin Todder of Todder's Original Patent Starch; once again, also, the juxtaposition of a sentimental love scene with a noisy quarrelsome one.

The faults of the Robertson style are magnified in *School* (1869), and it is a tribute to the Bancrofts that they made the play so popular in spite of their material. The plot concerns the love affairs of Bella and Naomi,[1] two girls in Dr. Sutcliffe's Academy, with Lord Beaufoy and Jack Poyntz. Because of its setting the *dramatis personae* include a large number of young girls, who are idealized *en masse* in a dreamy fantasy of English womanhood.[2] The langorous femininity of *School* and the utter fatuity of the young men give the love scenes, which are nevertheless written with some charm and skill, a sickly sweetness previously incipient in Robertson's sentimentality but now openly emergent. They can be compared unfavourably with the scene between Maud and Daryl in the first act of *Society*. It seems that, unable to develop as a dramatist after *Caste*, Robertson simply repeated himself; what was originally delicate and subtle coarsened through unvaried use.

Progress (1869) is thematically more significant than *School*, and begins promisingly. In Act I there is a confrontation between Arthur, son of Lord Mompesson, and Ferne, a railway engineer who has come to Mompesson Abbey to plan its demolition in order to make way for a railway and station. Arthur, the aristocratic traditionalist, stands for the old order and condemns 'progress':

That is the modern slang for the destruction of everything high and

---

[1] Clearly Mrs. Bancroft's playing of Naomi, her best-known and most popular Robertson part, was fundamentally escapist and idealist in appeal, in keeping with the author's conception of the character: 'The artless simplicity and sunny nature of "Nummy", the utter ignorance of the existence of any sadness in the whole world except what school discipline enforces, her fearless and open avowal of her romantic adoration for Jack Poyntz, make her a lovable thing. . . It was a delight to act Naomi Tighe; she is as fresh as country butter, and every word she utters breathes the unladen atmosphere of a bright, green spot "far from the madding crowd".' (*Mr. and Mrs. Bancroft On and Off the Stage*, ii. 413.)

[2] *School* concludes with an apostrophe to the 'true lady' as Dr. Sutcliffe and the eccentric old Farintosh sum up between them her qualities. They make an interesting list: 'nobility of feeling', 'a kind heart', 'a noble mind', 'modesty', 'gentleness', 'courage', 'truthfulness', 'birth', 'breeding', and—'above all'— 'School'. This arrangement of ending a play with the consecutive enumeration of necessary qualities of character is taken directly from *Money*.

noble, and the substitution of everything base and degrading. . . .
Horses, which in my youth were considered noble animals, are
abolished for engines that smash, for trains that smash, for velocipedes
that smash; and the débris of broken wheels, boilers, bones, and shat-
tered human beings, you call progress! . . . As to manners, progress
has indeed altered them. Everyone is much too occupied to think, to
feel, to love, or to improve. Progress does not permit sleep, or sentiment, or accomplishment, or leisure. . . . Nowadays you eat rapidly,
you drink rapidly, you make love rapidly, you marry rapidly, you go
through the Divorce Court still more rapidly. Luxury everywhere,
comfort nowhere.

Ferne replies with his *credo*:

We have changed from the worst to the better—we are changing still,
from bad to best; and during this transition I am proud to know that
it is I—the engineer, the motive-power—who leads the way. 'Tis
I who bring industry, invention, and capital together; 'tis I who
introduce demand to supply. 'Tis I who give the word—'tis I who
direct the train that flies over valleys, through mountains, across
rivers—that dominates the mighty Alps themselves. 'Tis I—the
engineer—who exchanges the wealth of one country against the
poverty of another. I am broad, breathing humanity, that whirls
through the air on wings of smoke to a brighter future. I spread
civilisation wherever I sit a-straddle of my steed of vapour, whom I
guide with reins of iron and feed with flames. As for the tumbledown
old ruins I knock down in passing, what matter? Where I halt towns
rise and cities spring up into being. 'Tis the train that is the master
of the hour. As it moves it shrieks out to the dull ear of prejudice,
'Make room for me! I must pass and I will, and those who dare oppose
my progress shall be crushed!' Its tail of smoke is like the plume of
a field-marshal; and the rattle and motion of its wheels are as the
throb and pulsations of the progress of the whole world.

After the first act, however, there is little reference to the theme
of progress. Arthur returns from London, having saved the
Abbey from the railway but enthusiastic about the new joys
of travelling by rail, wearing new clothes, and ordering new
furniture. His niece Eva falls very ill and he curses because he
cannot quickly obtain a medical consultant, since he has been all
too successful in banishing the nearest railway and telegraph
station to a distance of sixteen miles from the Abbey. The plot
becomes involved with the ups and downs of Ferne's love affair
with Eva, and by the end of the play 'progress' merely means the

attainment of individual happiness. Eva says, 'My path must lead to happiness when love and hope conduct me, and affection and experience guide me—[*Smiling.*] that's Progress!' Prominent among the characters are the Bunnythornes, vulgarian father and tippling son; old Bunnythorne comically upholds traditional values. Robertson's predilection for melodramatic effect is again evident, notably at the Act II curtain when the ailing, lovesick Eva tries to kill herself by rushing out into the freezing wind and snow, and is carried fainting inside.

This tendency to heavy drama overwhelms *Birth* (1870), nominally a comedy, and like *Progress* not acted by the Bancrofts. The theme is class antagonism between the proud Earl of Eagleclyffe and the factory owner Paul Hewitt, whose works are contiguous to the Earl's estate. The Earl has been forced to sell his estate to Hewitt, piece by piece, until he is entirely dispossessed and Hewitt moves into the castle. Once again potential significance of theme is frittered away after the first act in trivial love complications and irrelevant melodramatic incidents. The author evades a real development of his theme by patching up the whole affair with an engagement between Hewitt and the Earl's sister and another between the Earl and Hewitt's sister. *M.P.* (1870), Robertson's last comedy to be performed by the Bancrofts, is also taken up by two love affairs. As in *School* there is a moonlight scene for two couples, but the love scenes between the Quaker girl Ruth and Chudleigh Dunscombe are feebly trivial and enervatingly sentimental. Again the well-bred gentleman defeats the *nouveau-riche* schemer; this time the schemer is a villain rather than a vulgar fool.

Robertson's success in adapting his drama to the taste of his middle-class audience, and the Bancrofts' skill in working with their playwright to find a performance style that exactly suited his comedies, reveals much about the plays themselves. Writing of *Society*, Bancroft said that Robertson 'rendered a public service by proving that the refined and educated classes were as ready as ever to crowd the playhouses, provided only that the entertainment given there was suited to their sympathies and tastes. . . . The return to Nature was the great need of the stage, and happily he came to help supply it at the right moment.'[1] The smallness of the Prince of Wales's was a great

1 *The Bancrofts*, p. 83.

advantage in the cultivation of an intimate, controlled acting style that so satisfactorily provided the illusion of domestic realism and a 'return to Nature'. Dutton Cook commented on the first presentation of *School*:

A story gains in strength and significance by being brought so close to the view of the spectators; and the players are not constrained to unnatural shouting and grimacing in order that their speeches may be heard and the expression of their faces seen from the distant portions of the house. Both author and actors are thus enabled to avoid the exaggeration of language and manner which has long been a prominent failing in dramatic writing and representation.[1]

Writing in 1881, Henry James remembered the Prince of Wales's as 'a little theatre':

The pieces produced there dealt mainly in little things—presupposing a great many chairs and tables, carpets, curtains, and knicknacks, and an audience placed close to the stage. They might, for the most part, have been written by a cleverish visitor at a country house, and acted in the drawing-room by his fellow inmates. The comedies of the late Mr. Robertson were of this number, and these certainly are among the most diminutive experiments ever attempted in the drama . . . This gentleman's plays are infantile, and seem addressed to the comprehension of infants.[2]

Current critical opinion was much friendlier to Robertson than this, although there was some dissent, which grew in the 1880s and 1890s, from the general praise with which the comedies were received. 'Realism', 'truth', 'nature', and 'plausibility' were terms repeatedly used in this praise; there was a strong feeling that the comedies were a much-needed departure from contemporary practice, and critics quickly perceived how much Robertson was indebted to the Bancrofts and to the sizeable public ready and eager to support him.

After a perusal of Robertson's comedies one sees that he owed much more to previous dramatists than either his contemporaries or modern critics realized. His debt was in both theme and form. Wealth, the ideal woman, social ambition, the importance of privilege and birth, the aristocrat and the parvenu, the virtues of simplicity and domesticity—all this was inherited material.

---

[1] *Nights at the Play*, pp. 69–70. The Bancrofts' move to the larger Haymarket did not, however, adversely affect the popularity of Robertson's comedies.

[2] 'The London Theatres', *Scribner's Monthly*, xxi (January 1881), 363–4.

Similarly, the reliance on eccentric and even low comedy, the mingling of the intensely pathetic and serious with the lightly comic,[1] the recurrence of stumbling and often unbelievable plots, the pervasive sentimentalism—these too were familiar aspects of comic technique before the 1860s. One tends to forget that before he became prominent as an author of comedies Robertson had a long apprenticeship in melodrama and farce (his first play was performed in 1845, twenty years before *Society*), and even after fame reached him he continued to write lurid melodramas such as *The Nightingale* (1870); it was easy for him in his comedies to slip into traditionally melodramatic ways—and he did.

It is my opinion, then, that Robertson confirmed existing trends rather than created new ones, that his comedies represented the exhaustion of an established tradition of writing rather than a new approach to comedy. In comparison with the greatly varied, vigorous, and inventive comedy of his contemporary Taylor, Robertson's plays lack blood and spine. The erratic energy and bursting life of an older comedy was not Robertson's. Nevertheless, he was an important dramatist who made a most significant contribution to the development of nineteenth-century comedy, even though a large part of that contribution came already prepared to his hand. He had considerable talent in the creation of credible characters and dialogue, a genuine simplicity and freshness, and powers of restraint and economy—when he chose to exercise them. But much more important was his domestication of everything he touched; the romance, the rhetoric, the morality, the sentiment of nineteenth-century comedy became, in Charles Lamb's phrase, the 'fireside concerns' of Robertson. 'Domestic and commonplace, dealing only with the superficial phases of an over ripe civilisation, calling upon no great powers of genius in the actors, indeed, scarcely elevating them beyond the tame emotions of every-day existence' was the description H. Barton Baker applied to the theatre of Robertson.[2] The appeal of the domestic,

---

[1] Boucicault's well-known advice to Bancroft in 1868 that the public preferred broadly comic domestic drama, 'a sentimental, pathetic play, comically rendered' to pure comedy, could well describe Robertson's comedies, as Boucicault himself recognized. (*Mr. and Mrs. Bancroft On and Off the Stage*, i. 245–6.) But it was only what comic playwrights had been doing since the nineteenth century began.

[2] *Our Old Actors* (1878), ii. 370.

the appeal of the normal, the ordinary,[1] the quiet, the simple, the seemingly matter-of-fact, an appeal embodied in carefully chosen middle-class contexts; and attitudes, sentiments, and characters chosen with equal care for their attractiveness to middle-class sensibilities and homely but romantic ideals—this was the appeal that made Robertson so popular and the Bancrofts so rich. The results of Robertson's success in domestically taming and shrinking the content and scope of the older comedy was to impel comedy firmly in the direction of a commonplace domestic realism, a direction it has never entirely abandoned. After an uncertain interlude, the playwrights of the 1880s and 1890s strengthened and intensified this realism in better-made plot structures than Robertson could ever manage, and rooted it even more deeply in middle-class soil.

Robertson's influence on the comedy of the seventies was immediately evident. The only dramatist who stood quite apart from him and developed a different vein of comedy was Gilbert; on the other hand James Albery was a direct imitator. His first and best comedy, *Two Roses* (1870), carries Robertson's sentimental idealism to extreme lengths, and Albery's domestic romanticism is syrupy beyond anything seen before. The haughty but poor Digby Grant comes into a fortune, contemptuously pays off those who befriended him, and forbids his sweet and beautiful daughters Ida and Lotty (the two roses) to associate any more with their penurious young men, Wyatt and the sentimentally conceived Caleb Deecie, who is blind. Of course the girls continue to love them, and the old-fashioned dénouement employs melodramatic plot machinery: Deecie is discovered to be the lost heir to the fortune, and virtuous poverty is rewarded by beauty as well as riches. The first entrance of Lotty and Ida characterizes their appeal; they appear framed in a window counting roses: '*They smell first one, then the other, till at last they run their faces together, when they both laugh, throw their*

---

[1] For instance, when Hawtree in *Caste* says, 'I don't pretend to be a particularly good sort of fellow, nor a particularly bad sort of fellow. I suppose I'm about the average standard sort of thing', he must have gone right to the hearts of his audience. Naturally he is a sympathetic character, an ideal of quiet manliness, decency, good humour, and true friendship, a superior version of the mildly idiotic, eccentric 'swell' with a heart of gold who was so popular in the comedy of the seventies and eighties—the lineal descendant of the fops Lewis used to play at the turn of the century.

arms round each other's necks and kiss, then leave the window. . . .
The Girls come in, the bright light falling on them as they pause at
the door . . . both flushed with health.' Although Albery's sentimentalism is excessively sweet, it is skilfully counterpoised by
the richly comic figure of Digby Grant, simultaneously paternal,
tender, proud, hypocritical, posturing, and sybaritic. Low comedy
is present in Our Mr. Jenkins, a travelling salesman, and his
tyrannical wife.

The most prolific playwright of the decade was H. J. Byron,
who began to write in the fifties and had already achieved a
considerable reputation in extravaganza and burlesque. In the
1870s and 1880s he was the author of numerous comedies,
dramas, and farces; his output was so large and its quality so
generally poor that William Archer, a sworn enemy to Byron,
considered that 'he has done more than any other man to hinder
the development of a worthy modern drama in England, by
fostering a taste for frivolous and puerile work'.[1] Yet Byron
did attempt something more serious in several comedies, full
though they are of puns, jokes, and wildly improbable plots,
characters, and human relationships. Unlike Robertson, Byron
in these plays dealt with unhappily married couples rather than
sweet young lovers; he was not original in this, but such a shift
of focus became fundamental to the comedy of the 1890s.

In *Cyril's Success* (1868), a successful novelist and dramatist
pays little attention to his wife, and the well-written first act
vividly conveys her loneliness as she broods on being neglected,
her husband's preoccupation with writing and business, and the
tensions developing between them. After that, however, all is coincidence, unbelievable misunderstanding, and mistaken identity.
In *Partners for Life* (1871) a husband has separated from his wife
because he found his independence corrupted by her fortune. They
meet again and are reconciled. The play is of little interest,
but the ideal of home and hearth is strong even in their misery:

FANNY. I would rather lead a domestic life, if I had the opportunity
—the pleasant late dinner with the curtains closed and the gas
lighted—the music and the chat, and the cozy hour or two with
coffee, and one or two of my husband's old friends smoking a cigar
and talking of their old bachelor days—the calm pleasant close to
the long day; how charming is the picture if it could but be realized.

[1] *English Dramatists of To-day* (1882), p. 121.

TOM. [*Aside.*] By Jove, how true her words are! What a waste my life is. What are *my* evenings? Soda and brandy, and bitter thoughts.

Married in Haste (1876), more drama than comedy, is concerned with a young artist's jealousy of his wife's talent. Cut off by a rich uncle, Vere resorts to painting for his living; but his wife is the better painter and he will not permit her to sell her work. Since he has quarrelled with the only potential purchaser of his own paintings, the couple are reduced to poor circumstances and the wife leaves, partly because she cannot stand bickering and being in debt to tradesmen and partly because Vere has been keeping feminine company. In the last act Byron evades the issues in the credible and difficult domestic situation so far portrayed. The rich uncle buys the wife's paintings and is reconciled with his nephew, who has worked hard and attained success by being hung in the Royal Academy. Husband and wife are brought happily together again, and the problem of his artistic jealousy is left unresolved and unmentioned.

Even a comedy like the immensely popular *Our Boys* (1875), which ran for over four years, was built around contemporary thematic material, as well as absorbing large quantities of Robertsonian sentiment. Comic tension, slipshod and crude though the presentation is, arises from class hostility between the wealthy retired grocer Middlewick and the arrogant baronet Sir Geoffrey Champneys. Their sons, Charles and Talbot, have returned from a European tour together, and Sir Geoffrey designs Talbot for the heiress Violet Melrose. But Talbot loves poor Mary Melrose and Charles loves Violet. Middlewick will not let Charles marry Violet because she despises the butterman for his class. The sons defy their fathers and retreat to London, where they live together in humble lodgings; finally the fathers come after them and relent. Humour arises from the contrast between the extreme haughtiness of Sir Geoffrey and the profound cockney ignorance of Middlewick, as well as the effete foppishness of Sir Geoffrey's son. Middlewick, a fine comic creation, is innately noble and golden-hearted despite his ignorance, as indeed are Charles and Talbot and almost everybody else in the play. Puns abound, and the extremely banal and watery love scenes are patterned upon Robertson's. *Our Boys* was despised by many critics for farcical exaggeration, but it is right in the mainstream of Victorian comic development.

Talbot Champneys in *Our Boys* is dressed in 'velvet coat and vest, light pants, eye-glasses, blonde wig parted in centre, blonde side-whiskers and small blonde mustache'. Such a character, one of many modelled on the Lord Dundreary of E. A. Sothern in Taylor's *Our American Cousin* (1858)—and with another ancestor in Sir Frederick Blount of *Money*—is an example of the dependence on eccentric comedy in the 1860s and 1870s, a phenomenon worth noting. Robertson's fops and eccentrics are mild in conception compared to Byron's. These required appropriate acting techniques, and the joyful indulgence of many actors in comic excess easily toppled the comedies in which they appeared into purely external farce. Percy Fitzgerald objected that the taste for 'sensation' in comedy now meant that the characters, in order to 'draw', must be 'of that startling "raree-show" description popularized by burlesque, laid in such staring gaudy colours as all who run may read'.[1] Byron's performance of Sir Simon Simple in his own comedy, *Not Such a Fool as He Looks* (1868), drew Fitzgerald's fire:

Mr. Byron . . . worked on the surface, merely following to the established principles of the day. The first object was the creation of a purely eccentric character, who would stand alone, and whose oddities of dress, speech, and manner might cause laughter. A great deal of effect is produced by a dull sheepish manner, an eye-glass permanently fixed in the eye, sleek yellow hair, &.c. Nearly every speech he utters is written to produce a point and convey variety.[2]

To Fitzgerald such writing and acting was pernicious, and destructive of real characterization and true comedy; much of it, he thought, was the legacy of Robertson, not only of his characters but also of his inclination for 'forced quips' and epigrams for their own sake.

The actor introduces himself, his fun, his gags, and his vanity into the part, quite regardless of whether any be appropriate to, or at variance with, the character. In the same fashion, the writer only thinks of what he considers the 'good things' that will tell on the audience, never considering whether his 'sparkling epigrams' are suitable to the situation, or ridiculous in the mouth of the particular actor.[3]

---

[1] *Principles of Comedy and Dramatic Effect* (1870), p. 82.
[2] Ibid., pp. 83–4.   [3] Ibid., p. 103.

Thus the objection was to character fabricated out of external
bits and pieces, 'strange-coloured hair, false forehead, comically
cut coats, parti-coloured trousers; also out of tricks of elocution,
of strange sounds, and jerks of manner. . . . These are what
make up character-parts—strange beings formed on no human
model, wearing clothes seen in no known street, talking as no
human beings ever talked: and these are the creations that
figure in the pieces where anything comic is required.'[1] What
distressed Fitzgerald so much died away in the 1880s and
1890s, when dramatists depended far less on eccentric comedy
and hardly at all on low comedy.[2] The last flowering of eccentric comedy in Robertson and Byron had its roots in the vigorous
eccentricity of the Colman–Reynolds school, and this kind of
humour had provided English comedy with essential material
since the beginning of the nineteenth century.

Byron was still writing comedies in the eighties, but the best
comic work of the decade was being done by Gilbert and
Sullivan in the Savoy operas. Since opera and operetta are
outside the bounds of these prefaces because of their primarily
musical content, we are left with dramatists of merit and reputation such as Sydney Grundy, Henry Arthur Jones, and Arthur
Pinero. I am omitting Wilde and Shaw in the nineties (whose
plays, because they are so generally available in print, are
excluded from discussion): Wilde because *Lady Windermere's
Fan* (1892), *A Woman of No Importance* (1893), and *An Ideal
Husband* (1895) are not comedies at all, but thoroughly conventional Society dramas with comic additions that one would
say were uniquely Wilde's if one forgot how much he was influenced by Gilbert, even to the extent of his ironic viewpoint
and dialogue. His famous epigrams are the ultimate refinement
of an earlier comic technique (seen at its worst in Robertson and
Byron); his wits, both male and female, are aristocratic developments of the comic men and women of an earlier drama. *The*

---

[1] Ibid., pp. 64–6. During the rehearsals of *Caste*, Bancroft surprised everybody
by refusing to adopt the conventional fop's blonde wig and long flaxen whiskers
for Hawtree, instead appearing as 'a pale-faced man with short, straight, black
hair', dressed 'in the quietest of fashionable clothes'. (*Mr. and Mrs. Bancroft On
and Off the Stage*, i. 230.) Thus even the extravagant 'swell' was tamed and
quietly domesticated in productions of Robertson.

[2] The last traditional low comedian of repute, J. L. Toole, retired in 1895.
He performed in new comedies by Byron until 1885.

Importance of Being Earnest (1895), Wilde's only comedy, is too well-known to require discussion. Undoubtedly it is a comic masterpiece, yet again one must point out its heavy debt to Gilbert's *Engaged* (1877) and the whole tone of the Savoy operas. Shaw, too, hardly needs comment; his work has received elaborate critical treatment. However, it is worth noting two things. Firstly, that the duality of the comic and the serious, basic in such plays as *Major Barbara* and *Heartbreak House* (to name only two), and clearly apparent in early comedies like *Arms and the Man* (1894) and *Candida* (1895), is of central importance in the development of nineteenth-century comedy. Secondly, and the point is a similar one, Shaw's material and techniques in his early plays—and not only the early ones—originated in existing traditions in the writing of nineteenth-century comedies.[1] Thus neither Wilde nor Shaw can be isolated from his immediate dramatic heritage.

The contrast between Grundy on the one hand and Jones and Pinero on the other is instructive. Grundy adapted widely from the French, and his best comedy, *A Pair of Spectacles* (1890), is one such adaptation. Jones and Pinero used French sources very little; the effort to be original was characteristic of authors in the last two decades of the century, in contrast to the wholesale and legally unrestricted pilfering from French and German plays that had gone on for many years, and in which Taylor and Robertson, for example, both indulged. In structure and outlook *A Pair of Spectacles* is also of an older school of playwriting. The plot concerns the change of character that the philanthropic Goldfinch undergoes when he breaks his spectacles and borrows those of his flint-hearted brother Gregory. Previously generous to all in distress, he becomes suspicious and miserly. He is made himself again by the restoration of his mended spectacles, and his eyes are further opened by numerous offers of money and service from all those he treated badly, who mistakenly think him ruined. Even the miserable Gregory, shaken by the arrest for debt of his starving son, reforms to the point of liberality. The play has the appeal of a wholesome fairy tale: the good brother and the cruel brother, the rich son and

---

[1] This debt has been fully explored and documented in Martin Meisel, *Shaw and the Nineteenth Century Theatre* (1963).

the poor son, the magic spectacles, the procession of gift-givers in the last act. *A Pair of Spectacles* is suffused with goodness and benevolence, and its sentiment, unlike the delicate romantic sentiment of *Two Roses*, hearkens back to the strenuous, militant sentiment of Colman, Reynolds, and Morton.

That there was still a large audience for a good wallow in sentiment and the sunny side of human nature is indicated, not only by the success of *A Pair of Spectacles*, but also by the great popularity of Pinero's comedy-drama *Sweet Lavender* (1888). In this play, which relates the removal of obstacles to a union between a young barrister and the daughter of his laundress, and the reformation of his seedy, hard-drinking, but generous friend, every character is steeped in emotional sensibility and warm washes of goodness. The publishers of *Sweet Lavender* declared that 'it deals with no "problems", nor does it pretend to mirror the often sordid realities of life . . . a Victorian Fairy Tale of the Temple'. Clement Scott was loud in praise of *Sweet Lavender* for reasons central to his view of the whole purpose of drama: 'We all know how sad life *must* be as a rule; let us sometimes, even in a despised theatre, dream how happy and ideal and beautiful it *might* be. Rose-coloured spectacles are so much more soothing than the bare white glass, which only magnifies and seldom hides the defects of this ofttimes unlovely world.'[1]

The fact that Jones and Pinero were popular and successful dramatists of the 1890s shows that they appealed to more than a minority *avant-garde* audience that rejected rose-coloured spectacles. Their audience was the middle- and fashionable upper middle-class *cum* aristocratic audience of the St. James's, the Court, the Garrick, and the Criterion, theatres controlled by highly respectable and respected actor-managers: George Alexander, John Hare, and Charles Wyndham. This audience was prepared to accept more intellectual and serious comedy provided it did not offend social convention, and provided that its settings and characters were largely taken from the society with which it was comfortably familiar. Thus the comedy of Jones and Pinero employed social themes in settings which, like the settings of all late nineteenth-century middle-class drama,

---

[1] *The Drama of Yesterday and Today* (1899), ii. 189.

were increasingly elaborate, realistic, and socially elevated; the social class of their *dramatis personae* was correspondingly raised The growing sophistication of comedy and its tendency to stay in Mayfair meant a declining interest in rural settings and characters and the moral value of country simplicity and virtue. This kind of comedy was not an entirely new comedy, however, and, like Wilde and Shaw, Jones and Pinero assimilated subject-matter and techniques from their English predecessors.

Two significant characteristics of the comedy of the nineties are the improvement in plot construction and the more skilful intermingling of serious and comic elements; so-called comedies such as Jones's *The Crusaders* (1891) and Pinero's *The Benefit of the Doubt* (1895) are indistinguishable from dramas. Again this is nothing new, but dramatists had learned to blend comedy with pathos and potential tragedy rather than alternate them. Furthermore, comedies were written about marriage rather than courtship. Marital incompatibility and even sexual problems became thematically important and more prominent than before.

Henry Arthur Jones treated marital difficulties in *The Case of Rebellious Susan* (1894) and *The Liars* (1897) with an unqualified, burning moral conservatism and domestic idealism that condoned no departure from socially accepted *mores*. In the former play the *raisonneur* Sir Richard Kato persuades Lady Susan to return to her husband two years after she left him because of his infidelity. During that time she has fallen in love with Lucien Edensor, but Jones avoids allowing her a genuinely free choice by suddenly marrying off Edensor to another woman. In Jones's view Susan clearly does right to return to her worthless husband. The hero is obviously Kato himself, dispensing moral law with the authority of Jehovah. In a more overtly comic sub-plot, Jones condemns the New Woman in Elaine Pybus, a militant intellectual feminist who ruins the domestic life of her ineffective husband.[1] Kato lectures her fervently when she claims 'an immense future for Woman'. 'At her own fireside', he replies:

There is an immense future for women as wives and mothers, and a

---

[1] Very like Elaine, and given the same satirical treatment, is Miss Crane in Taylor's *Victims*. In 1857 Miss Crane is a repellent advocate of Female Emancipation.

very limited future for them in any other capacity. While you ladies without passions—or with disturbed and defeated passions—are raving and trumpeting all over the country, that wise, grim, old grandmother of us all, Dame Nature, is simply laughing up her sleeve and snapping her fingers at you and your new epochs and new movements. Go home! . . . Nature's darling woman is a stay-at-home woman who wants to be a good wife and a good mother, and cares very little for anything else. Go home!

While the marriages of all about him who disobey Jones's moral and social code are in pieces, it is fitting that the righteous man of principle, Kato, is the only one to receive a reward: the person and fortune of a wealthy young widow. Similarly, Sir Christopher Deering of *The Liars*, another *raisonneur*-hero, wins the hand of another beautiful widow while forcing the gay and clever Lady Jessica Nepean to stay with her unpleasant and boorish husband Gilbert. What prevents her running off with Edward Falkner is a terrible fear of the consequences of social disgrace. This is a powerful weapon in Deering's hand; indeed, intense social awareness and social apprehension are distinguishing features of the Mayfair dramas and comedies of the nineties. Yet Deering has no better marital advice for the reluctantly reconciled couple than to tell Gilbert to take his wife to a good dinner at the Savoy. *The Liars* is ingeniously constructed, with an extremely clever penultimate act in which character after character becomes involved in a lie to save Lady Jessica's reputation. The view of Society taken here is much more trenchant and sardonic than in *The Case of Rebellious Susan*; thus the wit and intrigue are considerably more entertaining, although there is no questioning of Society's moral and social dictates. The weakest thing in the play is the incredible marriage of Lady Jessica and Gilbert: the whole plot depends upon their hopeless incompatibility, but it is difficult to believe that such a pair could have married in the first place.

The Manoeuvres of Jane (1898) is, for Jones, an unusually light comedy of young love bordering on the farcical, but two earlier plays, *The Crusaders* and *The Triumph of the Philistines* (1895) are sterner stuff. *The Crusaders*, a one-sided attack against puritanism, social philanthropy, and fashionable intellectualism, contains comic caricatures of a moral fanatic and a pessimist philosopher as well as the idealized figures of a social reformer and a saintly girl who adores him.[1] Jones was, in fact, a passionate idealist about men and women; several characters in his comedies and dramas partake of a spiritual and fanatic devotion to Duty and Goodness. In *The Triumph of the Philistines* a hypocritical puritan tries to drive Art and Gracious Living from Market Pewbury, but fails. Jones savagely condemns the hypocritical morality of the puritans but conveniently overlooks the narrow base of his own. Female evil is the sole province of an alluring French model and entirely remote from the kind of idealized Englishwoman (like the heroine) of whom the *raisonneur*-hero states, 'We know there are two kinds of women. And it's you, and not the others, that we will have at our firesides. It's you and not the others, that we will have for our mothers, and sisters, and wives.'

Having learnt more from French methods of construction, Pinero was a better craftsman than Jones, and, although by no means excusing his characters from meeting social standards and abiding by judgements dictated by social convention, did not possess Jones's penchant for tub-thumping social morality. Pinero did not develop a reputation or a distinctive style of his own until the Court Theatre farces of the 1880s. The last but one of these, *The Cabinet Minister* (1890), is less a farce than an ironic comedy showing the influence of *Engaged*, with bitter overtones foreshadowing *The Benefit of the Doubt*. The household of the cabinet minister, Sir Julian Twombley, sinks deep into debt through sumptuous living. The Moorish conservatory of the first act displays '*elaborate Algerian magnificence*'; the morning-room of the second, '*handsomely decorated and furnished*', exhibits '*every evidence of luxury and refined taste*'. In order to avoid ruin, Lady Twombley is compelled against her will to introduce into Society the oilily unpleasant Jewish money-lender Joseph Lebanon and his socially ambitious sister, who are secretly supplying her with money and at the same time threatening exposure. The plot unfolds Lady Twombley's struggle with them and her efforts to marry her daughter to a fortune before the crash comes. Pinero's moral position is typically ambivalent. Lebanon, the vulgar lower-class black-

---

[1] Taylor's *Victims* not only satirizes Female Emancipation, but, anticipating *The Crusaders*, presents caricatures of an economist, a poet, a literary editor, and a metaphysician.

mailing bounder, part villain and part low comedian, receives appropriate retribution; much humour is obtained from his manners in a social set quite beyond and above him. But Lady Twombley, who is responsible for her family's financial predicament in the first place and who sells a cabinet secret to Lebanon in order to preserve herself, is given only the gentlest moral rebuke; the dénouement permits her to save the household and make a great deal of money at the same time. There is no disapproval of extravagance and fashionable living. And Lady Twombley's daughter accepts her true love—an explorer who had earlier appeared bearded and 'roughly dressed' in his humble position of gamekeeper—only when he appears in the last act 'trimmed, shaven, and in immaculate evening dress'.

The nouveau-riche of The Times (1891) is not a villain but a rich linen-draper, Bompas, who schemes to marry his daughter to the son of a peer as part of his plan to 'get on' in Society. The character type is a familiar one in Victorian comedy, but the tempestuous, drivingly ambitious, though basically simple and good-hearted Bompas is portrayed with some complexity and tragi-comic force. Largely because of his stupid son's untimely marriage with the coarse daughter of a low-class Irish widow, he learns that the past can never be hidden (there is an Ibsen influence here), fails in his marriage scheme, resigns from Parliament, and resolves to live a simple life abroad. In a genuinely affecting scene, Bompas and his wife, their hopes in ruins about them, talk quietly of how they lived in the old, unpretentious days; ironically, the sofa they sit on is part of 'a richly decorated and sumptuously furnished room . . . wealth and luxury are evident in all the appointments'. Society cruelly rejects the Bompases, but its standards are never criticized. The moral might well be that linen-drapers should not 'get on' in Society; in fact Bompas himself says that 'there ought to be a law to stop men like me from "getting on" beyond a certain point'. In a sentimental compromise that weakens the end of the play the peer's son declares that he will marry Bompas's daughter anyway. Pinero's audiences were often able to have their cake and eat it too.

The Benefit of the Doubt (1895) is a much darker play, a drama rather than a comedy. The failure of two marriages is depicted with considerable emotional power, the more forceful for being tightly disciplined. What social comedy exists is bitterly ironic, and the play is comically enlivened by the presence of a foolish and pompous M.P., a character type whose long line of descent in nineteenth-century comedy culminates in the satirical excellence of this portrait. The weight of high society crushes Pinero's next comedy, *The Princess and the Butterfly* (1897), despite a serious theme of the fear of age and unattractiveness. Princess Pannonia and Sir George Lamorant, a fashionable pair approaching middle age, turn to each other for comfort but at the last moment follow the impulses of their hearts ar.d marry much younger people. The plot is thin and spun out to great length, and its tedium is heightened by a superfluity of uninteresting characters from high life who indulge in a superfluity of banal dialogue. *Trelawny of the 'Wells'* (1898) is far better, a superior exercise in the nostalgic and sentimental recreation of the theatre of the sixties, the best nineteenth-century play written about the theatre. *The Gay Lord Quex* (1899) pits a reformed middle-aged profligate against a wily Bond Street manicurist in a struggle between his determination to behave impeccably during his engagement to an idealistic young woman and the manicurist's equal determination to sabotage the match. In spite of undoubted merits of characterization, dialogue, and situation, *The Gay Lord Quex* illustrates the dangers of a too careful attention to the plot requirements of a well-made play: the first two acts exist mainly to lead up to the excellent *scène à faire* in Act III, where Quex finally confronts his opponent in a bedroom at midnight, and the anti-climactic fourth act is there to resolve the questions arising from this scene.

Thus the comedy of the nineteenth century, in common with its tragedy and 'drama', ended in a decade emphasizing craftsmanship, social elegance, a considerable degree of economy and restraint, a great respect for social conventions, and an often elaborate verisimilitude of setting that formed the logical environment for a greater and more credible realism of characterization and dialogue. In 1900 comedy was even more solidly a middle-class and fashionable taste than it had been in 1800, and over the course of a century it gradually brought order and refinement out of the social and comic sprawl inherited from Colman and Reynolds and their successors. However, it preserved in its new decorum much of the theme material, moral viewpoint, and comic technique of those days and of the dramatic generation from the 1840s to the 1860s. No author of nineteenth-century comedies departed sharply from the practice and subject-matter of his immediate predecessors. Despite the great variety of work done and the apparent jumble of styles and materials, one can observe a remarkable continuity of development over a hundred years of comic writing.

How to Settle Accounts with your Laundress. Widgetts discovers a 'suicide'.
British Museum

IV. FARCES

For much of the eighteenth century, and especially after the Licensing Act of 1737, the performance of farce in London was a matter for the two or three theatres legally and regularly open. Thus the output of farce, while considerable, was not immense, and the scholar can examine it thoroughly. With the nineteenth century, however, and the enormous increase in population and the number of theatres, both in London and the provinces, the writing and performance of farce became an aspect of mass marketing. In quantity and popularity farce ranked second only to melodrama, and appeared on virtually every playbill until at least the 1870s. Like the study of any form of nineteenth-century drama, therefore, the study of farce can only be selective rather than totally comprehensive; this inevitable limitation apart, a selection of the kind contained in this volume, together with a brief introduction, should illuminate at least to some degree a form of nineteenth-century theatre that has in the past been consigned almost entirely to the outer darkness of history and criticism. On the strength of its contemporary popularity and dramatic significance nineteenth-century farce certainly deserves a volume to itself.

A discussion of the considerable change that came over farce in the nineteenth century and the nature and characteristics of that farce is best prefaced by a glance at the previous century's farce and the social factors producing such a change. Socially, the eighteenth-century patent theatre audience was remarkably stable: the fashionable aristocracy and upper middle class in the boxes, the middle class, professional and literary people in the pit, and the lower middle class, servants, journeymen, apprentices, sailors, etc. in the galleries. This pattern was preserved with little change until the next century. The content of the one- or two-act farce afterpiece reflects the tastes and composition of this audience. Its settings and characters are commonly middle, upper middle, and aristocratic in class: the father or guardian, the young lady or pair of young ladies, the lover and his friend (who may also be a lover), the foolish rival, the clever manservant and scheming chambermaid—a pair necessary to keep the upper gallery interested and allow it to identify enthusiastically with its class representatives on stage, whose intelligence and ingenuity much exceed their masters'.[1] These stock character types repeat themselves again and again. The plot range is also narrow. By far the most popular plot is that in which the favoured lover, often by the aid of his servant or his lady's maid, or both, gulls a parent or guardian as well as a rival out of the hand of the heroine. The rival may be a fop, a blustery coward, or a doting old man; the father (or guardian) may be a traditional Jonsonian 'humours' character with a dominant eccentricity. The countryman can sometimes appear as the rival, and also separately as a character actor; he is often satirically treated, but sometimes his moral worth and superiority to the corruption of the town are vigorously asserted—as, for instance, in Garrick's *Bon Ton* (1775). The general tone of eighteenth-century farce, concerned as it is so frequently with aristocratic and upper middle-class love intrigue, is relatively elevated and refined, and comic physical business is not abundant.[2] Well before the end of the century sentimentalism reached farce, and plot resolutions were increasingly dictated by moral and sentimental standards of stage behaviour.

This kind of farce persisted into the nineteenth century, even though it became steadily less genteel. The plot of the successful lover outwitting his rival and the heroine's father was still popular, as instanced by James Kenney's *Raising the Wind* (1803), Charles Mathews's *Patter versus Clatter* (1838), and William Murray's *Diamond Cut Diamond* (1838). In Thomas Dibdin's *Past Ten O'Clock and a Rainy Night* (1815), Harry Punctual and Charles Wildfire deceive the guardian of two

---

[1] Obvious examples are Fielding's *The Intriguing Chambermaid* (1734) and Garrick's *The Lying Valet* (1741).

[2] A farce like James Cobb's *The First Floor* (1787), with its characters rushing in and out of hiding, concealing themselves in bedrooms, and stealing to and fro in the dark, is unusual for the century.

clever young women and make off with them, thus frustrating his plans to marry one to Punctual's father and the other to his own foppish son. The traditionalism of this plot is blended with more low comedy than an eighteenth-century farce would normally have possessed. Humour arises from the drunkenness of two servants, Dozey and Squib (the former a renowned part of Munden's) and from the physical business of the dual elopement. In the same author's *What Next?* (1816), Major Touchwood impersonates his uncle Colonel Touchwood in a complicated plot to marry the Colonel's daughter and frustrate his rival Colonel Clifford, who is, however, loved by the other lady in the case. The major is aided by his inventive servant, Sharp, who devises the intrigue, gets drunk, and enjoys himself thoroughly. All this is conventional, inherited farce machinery. In John Poole's *Deaf as a Post* (1823), Templeton makes an utter fool out of his Sophia's booby fiancé and thus persuades her father to break off the match. What humour there is in T. G. Rodwell's *The Young Widow* (1824) arises from the schemes of two servants, Splash and Lucy, to outwit each other and the opposing master or mistress. J. B. Buckstone's *A Dead Shot* (1830) displays Louisa's ingenuity in evading the command of her uncle to choose within an hour between two unattractive suitors; Timid, who seeks a quiet, domestic wife, and Wiseman, who wants a delicate and refined one. She plays the virago with the terrified Timid and the hearty, mannish sportswoman with the disgusted Wiseman; in consequence neither will marry her, and her lover Frederick wins her by pretending to have been shot in a duel and marrying her on his 'deathbed'. The farce here arises out of characterization rather than situation; it should not be thought that the nineteenth-century farce writer could only create amusing contretemps. As the farces in this volume surely testify, he was also capable of inventing excellent comic characters. Certainly the main plot ideas and much of the apparatus of eighteenth-century farce survived the turn of the new century by many years, and it took some time before love intrigue ceased to be the centre of concern. After the 1830s, however, it played a less significant role in farce's increasing variety of subject-matter and social range.

The number of minor theatres in London had been growing since the last decade of the eighteenth century, and at the

time of the abolition of the patent monopolies in the Theatre
Regulation Act of 1843 there were not only several important
ones in the West End, such as the Adelphi, the Strand, the
Olympic, and the St. James's, but also neighbourhood working
and lower middle-class theatres on the South Bank, in the East
End, and on the fringes of the West End. The audience distributed over these theatres was not socially as stable as it used
to be, and the concept of the same theatre for all classes of patron
had disappeared. Even in the established patent theatres seat
prices were lowered to attract a wider audience, and boxes were
on the whole poorly attended. Managers and playwrights were
appealing to a different class (or classes) of patron from that
which had previously dominated the compact and ordered society
of the eighteenth-century patent theatre audience. Different
kinds of farce were now written for different kinds of theatres; the
extent of the survival of the upper middle-class and aristocratic
farce of an earlier period depended upon the particular theatre of
performance and the constitution of its audience. The content
and style of nineteenth-century farce, like that of other forms of
contemporary drama, were largely determined by the taste of its
audience—or, one should say, audiences. Changes in the social
composition of these audiences ensured changes in the character
of farce.

Before examining the nature and attributes of this farce—an
examination that will offer an aggregate description of nineteenth-century farce in place of a general and single definition
impossible to frame satisfactorily—we might find it useful to
consider those areas of attitude and subject-matter that farce
shares with comedy. The two forms were not remote from each
other. The problem of identification and definition involved in
the attempt to distinguish 'comedy' from 'drama' can also
attend the effort to separate 'farce' from 'comedy'. Undoubtedly
farce has special characteristics comedy does not possess—these
will be discussed below—but it is surprising how much they
have in common. A two-act piece called a 'farce' or 'comic
drama', such as Buckstone's *A Rough Diamond* (which was
called both) has all the characteristics of the *petite comédie*
popular at Vestris's Olympic in the 1830s; it was in fact per-

formed at the Lyceum under Vestris and Mathews in 1847. On the other hand, the same author's *Married Life*, played at the Haymarket in 1834 and termed a 'comedy', is much more farcical. For most of the century the standard farce was in one or two acts, and its very shortness automatically distinguishes it from the three-act comedy. However, this distinction is not helpful when one is confronted with the two-act 'comedy' as well as the two-act 'farce', not to mention the two-act 'comic drama'. Later in the century the three-act 'farcical comedy' is usually identical with the 'farce' itself As in the muddling of the categories of 'comedy' and 'drama', contemporary nomenclature does not really assist us in framing definitions—Victorian dramatists and their publishers were not legal draughtsmen—and there is much overlapping. As in the case of comedy and drama once again, it is wiser to forget about definitions and instead investigate those areas where farce resembles comedy and where they markedly differ.

Several main features of nineteenth-century comedy are apparent in farce: the blending of serious and comic material, the moral and sentimental motivation of behaviour, the glorification of the domestic ideal, and the assertion of the husband's rightful authority over his wife. Buckstone's farces are good illustrations. The heroine of *A Rough Diamond* is Margery, a simple, jolly country girl; her husband, Sir William, is reduced to despair by the failure of his repeated efforts to improve her conversation and make her into a fashionable society woman like the young wife of his uncle, Lord Plato. Audiences no doubt laughed at Margery's rustic gaucherie, country prattle, and hearty affection for her cousin Joe. However, Sir William revises his opinion when he observes the educated and sophisticated Lady Plato secretly renewing an affair with a former lover. Sir William, Lady Plato, her husband, and her lover are purely serious characters; they serve only to underline both the comedy and the moral superiority of Margery and Joe. The moral and sentimental lesson is that true virtue is resident in the country; this is reminiscent not only of the characters and sentiments of many comedies, but also directly relates to the moral dogma of melodrama, which is always contrasting rural innocence with

urban vice, the virtuous peasant with the corrupt aristocrat.
The country is also idealized in Charles Selby's *Peggy Green*
(1847), whose heroine sings 'Home of my Childhood' and
declares, 'Oh, London, London—smoky, foggy, noisy, toiling,
dissipated London, how glad I am that I have exchanged your
fatiguing pleasures for the peace and quiet of this sweet paradise'
—a speech that could have come out of any village melodrama
between 1820 and 1870.[1] In another of Buckstone's farces, *An
Alarming Sacrifice* (1849), moral and sentimental assumptions
are the basis of conduct. The thoughtless and extravagant Bob
Ticket discovers his uncle's will, which to his horror leaves the
whole estate to the housekeeper, Susan Sweetapple. Bob
struggles with his conscience as he looks in the mirror:

Now, let my face tell me what I ought to do. I'll destroy the will; I'll
burn it. Susan shall never know such a document ever existed. I will—
I will—and enjoy my property, and—oh, what a demon I do look!
I'd no idea I could ever be so frightful. I'll try again. I'll be a man; I'll
do the right thing; I'll tell the poor girl of her good fortune—put her
in the possession of all. My heart will approve of my conduct, and I
shall be one of the noblest works of creation, an honest man! Oh, what
an angel sweetness beams in every feature; what a handsome fellow
I am. Yes, and I'll behave as handsome. The struggle's over—an
alarming sacrifice *shall* be made!

This struggle is comically portrayed, of course, but the moral
decision arrived at is a serious one. After Susan gives Bob a place
as a servant and forces him to run around waiting on table,
she burns the will in a fit of conscience and good-heartedness;
the now thoughtful Bob offers to marry her, partly out of
gratitude and partly out of respect for her virtue.

Sentimentalism in farce was admirably suited to the character
of the stage Irishman, who had been a comic and sentimental
type for generations and flourished vigorously throughout the
century in melodrama, drama, and comedy as well as farce. The
nineteenth-century stage Irishman was a clever, improvident,
hard-drinking, credible rogue with a heart of gold, despite his

---

[1] We are not, however, to take this too seriously, since she is quite happy to
return to London as the wife of the dashing town gallant, Roverly. The countryside
in this play is represented with more farcical truth by the booby ploughboy,
Nicholas. Nevertheless, the speech, the song, and the sentiment are there all the
same.

innate capacity for deception and anti-social behaviour. Primarily he was a stereotyped character mechanism for extracting laughter out of low-comedy situations. A comedian like Tyrone Power stood at the head of his profession for his ability to do just this.[1] Power played the journeyman tailor Tom Moore in Buckstone's *The Irish Lion* (1838), who is mistaken for the poet of the same name, invited to an elegant party of fawning admirers, and disports himself with singing, dancing, and whisky punch. It was Power also who made his first entrance as the valet Larry Hoolagan in T. G. Rodwell's *More Blunders than One* (1824) singing 'Oh Erin, sweet Erin, the land that we live in'. Hoolagan spends the whole play blundering out of one scrape into another, but like all Irishmen in farce is tolerated and forgiven. Both Moore and Hoolagan are used only for good-natured low comedy, but in a secondary role the Irishman could also fulfil a moral and sentimental purpose—like the low-comedy countryman in the comedies of Colman, Reynolds, and Morton. Two other characters originally performed by Power can serve as examples. In George Rodwell's *Teddy the Tiler* (1830), the workman Teddy is mistaken for the heir to Lord Dunderford and behaves ludicrously in socially elegant surroundings and dress. A fire breaks out across the street, trapping the real heir in a garret; Teddy rushes up a ladder and plunges into the flames to rescue him. The others try to stop this precipitate action, but he declares, 'If I'm not to go to a fire because I'm a nobleman, the sooner I throw up my peerage and become a commoner again the better.' 'What mean you?' asks Lord Dunderford, and Teddy replies, 'Why, I mane that if I can save a fellow creature's life, I'll do it. There's rale nobility for you!'—and dashes off. O'Callaghan, the down-at-heels scapegrace of W. B. Bernard's *His Last Legs* (1839), impersonates a doctor in order to win a meal and a fee. At the end of a series of complications and misunderstandings he is responsible for reconciling the real doctor with his wife and making possible the engagement of O'Callaghan's erstwhile patient with his loved one. The delighted O'Callaghan tells his

---

[1] 'Power was the best Irishman I ever witnessed on the stage. He was entirely divested of those vulgarities, too often adopted by the representatives of Hibernian character, and possessed the refined and happy art of making them equally droll and amusing without resorting to such coarse material.' (Edward Fitzball, *Thirty-five Years of a Dramatic Author's Life* (1859), ii. 21–2.)

new friend that the latter sees before him 'the human mind, sir, in its finest aspect, sympathizing with the happiness of others'. Thus, in the single character type of the Irishman, that curious mixture of low comedy and sentimental morality so typical of nineteenth-century farce is strikingly apparent.

Sentimentality and moralizing would not appear to be the province of farce, but they are prominent in a great many nineteenth-century farces. Neither would one think that the often militant advocacy of domestic ideals—or indeed the upholding of any ideals—properly belonged to farce. Such is the case in the nineteenth century, however, and subject-matter of this kind is again held in common with comedy and drama. The sole purpose of Mildman, an allegorical figure in Charles Dance's *Kill or Cure* (1832), is to reconcile the perpetually quarrelling Browns. He finally does so, though not until Brown has been carried off to be stomach-pumped for drinking milk that he thought was poison; the farce passes immediately from this strongly physical incident to a final scene in which the benevolent Mildman, a true fairy godfather, orchestrates an ecstasy of domestic reconciliation. The Browns soon intrude their bickering upon *Kill and Cure*, but many farces begin with a picture of apparently ideal domestic bliss, proceed to shatter it, and conclude by reaffirming it. One such farce is Charles Mathews's *My Wife's Mother* (1833). The opening lines are spoken by the husband, Bud, and reflect an exclusively male conception of domestic felicity: 'My dear Ned, I'm the happiest of men. You must see I am yourself; how comfortable everything is about me! Arm chair, dressing gown, and slippers— well ordered breakfast table, good fire, clean room—everything cheerful and smiling. There's nothing like a wife for managing these matters, and I flatter myself there are not many like my Ellen. Ah, you bachelors are wretched dogs.' However, his contentment is soon destroyed. Bud's mother-in-law, the fearsome Mrs. Quickfidget, arrives to stay and completely disrupts the household: she persuades Mrs. Bud that her husband is unfaithful, disturbs the regular habits of old Uncle Foozle, and antagonizes the servants into giving notice. Finally she is asked to leave and peace is restored. Bud's bachelor friend Waverly, wondering whether or not to marry, acts as chorus and comments enthusiastically or dispiritedly on the married state. Similarly, the happiness of the Southdowns in Tom Taylor's *To Oblige Benson* (1854)—a play from the French labelled a 'comedietta' and possessing the characteristics both of farce and of *petite comédie*—is marred by their attempt 'to oblige Benson' and awaken Mrs. Benson to her folly in corresponding secretly with Meredith. Moral pronouncements and a general elegance of tone and setting are mingled with comic business in Southdown's pretended rage at his wife—acted at her prompting for Mrs. Benson's benefit—that turns into a real furniture-smashing tantrum when he comes to believe that Meredith's letter was meant for Mrs. Southdown. The play ends in perfect domestic harmony for both couples, and all characters indulge in dreadful warnings of the possible consequences of a wife's indiscretions; little slips are not to be condoned.

The expression of the domestic ideal in farcical terms meant that the wife, of necessity subordinate to her husband since such subordination was essential to the ideal, can be either a sweet insubstantial being like Mrs. Bud, who doubts her husband only because of misunderstanding and the suspicions of her nasty mother, or a seemingly strong-willed woman with her own weaknesses and indiscretions who sees the light before the final curtain and crumbles into submission.[1] Husbands and wives frequently quarrel in farce, but such quarrelling is easily patched up and never destructive. The wives only temporarily resent the sort of treatment typified by Mr. Mammoth's declaration in Douglas Jerrold's *Law and Lions* (1829) that 'we of the better sort of creation only associate wives with household affairs, connubial love and a shoulder of mutton'. More often than not in domestic squabbles it is the wife who confesses to error, like Mrs. Hussey in Thomas Bayly's *The Culprit* (1838), who after discovering that her husband's secret infatuation is with a Turkish pipe (she abhors smoking) rather than another woman admits that 'when I married, I expected

---

[1] In many farces a wife was not needed at all. Of the farces mainly discussed here, only *The Magistrate* contains a wife in a leading role, and *Tom Cobb* is the only other to number a wife in the *dramatis personae*. Such an absence of wifely representation is coincidental and not truly characteristic of the general domestic scene in farce, especially Victorian farce, which like Victorian melodrama, 'drama', and comedy is much more domestic than the drama of the first part of the nineteenth century.

too much. I required my husband to give up an innocent indulgence which long habit had rendered essential to his comfort.' The exonerated Hussey triumphantly installs the hookah in his own home. On a more serious note, the wife in J. P. Wooler's *A Model Husband* (1853) confesses her weakness in being tempted by the attentions of a flashy young man: 'No more jaunts without my husband—no more amusement but *with* my husband—no more care but *for* my husband.' 'You are master and shall be,' she tells him, 'and I will try to be a good and dutiful wife.' Even in farce, therefore, the stage doctrine of the husband's marital superiority—no matter how much of a fool he might look in the midst of comic domestic confusion— goes basically unchallenged.

Attitudes toward marriage and the domestic ideal expressed in farce are held with undoubted conviction. The nearest a nineteenth-century farceur comes to placing these subjects schematically on a plane of thematic significance is Buckstone. *Second Thoughts* (1832), *Married Life* (1834), and *Single Life* (1839) are described as comedies on their title-pages, but they are strongly farcical. In *Second Thoughts* the impulsive Sudden quickly resolves to marry Mrs. Trapper, has his usual second thoughts when he thinks that she has poisoned her first hus- band, withdraws, is sued for breach of promise, decides to flee England, and is caught by Mrs. Trapper and her bailiffs. His problems are solved by the timely arrival of the very much alive Mr. Trapper from America. This plot is entirely farcical; Sudden is a 'humours' character with an obsession about 'second thoughts', and his eccentric and gossipy friend Jabber makes a living imitating musical instruments at society parties. However —and unusually for a two-act farce—there are two sub-plots, and here serious matters are introduced. Mrs. Trapper tries to find husbands for her three daughters, who have pleasant but useless hobbies hardly calculated to improve their marital chances: reading novels, collecting autographs, making knick- knacks. In the other sub-plot Sudden attempts to prevent his ward from marrying an attractive young man, Cecil. Under- neath the farcical events and eccentric characterization in which the theme of marriage is initially developed is a current of seriousness and pathos, at first evident only in the second sub- plot, in which Cecil and Sudden's ward are quite devoid of humour, but dominant in the second act with the discovery that Cecil is Sudden's long-lost nephew and the suffering of Mrs. Trapper's now married daughters. Because of her insistence on husbands for the sake of being married, the daughters make unfortunate matches: one marries a footman, one a rich business-man who is exposed as a fraud and sent to Newgate, and one a poor miniature-painter struggling with poverty. In so far as *Second Thoughts* was written to express a serious theme, Buck-stone appears to be saying that the borderline between comedy and disaster in marriage is a narrow one, and that what seems to be merely amusing in marital complications may mask wrong attitudes toward marriage that if persisted in lead to serious harm and personal sorrow.

Married Life and *Single Life* are early examples of the three-act farce popular in the last quarter of the century. The former contains four comic couples who fall out for various reasons: Coddle complains of the cold and draughts; Mrs. Coddle is always too hot; the Younghusbands perpetually contradict each other; Dismal is rude and surly to his wife; Dove, a former footman, irritates his middle-class wife by forgetting his elevated station and running to answer the door whenever he hears the bell; Mrs. Dove annoys Dove by continually correct-ing his footman's vocabulary and pronunciation. The farcical climax of the play comes when five spouses rush out of the room, one after another, after each has had a vigorous altercation with his or her partner. The fifth couple, the Lynxes, are intense and melodramatic characters, and their part in the plot and the sequence of misunderstanding and marital discord is entirely serious.[1] Mrs. Lynx is obsessed with suspected infidelity on her husband's part, but not in a comic way, and utters powerful and disordered speeches on the subject. Lynx is protecting the identity and honour of a mysterious young girl who turns out to be his dead sister's daughter. The emotional scenes between them come from melodrama, not farce, as does Lynx's rescue of his wife from the assault of an off-stage villain. The potentially

---

[1] A practical explanation of their presence in a farce might be that Mrs. Lynx was played by Helen Faucit, whose forte was not comedy, and who, being in the Haymarket company at the time, presumably had to be employed. A theatrical reason might be the answer, or part of it, in this particular case, but nevertheless the inclusion of purely serious characters in comedy and farce was a characteristic of the age.

tragic treatment of marriage in the Lynx relationship parallels the purely comic but nevertheless full development of the same theme in relation to the other couples. Mrs. Lynx is reconciled to her husband; both confess faults and agree to let 'mutual confidence henceforth secure to us that happiness to which we have so long been strangers'. Miserable, repentant wives are reunited with miserable, repentant husbands, and Coddle delivers a final harangue to the audience on the principal subject of the play, a speech so solemn in content and so glowing with domestic idealism that it is worth quoting in its entirety. It is prefaced by a piece of comic though none the less idealistic stage business. Coddle addresses the assembled married couples:

CODDLE. Whenever a disagreement breaks out among you in future, recall the memory of those inducements which first led you to think of each other, and you will find it to be a wonderful help to the restoration of peace. Do you all agree to this?

ALL. Yes, yes!

CODDLE. Then follow my example, and ratify the agreement by a hearty conjugal embrace; I will give the word of command. Make ready! [As CODDLE puts his arm round his wife's waist, each of the husbands do the same to their wives.] Present! [CODDLE takes his wife's chin between his fingers and thumb, and prepares to kiss her; all the husbands do the same.] Fire! [They all kiss and embrace at the same moment.] There, this is the way that all matrimonial quarrels should end—and if you are of the same opinion [To the audience.] then, indeed, will our conjugal joy be complete, and our light lesson not have been read in vain. You have seen the result of perpetual jealousy in the case of Mr. and Mrs. Lynx; of continual disputes and contradiction in that of Mr. and Mrs. Younghusband; of a want of cheerfulness in Mr. and Mrs. Dismal; of the impolicy of public correction in the instance of Mrs. Dove; and of the necessity of assimilating habits and tempers in the singular case of Mr. and Mrs. Coddle; and though these may not be one half the causes of quarrel between man and wife—yet even their exposure may serve as beacon lights to avoid the rocks of altercation when sailing on the sea of matrimony. So think of us, all ye anticipating and smiling single people; for you must, or ought all to be married, and the sooner the better—and remember us ye already paired; and let our example prove to you that to mutual forbearance, mutual confidence, mutual habits, mutual everything, must we owe mutual happiness. And where can the *best* of happiness be found, but in a loyal and affectionate married life?

It would seem that Buckstone deliberately exceeded both the usual length and the ordinary moral proprieties of the comic tag —the one that ends *Married Life* must be the longest in any nineteenth-century play—in order to emphasize his theme.

In *Single Life*, which Buckstone intended as a companion piece to *Married Life*, five bachelors, all with different attitudes to marriage, are eventually united to five spinsters. Niggle desperately wants a wife, but has always been prevented from marrying, sometimes forcibly, by his misogynist friend Damper, who despite himself is attracted to a professed man-hater, Miss Macaw. Pinkey loves Miss Skylark, but is too bashful to propose and instead copies love letters for her from *The Complete Letter Writer*. The elegant Narcissus Boss, who spends much time admiring himself in a mirror, becomes engaged to the equally self-admiring Miss Snare. The serious interest, slighter than in *Married Life*, is provided by Chester and Miss Meadows, each afraid of being married for money, each pretending to poverty and concealing wealth. The play opens with an excellent and truly farcical scene in which Niggle, in a feverish hurry to slip away to church for a secret marriage with Miss Coy, is prevented from doing so by a steady stream of callers. Scenes in which marriage is a subject for irony are followed by scenes in which it is considered beautiful and romantic; on the whole, as in *Married Life*, marriage is more praised than derided, even though, as in the earlier play, all five couples quarrel and are reconciled. Together with *Second Thoughts*, *Married Life* and *Single Life* constitute the fullest and most 'serious' examination of marriage and the domestic ideal undertaken by any single author of nineteenth-century farce. And clearly, farce and seriousness are not entirely incompatible.

The basically sentimental outlook of nineteenth-century farce, despite its necessary plot machinery of intrigue, deception, misunderstanding, and coincidence, is closely allied to the overwhelming domesticity of this and other kinds of nineteenth-century drama. The best farce is the disciplined expression of moral and domestic anarchy, the plausible and logical presentation of a completely crazy world that all the characters take with the greatest seriousness, a world in which extraordinarily absurd and fantastic pressures on the ordinary individual drive him to the very extremity of his resources and his senses, a world in which he can survive only by pitting the ingenuity of his own insanity against the massive blows of hostile coincidence and a seemingly remorseless fate. Such a world is the world of the best French farce, the world of Labiche and Feydeau, whose undoubted domesticity is uncompromisingly ruthless, savage, and anti-familial, whose very chaos and controlled violence is a kind of inverse moral order of great rigidity. Labiche and Feydeau are not sentimental, nor do they write on that level of domesticity concerning the trivia of home, hearth, and daily living that cram the English farce to bursting. One might say the domesticity of French farce is hard and sharp-edged, the domesticity of English farce soft and well-disposed. The difference occurs because the farce of Labiche and Feydeau is anti-idealistic and satirical in aim, whereas the purpose of its far less aggressive Victorian counterpart is to amuse in a jolly and properly moral way, to cast a friendly, avuncular eye on the minor vicissitudes of home and family.[1] The ideals of love, marriage, and household that enervate so much serious nine-teenth-century drama also debilitate nineteenth-century farce, yet simultaneously give it a sort of homey charm that the French farce eschews.

Charm, sentiment, and a sense of fun, all expressed in the proper moral spirit, are distinctively characteristic of nineteenth-century English farce, but of course that is not all this farce had to offer. One must also take note of those characteristics that separate it from comedy and other forms of theatre, those seemingly more appropriate to its peculiar province than the ones already discussed.

Several major techniques of farce—the repetition and accumulation of misunderstanding and coincidence, the reversal of normal expectation, the surprise entrance, the bringing together of characters who at all costs should remain apart, the extreme eccentricity of a minority of characters, the truncation of time so that comic events follow one another with ludicrous rapidity—are too familiar to require elaboration and are part of

---

[1] The Examiner of Plays and public opinion prevented Victorian farceurs from writing—even if they had wished to, which is most doubtful—as witheringly about love and marriage and as openly about adultery as the French playwrights did.

the conventional machinery of all farce; they are much in evidence in this volume. One could also mention another aspect of technique illuminating not only the way in which nineteenth-century farce works but also the nature of the world it creates. All farce is fantasy; all farce must involve its audience in this fantasy as well as indicate clearly that it *is* fantasy. Nineteenth-century farce does this through technique as well as subject-matter.

One of the ways in which the farce author involved his audience was by addressing it directly, confiding in it, appealing for approval, and frankly stressing the non-realistic nature of his genre by directing attention to the strings on which his puppets dance. Soliloquies and informational asides are standard procedure in nineteenth-century drama, but farce goes much further than this. A common device is a speech near the beginning, sometimes opening the play, sometimes of great length, relating to the audience the events that have happened already, the precise situation in which the character speaking finds himself, and how he got there. The longest speeches of this type were assigned to comedians of great skill who could hold their audiences with such narrations. For example, J. M. Morton's *Grimshaw, Bagshaw, and Bradshaw* (1851) begins with a two-page rambling account from Grimshaw—originally played by Buckstone—stating how sleepy he is, how early he has to get up, what his employer is like, that he must put on dressing-gown and slippers, how he went to Cremorne (a Victorian pleasure-garden in Chelsea) three weeks ago to watch a man go up in a balloon with a donkey, how it rained, how he met the delightful Fanny and took her home, that he had better go to bed. Similarly, Charles Mathews in *Little Toddlekins* (1852) wrote a three-page speech for himself as Brownsmith, explaining his whole history and particularly how he came to be the father of a daughter eighteen years older than himself. Brownsmith appeals directly to the audience for assistance ('Is there anybody who'll take her off my hands?') and sympathy ('There, now you've seen her! Well, what do you say?') Muddlebank in W. E. Suter's *Our New Man* (1866) swears the audience to secrecy before providing it with an involved explanation of how he came to be at Cremorne without his wife and how he had tea with a charming young lady. Such speeches are simple and naïve in intention and effect; there is no attempt to develop exposition by the frequently clumsy device resorted to in other forms of contemporary drama whereby two characters ignore the audience and carry on an opening dialogue that conveys necessary information which both characters usually know anyway. The peculiar flavour of the longer expository speeches in farce—they can scarcely be called soliloquies, since their speakers are not engaged in self-communion—can be gathered from *Going to the Dogs* (1865), by William Brough and Andrew Halliday, in which Fidge explains to the audience how it is that he is afraid of being arrested as an accessory in the crime of dog-stealing:

The other day, just as I was leaving the quoit ground at the Welsh Harp, the landlord, Mr. Groggins, comes up to me and tells me a confounded story about a dog—hang Groggins and his stories! It seems my friend Captain Lightfoot bought a dog of a man in Regent-street. Well, one day, walking along with the animal, up comes one Boodle, a cowkeeper, and claims the dog as one that has been stolen from him. Lightfoot refuses to give up the dog, and Boodle gives him into custody for the theft. Magistrate discharges Lightfoot, of course, but orders dog to be given up to Boodle. Then, what does Lightfoot do but go and bribe the fellow of whom he first bought the dog, to steal dog back again from Boodle. . . .

and so on, for as many lines again.

Shorter speeches of this kind were more common than longer ones. To give only one example, in *More Blunders than One* the maid Susan opens the play by admiring herself in the glass, declares that 'I'm in momentary expectation of the arrival of Mr. Larry Hoolagan, valet de chambre to my mistress's intended', and praises him rapturously. Henry Melbourne begins the second scene with 'Now I am alone, let me again read my uncle's letter', which he does; the uncle shortly arrives with 'Well, here I am, once more in my native land, and under the very roof, too, with the only relation I have in the world.' Just before his entrance the bailiff Trap comes on and says, 'I've gammon'd 'em so far, however. How lucky I happened to hear of the expected arrival of old Melbourne from India. In this disguise of his uncle I shall bring him down.' In the third scene Hoolagan enters with 'So, here I am once more under the same roof with my little darling. I've sneaked in this afternoon to wish her good morning. My master sent me somewhere else, but I preferred coming here because it was more agreeable.' The fourth scene opens with a speech from the now tipsy Hoolagan beginning 'My master discharged me, but I won't go.' To cut summary short, there are nineteen speeches like this in the one-act farce, apart from the ordinary confidential asides when more than one person is on stage.

More Blunders than One ends with Larry Hoolagan asking the audience to bestow their favours 'on poor Larry's "More Blunders than One" ' so that the piece can continue its run. A final brief speech or tag, addressed directly to the audience, usually by the principal comic actor, with the rest of the cast on either side of him straight across the front of the stage, or disposed in a semicircle, was the ritualistic conclusion of virtually every farce acted until the 1870s. This tag commonly begged the audience's blessing and often included the title of the play. Such an ending was frankly artificial and made the same appeal to the house as the prologue and epilogue of an earlier age. Sometimes the tag was ingeniously varied in a way that made the audience even more aware of the workings of a comic mechanism. When the curtain rises upon J. M. Morton's *Slasher and Crasher* (1848), the characters are lined up across the stage and Blowhard is about to deliver the tag to a play presumably just finished, in which Slasher and Crasher have been successful suitors for Blowhard's sister and her niece. He is then handed a letter informing him that Slasher and Crasher are really cowards. He goes no further with the tag, orders them out of the house, and the farce proper begins. When Slasher and Crasher have been successful at last and the play ends, the characters resume their opening positions and the interrupted tag proceeds to its conclusion. Slasher and Crasher were played by the Adelphi's low comedians, Wright and Bedford; the same actors took the parts of the Intruder and Snoozle in the same author's *A Most Unwarrantable Intrusion* (1849), whose full title is *A Most Unwarrantable Intrusion Committed by Mr. Wright to the Annoyance of Mr. Paul Bedford*. This kind of theatricality is emphasized at the end of the piece when Wright as the Intruder repeats a cue for Bedford as Snoozle, and Bedford as himself declares that he has no more in his part; Wright as himself replies that neither has he. The prompter is summoned and asked where the tag is; he explains that the author did not write one because 'Wright always spoke his own'. Wright then does speak 'his own' and the curtain comes down. The conclusion of Blanchard Jerrold's *Cool as a Cucumber* (1851) is equally inventive. Old Barkins refuses to support the young lovers if they marry without his consent. The comic lead, Plumper, angrily orders the curtain down behind him, cutting off the other characters from the auditorium; he then abuses Barkins to the audience. From behind the curtain Barkins cries out that he relents; Plumper orders the curtain raised, pronounces the piece properly finished, and calls for red fire and a tableau as the young couple kneel before Barkins in a parody of a conventional melodramatic finale. J. S. Coyne's *Binks the Bagman* (1843) concludes with Binks, a commercial traveller, distributing among the audience cards announcing that his business will continue at the Adelphi every night at nine o'clock. As the weary Dabchick of William Brough's *How to Make Home Happy* (1853)—a title typical of contemporary domestic farce—persecuted by his wife's groundless jealousy but now reconciled with her, steps forward to speak the tag, Mrs. Dabchick asks, 'Who is that lady in the dress circle you are looking at?' and becomes jealous again, especially when Dabchick says that he hopes to see the audience again tomorrow night at the same time. 'An appointment! Before my very face!' she cries. In such ways the farceur involved his audience by placing it in communion with his characters and establishing a direct and sympathetic bond between stage and auditorium. Simultaneously he distanced this audience by making it aware of the wheels and cogs of his own ingeniously constructed comic machinery. In a rather Pirandellian way, too, actors sometimes played actors playing characters. Nineteenth-century farce is not as utterly simple and artless as it might appear.

The attention to physical business is another technique of farce taken for granted: one vaguely assumes that all farce actors run in and out, knock each other over, hide in closets, and make a great deal of noise. As far as the nineteenth century is concerned, this assumption contains some truth. Farce of this type exists. However, although uproarious moments and situations where comic effects depend upon physical business occur frequently, they dominate few farces, and many are without them entirely. Physical comedy is more prevalent in the farce of the last quarter of the century, but it is not absolutely essential to the genre.

Comic business arising out of the preparation, serving, and consumption of food is very noticeable in nineteenth-century farce, especially in the twenty years around the middle of the century. The connection between low comedy and food and drink is an old one on the stage, and is particularly strong in nineteenth-century pantomime as well as farce. (One also remembers the comic uses of food in the silent film.) There are many comic inebriates in eighteenth-century farce—the stage Irishman of the eighteenth and nineteenth centuries could hardly have existed without his bottle—but it rarely resorted to the extended comedy of cooking, serving, and eating. The funniest scene of *Deaf as a Post*, an early example of 1823, is that in which Templeton, pretending to deafness, intrudes upon his stingy rival's private dinner party, takes his rival's place at table, eats his way unheedingly through his rival's capon, drinks his port and madeira, and blissfully departs. The best scene of *An Alarming Sacrifice* also occurs at table. Bob Ticket, in his new capacity of unwilling servant to his uncle's housekeeper, suffers the indignity of being forced to wait on what was a few minutes ago his own table:

---

[1] The reversal of roles and the degradation of the 'master' is a common feature of nineteenth-century farce, e.g. Widgetts serving at his own table in *How to Settle Accounts with your Laundress*, Mr. Posket's battered humiliation in Act III of *The Magistrate*, and the Dean of St. Marvell's imprisonment in the village jail in Pinero's *Dandy Dick*.

[DEBORAH *appears with a tray on which are three dishes, one of hashed mutton, one of hot potatoes, and the third roast duck.* PUG-WASH *takes cover off the dish before him.*

PUGWASH. Here, young man, take this cover.   [BOB *takes it.*

MISS WADD. Bob, some bread!

SKINNER. Bob, some ale!

PUGWASH. Bob, some pepper!

SUSAN. Bob, some butter!

MISS GIMP. Bob, some vinegar!

MISS WADD. Bob, some mustard!

SUSAN. Hot plates, Bob!

[BOB *brings the articles, as they are called for, from a table at the back.* DEBORAH *enters with hot plates;* BOB *takes them, burns his fingers, and drops them.*

Similarly, in Mark Lemon's *The Railway Belle* (1854), Greenhorne, so infatuated by the barmaid in a station refreshment room that he sits there every day ordering endless bowls of vile and undrinkable soup, seizes the chance to take the waiter's place when the need arises but is horrified to find himself waiting, quite incompetently, upon his fiancée and her hot-tempered father. The low-life Irish tinker of Samuel Lover's *Barney the Baron* (1857) is supposed to be amusing because in a German castle that he has won in a lottery he demands 'plenty of tripe and onions, and liver and bacon, and cabbage, and a big bowl of praties'. Peeled potatoes infuriate him, however; he throws them at the servants and is disgusted by a dish of sauerkraut. He carves clumsily, looks forward to breakfast on a few butter rolls and some boiled praties with the skins on them', and as a matter of course retires to bed to get drunk on a bottle of wine.

As can be seen, then, the use of food in farce is not general or suggestive, but extremely explicit. Detail is piled upon detail, and a piece of business can be so fully elaborated that it completely dominates the scene or even the whole farce. An example occurs in Charles Selby's *Hotel Charges* (1853), in which the waiters of a hotel, worried by the campaign 'A. Biffin' has been running in *The Times* against extortionate hotel charges, give extra-special food and service, at an incredibly low price, to a Captain Fitzchizzle whom they mistake for Biffin. The head-waiter, Sminker, is simultaneously concerned for the hotel's reputation and enraged to see his fiancée, the chambermaid Mary, flirting with Fitzchizzle. In the business that follows, seven waiters and a page are concerned in serving Fitzchizzle's meal:[1]

A WAITER *brings on a covered dish supposed to be the boiled fowl, and another the partridge; two others bring covered vegetable dishes which they place on the table; then* ROBERT *brings on haunch of mutton, which is passed from one* WAITER *to the other and placed on the table;* SMINKER *takes from sideboard a large carving knife and steel, and sharpens knife, looking ferociously at* FITZCHIZZLE, *who is coqueting with* MARY.

SMINKER. [*Flourishing knife.*] Oh, shouldn't I like to have a cut at him! [*Advancing.*] Mutton, sar! [*He takes hold of the shank of the mutton, cuts with savage flourishes two very small slices and puts them with some gravy, which he takes from dish with a large spoon, on a plate which* JAMES *holds. At this moment* SMINKER *sees* FITZCHIZZLE *offering* MARY *a glass of wine, and in his rage strikes the plate so violently with the spoon that it breaks;* JAMES *gives another plate and takes up the slice of mutton and places it before* FITZCHIZZLE; *the* PAGE *brings currant jelly from sideboard, taking by the way a sly spoonful, and gives it to* MARY, *who helps* FITZCHIZZLE *and returns it to* PAGE, *who eats the whole of it.* SMINKER *stamps and waves his hand;* JAMES *takes away the mutton and passes it to the other* WAITERS, *who pass it off; the* PAGE *takes away the fowl and* JAMES *the partridges, and as they are running off with them, meet, and the* PAGE *falls—a scramble and a bustle.* SMINKER *beats the* PAGE, *who goes off bellowing, pushed about by the* WAITERS: FITZCHIZZLE *takes advantage of the bustle to put his arm round* MARY'S *waist;* SMINKER *turns and sees him, and takes* MARY *up in his arms and carries her off.* WAITERS *enter and clear table.*

[1] A note in the text relating to the initial serving of the bread, soup, wine, and cruet, before the main meal begins, says that 'the whole of this business must be managed with great precision and rapidity, the idea being to show the division of labour practised in hotels'. An interesting anticipation of the stage business, if not the point of view, of Arnold Wesker's *The Kitchen*.

Comic business in farce, although a significant aspect of technique, cannot be easily separated from subject-matter and setting, even for the purpose of discussion. By the 1840s it arose directly out of the domesticity and materiality of early Victorian farce. A strong argument could be advanced for the contention that, aside from the farces of Pinero in the 1880s, the golden age of nineteenth-century farce was the forties, fifties and sixties: that is, when the tide of domesticity engulfed farce as well as other forms of drama, and finally swept aside the farce traditions inherited fron the eighteenth century. When one examines plays like J. M. Morton's *Box and Cox*, J. S. Coyne's *How to Settle Accounts with your Laundress*, and William Rough's and Andrew Halliday's *The Area Belle*—all performed between 1847 and 1864—one can see that what happened to farce in these years and did not happen to comedy was a substantial infusion of lower middle- and working-class material,[1] and therefore the appearance of comic techniques inseparable from this material. One has only to compare the settings, characters, and comic styles of these three farces with the same elements in *Raising the Wind*, *Patter versus Clatter*, and *Diamond Cut Diamond* to notice the change. The earlier farces have middle- and upper middle-class settings (except for the inn scene in *Raising the Wind*), protagonists of social and financial standing, and comic situations developed through intrigue, deception, and misunderstanding. Of course all farce is dependent to some extent upon intrigue, deception, and misunderstanding, but the world of the later farces mentioned above is markedly different from that of the earlier. Their protagonists—journeyman printer, journeyman hatter, lodging-house keeper, tailor, laundress, hairdresser, ballet dancer, policeman, soldier, milkman, housemaid—work for a living in relatively humble positions; the settings in which they move, like their occupations, are in that border area between working- and lower middle-class life: '*decently furnished*' lodgings, a tailor's showroom, a kitchen. Comic business is inextricably involved with *things*: a gridiron, a chop, a rasher of bacon, a penny roll, a water-butt, a tailor's dummy, a kidney, a laundry copper, a joint of mutton, a table-cloth. This materiality is overwhelmingly domestic, and omnipresent in mid-century

---

[1] The below stairs' farces of the eighteenth century come to mind here, but these are a very small minority, and the world of servants is always juxtaposed with a higher world of masters and mistresses.

farce. When the commercial traveller of *Binks the Bagman* opens his heart to Mrs. Crimmins, his expression of romantic sentiment in the metaphor of mercantile and domestic material-ism is utterly characteristic of the period: 'Has not your lovely image been printed in fast colours on the heart that beats beneath this Marcella waistcoat, never to be washed out, Mrs. C. ? . . . Embrace the present favourable opportunity—take advantage of the opening that now offers, and invest your valuable stock of charms in the arms of your faithful Binks.' Such a content and such a style tells us much about the taste of mid-century farce audiences,[1] and the result of all this is a farce whose healthy vulgarity, comic invention, naïve domesticity, and endearingly eccentric humanity make it one of the finest products of the nineteenth-century stage.

An important characteristic of farce is, for want of a better name, philosophical rather than technical, although developed through appropriate technical devices. This is the harassment of the ordinary individual beyond the bounds of reason, his entrapment in an incomprehensible and absurd situation, his unwilling involvement in an apparently mad world; in short, the farce of the preposterous and desperate predicament. To some degree, these things occur in all farce, especially in that of Labiche and Feydeau. In English farce of the nineteenth century they find characteristically homely expression, and their effect is softened by sentiment and friendly domesticity.

A failure to communicate is one of the first steps on the road to bewilderment and isolation. Templeton in *Deaf as a Post* reduces the stupid Sappy to sputtering rage by pretending deafness, eating Sappy's diner, and occupying Sappy's bed. There is no point of contact between the two; what Sappy takes as outrageously intrusive and anti-social behaviour the 'deaf' Templeton engages in as a matter of pleasant social intercourse

---

[1] Buckstone pointed out to the parliamentary Select Committee of 1866 that 'I can only keep on the Haymarket as a legitimate comedy theatre; and that class of entertainment is not so suited to the galleries.' (*Report of the Select Committee on Theatrical Licenses and Regulations* (1866), p. 126.) Comedy as such was not popular in the neighbourhood working- and lower middle-class theatres of the East End and South Bank, the taste of whose public ran mainly to farce, melodrama, and pantomime. The fact that the afterpiece farce of a West End theatre was usually calculated to begin at half-price time (9 p.m.) and thus attract an audience with a different character from the full-price patrons who had already seen a comedy or a drama, is also significant in any attempt to assess audience taste.

between amicable gentlemen of a like mind. In Buckstone's *Shocking Events* (1838), Puggs, mistaken (unbeknown to him) for a dumb man from whom the horse doctor Griffinhoof expects to make his fortune by discovering a remedy for dumbness, assumes the affliction for the sake of protection from an angry pursuer. Griffinhoof tries every means within his power to 'cure' Puggs, and since these means comprise a series of shocks calculated to make even the dumb cry out, Puggs finds himself inexplicably assaulted by a seeming maniac. The situation worsens when Griffinhoof decides that Puggs is a woman in disguise, addresses him without warning as 'dear Mrs. Perkins', and tells him to 'put on apparel more suitable to your sex'. 'It is a private mad-house,' declares Puggs, 'and that old fellow is one of the lunatics.' Griffinhoof continues planning to subject Puggs to a variety of shocks; at one point he *'comes from his room on tiptoe, produces a pistol which he discharges near* PUGGS' *ear.* KITTY *screams without, and a crash of china is heard. . . .* PUGGS, *stunned with the report, falls into a chair.'* Despite its apparent insanity, *Shocking Events* is anchored to normality and good humour by the solidity and plebeian matter-of-factness of Puggs; indeed, the more normal and down-to-earth is Puggs, the more insane the world in which he finds himself—which is how this kind of farce works. Alfred Highflyer's erroneous belief in Thomas Morton's *A Roland for an Oliver* (1819) that Sir Mark Chase's pleasant country estate is actually a lunatic asylum and Sir Mark a lunatic leads to similar complications, if not to the same sort of domestic rough and tumble. Jacob Earwig, the deaf boots of Selby's *The Boots at the Swan* (1842) is the cause of much misunderstanding and confusion in the first act, when the angry Higgins is simply unable to communicate with him. It is not surprising that the deaf or dumb character recurs; his affliction, pretended or real, represents the ultimate breakdown in communication and the damaging lack of comprehension at the centre of so many farce plots.

Truly farcical also is the situation which the central character may or may not understand, but which makes increasingly impossible demands upon him; a vain attempt to satisfy them may exhaust his physical and mental powers. Sometimes the situation is so extreme that he can be reduced to mindless and quivering helplessness, scurrying willy-nilly like a rat in a trap.

On the level of minor domestic harassment this is what happens
to Perkins Pocock in J. M. Morton's *An Englishman's House is
his Castle* (1857), who resolves to be master of his own house in
Bloomsbury Square but is besieged by a variety of extraordinary lodgers: the jealous inventor Dr. Bang, whose experiments
involve innumerable explosions and who, even while talking to
Pocock, walks about *'producing a number of explosions'*, the
fearful Mrs. Bang, the blustering Captain Connaught, the ever-
complaining maid-of-all-work, and Pocock's eccentric nephew.
Other lodgers make their presence felt by noises off: thumps,
a piercing bosun's whistle, 'God Save the Queen' practised on a
flageolet. Everything in the house goes wrong, including the
kitchen range. In Thomas Williams's *Ici on Parle Français*
(1859), Mr. and Mrs. Spriggins are forced by the sudden
departure of their overworked maid to wait upon their lodgers,
who request boots polished, stays laced, steak cooked, and
coffee made. More serious is the problem of Brownsmith in
Mathews's *Little Toddlekins* (1852). On the point of escaping
from Amanthis, a large and ugly stepdaughter eighteen years
older than himself, to a quiet marriage in Devon, he is horrified
by the arrival in his own house of the Babicombes, his fiancée
and her father, who wish to stay with him and transfer the
marriage ceremony to London. In a fever of anxiety Brownsmith tries to conceal Amanthis's existence from them (they
hear of his former marriage and, believing Amanthis an
infant—Toddlekins—bring her toys and a baby's bonnet) and
then, when the secret is out, desperately attempts to marry her
off, since his fiancée angrily refuses to be called 'mother' every
day by a woman twice her age. Brownsmith's seemingly
intractable difficulty is resolved by Babicombe himself agreeing
to marry Amanthis, and the play ends in complete bewilderment as the characters ponder the precise nature of their
relationships once the two couples are married. The main
character's ordinariness, emphasized by his name—John
Robinson Brownsmith—and complete conventionality are set
against a grotesquely ludicrous but thoroughly domestic
situation of extreme pressure; the tensions engendered by the
comic interplay between the two constitute farce.

One of the best farces treating the situation of the placid
individual invaded and imposed upon by an incomprehensible

outside force that pushes him to the limits of his sanity is Morton's *A Most Unwarrantable Intrusion* (1849), adapted like so many others of its time from the French, but domesticated, also like so many others, in a peculiarly English and Victorian way. Snoozle, relaxing quietly at home with his wife, daughter, niece, and servants out for the day, sees someone about to throw himself into the fishpond. He rushes out, drags him back inside—and finds him a perfect nuisance. The intruder sits in Snoozle's favourite easy chair, fiddles with the breakfast things, stirs the fishbowl with a toasting fork, sneezes into Snoozle's handkerchief, criticizes his clothes, puts on his dressing-gown, rearranges his furniture, decides to stay with his benefactor forever, abuses the portrait of his wife, touches up a picture of Snoozle standing on an easel, knocks over the book-case, accompanies himself on the piano, singing loudly and out of tune, snatches the cap off Snoozle's head and places it on his own, rummages through his drawers, hears his womenfolk come home and resolves to make love to them all. All this drives the frantic Snoozle—who has been rushing about trying to stop him, urging him to leave, and persuading him to drown himself—to distraction. Finally it transpires that this is a stratagem on the part of a rejected suitor for the niece's hand to force Snoozle's consent to the match. The despairing and baffled fury of the dazed, peace-loving Snoozle, fruitlessly expended against a situation quite out of his control, places him in the category of the quintessential farce victim, a placatory sacrifice to the household gods of a malicious universe.

Continual stress can make a farce hero doubt his own reality. Gilbert's Tom Cobb (*Tom Cobb*, 1875) does this; a much earlier character, Colonel Touchwood in Dibdin's *What Next?* (1816) is impersonated by a nephew he closely resembles. The Colonel's lawyer claims that he was summoned, post-horses are brought that he has not ordered, a dentist arrives unbidden to draw his teeth, and he is arrested for fighting a duel he knows nothing about. Touchwood, totally bewildered by the chaos around him, believes that his house and family are bewitched. Grim-shaw of J. M. Morton's *Grimshaw, Bagshaw, and Bradshaw* (1851), is mistaken for Bradshaw as well as Bagshaw and sub-jected to an inexplicable sequence of events in which he is turned out of his lodgings and various unknown people, popping in and out of doors and a secret panel, keep appearing and disappearing. When finally asked, 'Who the devil are you, sir?' he replies, 'Whoever you like, my little dear. The fact is that I'm in such a state of confusion that I neither know nor care who I am; but to the best of my belief I'm not Bradshaw—and I think I can take upon myself that I'm not Bagshaw, tho' I *have* paid his tailor's bill.' Like Tom Cobb and Colonel Touchwood, Grimshaw is reacting to a situation that questions his very identity, a situation that is the philosophical heart of farce.

The acting of nineteenth-century farce appears to have embodied its two main principles: the active and the passive, restlessness and solidity, the frantic energy that was one way of coping with farce problems and the grave, incredulous stillness at the centre of a fevered world that was the other possible reaction. Examples of the first principle can be found in the acting of Lewis, Munden, and Buckstone. According to Leigh Hunt, Munden over-reacted to comic situations:

Almost the whole force of his acting consists in two or three ludicrous gestures and an innumerable variety of as fanciful contortions of countenance as ever threw woman into hysterics: his features are like the reflection of a man's face in a ruffled stream, they undergo a perpetual undulation of grin, every emotion is attended by a grimace, which he by no means wishes to be considered as unstudied, for if it has not immediately its effect upon the spectators, he improves or continues it till it has.[1]

In a later generation Buckstone's acting seems in some respects to have been remarkably similar to Munden's. In the farces already discussed, it was Buckstone who created the roles of Box, Grimshaw, Bob Ticket of *An Alarming Sacrifice*, Coddle of *Married Life*, and Cousin Joe of *A Rough Diamond*. Certainly his acting personified the active principle of farce:

Buckstone, in all his characters, was metaphorically the trombone-player, calling attention to his humour by salient and very effective appeals to the audience, demonstrative, various, gesticulatory . . . His genial people were ultra-genial, his cowards thorough poltroons, his mischief-makers revelled in their sport; but it is quite true to say that characterization with him was quite subordinate to mirth . . . Never was there a face more fitted to excite mirth . . . the chief drawback from this favourite actor's striking merit was his love of exaggeration.

[1] *Critical Essays on the Performers of the London Theatres* (1807), p. 82.

He was accused by some critics of violating taste in certain characters by the breadth of his illustrations. This occasional fault was the result of the same animal spirits and enjoyment of frolic to which he was indebted for much of his success.[1]

On the other hand, the acting of Liston and Keeley was in some roles interpretative of the passive principle, of bewilderment and resignation on the part of the victim of farcical circumstance and the maleficence of fate. It was Liston who played Sappy in *Deaf as a Post* and Brown in *Kill or Cure*. According to Westland Marston, 'in almost every character he evinced quiet, intense self-satisfaction, and ludicrous gravity in absurd sayings and doings. His humour was often to seem insensible to the ludicrous, and a look of utter unconsciousness on his serene and elongated face would accompany the utterance of some absurdity or sly jest, and rouse shouts of laughter, while he stood monumentally calm.'[2] Keeley—the Puggs of *Shocking Events* and Jacob Earwig of *The Boots at the Swan*—'was usually phlegmatic, impassive, and pathetically acquiescent in the droll inflictions which fate had in store for him'.[3] The first kind of acting conveyed the vigour, bustle, pace, exaggeration, and not uncommon frenzy of farce; the second the puzzled incomprehension and fundamental helplessness of the farce hero who finds himself at the centre of an absurd world. The two kinds complemented each other; both were necessary to express the style and meaning of farce.

Many characteristics of the earlier farce can be found later in the century. There is less sentimentality and overt moralizing, less intrusion of serious matter and pathetic emotion, less direct addressing of the audience, less use of working- and lower middle-class material, and less insistence on the marital superiority of the husband; in fact he becomes even more of a comic butt than before. However, the basic machinery of misunderstanding, deception, intrigue, coincidence, and the inordinate rapidity of events is unchanged, and this machinery continues to operate in a cozy domestic setting, a setting that is socially elevated as the century progresses.

One aspect of farce intensified and elaborated in the later period is the use of physical comedy and comic business. The

[1] Westland Marston, *Our Recent Actors* (1888), ii. 88–91.
[2] Ibid., p. 292.   [3] Ibid., p. 88.

physical excess of J. M. Morton's *Drawing Room, Second Floor, and Attics* (1864) can hardly be found in the first half of the century. A plot summary is necessary to indicate the extent of the business, which indeed constitutes the whole play. Tripto-lemus Brown, a chemist's assistant, flees in terror from the violent pursuit of the jealous Captain Hardaport (whom he has never met); he is aided by his true love, the servant Phoebe. The play begins in an attic: Bunny, a retired furrier, enters and Phoebe's uncle accidentally knocks his hat over his eyes with the broom; Bunny then falls downstairs. Brown is perceived climbing out of a chimney-pot on the roof—where he took shelter during his first flight from Hardaport—and, exhausted and black with soot, gets through the attic window, wipes his face with clean linen, which is blackened, then clambers on to the roof again and hides in the other chimney-pot to avoid discovery by Phoebe's uncle. In the second scene he struggles to free himself as he hangs kicking above the fireplace a floor lower down, in the apartment of Arabella, Hardaport's sister; in this struggle he knocks the fire-irons over and does not succeed in dropping into the grate until a fire has been lit beneath him. When Hardaport tries to enter the room, Brown quickly puts on a dress of Arabella's over his torn and now even blacker clothes, and pretends to be a charwoman. In a fury Hardaport bursts open the locked door and struggles with Brown—someone carrying a tray of plates, glasses, and food is knocked over—who crashes through the window to the balcony below. In the next scene Brown emerges in the drawing-room looking more battered than ever and drenched with rain. He disguises himself in a ridiculous costume at an elegant party—other characters also appear in exaggerated dress—tries to avoid his drunken uncle, attempts to rush out when dis-covered, and in the ensuing scuffle pulls the cloth off a table loaded with '*pastry, cakes, decanters, wine glasses, &c.*' The precise character of the comic business is evident from a stage direction occurring when the wrathful Captain Hardaport finds Brown in Arabella's room:

TRIPTOLEMUS *here makes a sudden bolt, but is stopped by the* CAPTAIN. *In the struggle* TRIPTOLEMUS *slips out of his gown, which remains in* CAPTAIN'*s hands, and leaves* TRIPTOLEMUS *his trousers and waistcoat, with a very ample crinoline over them. He then makes a rush to the door, meeting* LUKE SHARP *as he enters carrying a tray, on which are a pie, plates, and glasses, upsets him and the contents of the tray.* The CAPTAIN *again seizes* TRIPTOLEMUS, *who retreats backwards struggling with the* CAPTAIN; *when close to the window,* TRIPTOLEMUS *loses his balance and falls backward through the window with great smash of glass.* ARABELLA *and* PHOEBE *each scream with all their might, and fall into different chairs.* LUKE SHARP *shouts 'Police', &c. &c.*

With its lower middle-class emphasis and jolly bouncing vulgarity, *Drawing Room, Second Floor, and Attics* belongs to the older variety of nineteenth-century farce. But its heavy indulgence in physical comedy is a mark of the newer farce. The banal dialogue and awful jokes of Charles Hawtrey's immensely popular *The Private Secretary* (1883) are accompanied by an enormous amount of violently physical business.[1] The unfortunate private secretary, Spalding—a timid, bewildered, uncomprehending character—is, among the innumerable physical indignities he suffers, pushed around, tripped up, shoved under tables, tied to a chair, hit by an umbrella, sat on, and stuffed into a chest. This kind of farce humour was much on the increase in the last quarter of the century, despite the refining influence of writers like Pinero and the gradual sophistication of other aspects of farce. One possible explanation is that, as the low comedian who could skilfully create character and a range of human eccentricities became rarer on the stage, his kind of comedy had to be replaced by one that did not require such powers of personal artistic creativity but could emphasize instead the much more easily attainable humour of general stage business and physical knockabout, a group effect rather than the power of an individual talent. Whatever the reason,

---

[1] Two examples of the quality of Hawtrey's jokes can be cited.
Gibson, a tailor, is talking to Cattermole:
GIBSON. That coat was made by an ijjot.
CATTERMOLE. It was not 'made in Egypt'. It was made in Calcutta.
GIBSON. What cutter?
CATTERMOLE. Calcutta.
GIBSON. I don't know him!
Douglas is showing the girls books in the library:
DOUGLAS. First of all, here's *The Vicar of Wakefield* . . . . .
EDITH. Oh, we know that—by heart.
DOUGLAS. No, by Goldsmith!

such farces abounded. Brandon Thomas's *Charley's Aunt* (1892) is one well-known example; its reliance on obvious physical effects—all carefully noted in stage directions—is extreme. Shaw recorded his disgust at this kind of farce when he reviewed *Never Again* (1897), an anonymous adaptation from the French:

In this play everyone who opens a door and sees somebody outside it utters a yell of dismay and slams the door to as if the fiend in person had knocked at it. When anybody enters a room, he or she is received with a roar of confusion and terror, and frantically ejected by bodily violence. The audience does not know why; but as each member of it thinks he ought to, and believes his neighbour does, he echoes the yell of the actor with a shout of laughter; and so the piece 'goes' immensely. It is, to my taste, a vulgar, stupid, noisy, headachy, tedious business.[1]

By 1897, plays of the general description of *Never Again*, adapted from the contemporary French boulevard farce, had been popular in the West End for twenty years. As in melodrama, drama, and comedy, adaptation from the French had been so widespread in farce, particularly since about the 1830s, that there is little point in treating it separately. The French farce that attracted English dramatists in the 1870s, however, was rather specialized, a farce that commonly dealt in bourgeois adultery or near-adultery, often involving both wife and husband, and placing the guilty parties in a series of compromising situations from which it would seem impossible to extricate them without the fatal discovery of the truth. To these ends the considerable abilities of the French farceur were directed, and the best results resemble precision machinery operating with inexorable and smoothly oiled inevitability. *The Wedding March* (1873), Gilbert's version of *Un Chapeau de Paille d'Italie* (1851), by Eugène Labiche and Marc Michel, really began the vogue of adaptation from this type of French farce. However, the major impetus to the movement on the English stage was *Les Dominos Roses* (1876), by Alfred Hennequin and Alfred Delacour, which spawned numerous English progeny over the next thirty years. The best of the immediately contemporary ones were Dion Boucicault's *Forbidden Fruit* (New York 1876, London 1880) and James Albery's direct adaptation, *Pink Dominos* (1877).

[1] *The Saturday Review*, lxxiv (16 October 1897), p. 417.

Both plays share the basic plot and comic complications of Les Dominos Roses. Two husbands plan a night out with ladies of doubtful character; the rendezvous is a restaurant of equally doubtful character at Cremorne, with a farcically convenient number of private rooms and doors opening onto the stage. By coincidence or design their wives appear in the same restaurant, to the confusion and horror of all. The pattern of development in farces of this kind is generally similar: in the first act a slow buildup of plots and counterplots; in the second (or third in the case of *Forbidden Fruit*) a fast pace with everybody arriving at the restaurant amid growing comic tension, and a climax with characters running in and out and hiding from each other; in the third act, set once more in the home, a painful unravelling of the tangled plot skein, a profusion of explanations and consequences, and peace made between all parties. In *Forbidden Fruit* Dove and Buster scheme to get away from their wives, and Dove invents a trip to Nottingham on business. Of course everything goes wrong: Dove's wife and her brother arrive at Cremorne when Dove is there, and Dove, not knowing the brother, suspects her of infidelity; Mrs. Buster discovers her husband with Mrs. Dove. Finally the brother intervenes to rescue Dove's reputation and the play ends happily. As in all farces of its type the plot is elaborate and complex; a full summary would occupy considerable space. In *Pink Dominos* Charles Grey-thorne, a quiet businessman from Manchester, and his friend Sir Percy Wagstaffe make assignations at Cremorne with two unknown ladies in pink dominos. The ladies are actually their wives engaged in testing their character. All four, as well as an old friend, Tubbs, his *'bright little lady'*, and Mrs. Tubbs's nephew with the Wagstaffe maid, gather in couples at the restaurant, whose head waiter is the unscrupulous Brisket. Many complications ensue: there is a steady stream of entrances and exits through the four doors to private rooms; partners are interchanged; the maid is involved with three men consecutively. Once again, in the third act, the characters extricate themselves with great difficulty from the consequences of their actions.

Without doubt this was a new farce on the English stage. Comic business concerning men and women hiding in bedrooms and closets had long been traditional, and examples could be offered from scores of comedies and farces. In the late eighteenth century and the first seventy years of the nineteenth century, however, such business was merely amusing and rather innocent; the naïveté of whatever sexual suggestion there was rendered it innocuous. Several critics of the 1870s, however, found the new farce alarming.[1] E. L. Blanchard, at first objecting to *Pink Dominos* on the grounds that the marriages depicted in French farce did not truly reflect 'the present conditions of domestic life in any capital where the slightest regard is paid to the "humanities" or where friendship, love, and truth have any distinct significance', finally made his protest specifically moral:

> It is yet right to assume that conjugal infidelity has not yet become recognized as a trait in the national character, and that husband and wife are not, in this country at least, passing their existence in trying to deceive, dishonour, and detect each other. . . . Of the very nature of the story it would hardly be excessive prudishness to withhold a description, for the same reason that no one in a family circle would think of explicitly detailing the plots of the plays of the Restoration.[2]

C. P. Newton suggested that English dramatic taste might have been 'depraved by a too close study of the dramatic works of our French neighbours and their views of domestic life', a taste that indulged itself in 'the worthless side of life' and 'the attempted invasion of married life and its obligations'.[3]

Nevertheless, even Blanchard had to admit that in English adaptations of the 'by no means squeamish' Palais Royal school 'a kind of deodorizing process has been usually deemed necessary before presentation to a London public of a theatrical dish compounded of such ingredients'.[4] Joseph Knight noted of French farces that 'complaint has been heard of the licence in which authors indulge in pieces of this class. As a rule, on the English stage at least, farcical comedy is skittish rather than indecent, and frequenters of the modern theatre have little of which to complain.'[5] Indeed, although the English adaptations had many more sexual implications than earlier farce, they were in all sorts of ingenious ways bowdlerized, sentimentalized, and generally rendered far less 'offensive' than the French originals.

---

[1] Before 1870 there was an almost total absence of critical comment upon farce.
[2] *The Daily Telegraph*, 5 April 1877.
[3] 'Frivolous Comedy', *The Theatre* (November 1881), pp. 268–9.
[4] *The Daily Telegraph*, 5 April 1877.
[5] *Theatrical Notes* (1893), p. xiii.

At the end of *Forbidden Fruit* the repentant Dove was made to say, 'I have tried the taste of forbidden fruit. I don't like it! A fast life looks charming to those who see it as spectators look at a play, but you have introduced me behind the scenes, and I prefer the illusion to the reality.' The *demi-mondaine* Foedora of *Les Dominos Roses*, picked up at the Variété and taken to the restaurant, became the virtuous Miss Barron of *Pink Dominos*, who innocently danced with Tubbs, could not find her friend afterwards, and 'promised ma to be home by one'.

The process of adaptation from the French and the adapter's methods of 'deodorizing' can be observed from a comparison of *Bébé* (1877), by Hennequin and Émile de Najac, with *Betsy* (1879), the English version by F. C. Burnand. In the French play Gaston, the son of Baron D'Aigreville, is treated as a baby by his parents; actually he is socially and sexually quite sophisticated, having had affairs with *cocottes* and the maid, Toinette. At present he is trying his best to seduce the wife of a family friend, De Kernanigous. One of the *cocottes* who come to visit him in his private part of the house, Aurelie, is also a mistress of De Kernanigous. From then on women are hidden in rooms, misunderstandings and misidentifications proliferate, Gaston's sexual proclivities are discovered, but De Kernanigous is talked out of suspecting his wife, who was on the point of surrendering to Gaston. Finally Gaston reluctantly agrees to marry a distant relative, Toinette is frustrated, and the play ends on a note of uneasy calm and hasty patchings up. The plot of *Betsy* is very similar; many of the same incidents and some of the same dialogue are used. But that is where the similarity ends. Characterizations and relationships between characters are fundamentally altered. The maid Betsy wants Adolphus (Gaston) to *marry* her, and Adolphus wants to *marry* the now perfectly respectable girl who was a *cocotte* in *Bébé*. The whole business of *cocottes* and sexual infidelity is excised from the English. Aurelie becomes Madame Polenta, a singing teacher, and McManus (De Kernanigous) takes private lessons from her. No doubt on stage this was made suggestive of McManus's intentions, but their relationship is totally innocent compared to the French. The only suggestion of impropriety between Adolphus and Mrs. McManus is contained in the following passage:

ADOLPHUS. If you call me dear child and little boy, and treat me as you used to, I'll treat you as I used to, and call you auntie, and give you a kiss. [*Kisses her.*

MRS. MCMANUS. Oh, for shame!

ADOLPHUS. Am I a boy now?

Not only are their relations and Gaston's intentions much more explicit in the French, but the same scene is much fuller, and passionate rather than playful:

GASTON. C'est de vous seule qu'il s'agit — de vous, si jolie, si bonne et si bien faite pour être adorée —

DIANE. Ah! Gaston, s'il rentrait!

GASTON. Mais puisqu'il est au couvent, votre mari. Ne parlons donc pas de ça! De vous que la cruelle destinée a unie à un être incapable de vous apprécier, de vous comprendre. [*Il la reprend dans ses bras.*

DIANE [*Voulant se dégager.*] Encore une fois, je vous en supplie!

GASTON. Oui! Incapable. [*Il l'embrasse.*] Tandis que moi! [*Il l'embrasse.*] Oh! Moi! [*Il l'embrasse.*

DIANE. [*À part.*] Ah, mon Dieu!

In *Betsy* McManus tells his wife that 'a flame of Dolly's' is hidden behind the door; the French is 'sa maîtresse', and translation of this kind is a matter of course in the English version. In *Bébé* Gaston's tutor discovers that Aurelie is the wife from whom he separated and to whom he pays an allowance that he cannot afford; he is delighted to find her a *cocotte* because he then possesses legal proof of her infidelity and will not have to pay the allowance. His English equivalent, Dawson, is happily reconciled with his wife at the end of the play. Adolphus eagerly rushes out for a marriage licence so that he can be speedily united with his beloved Nellie; Gaston has no desire to marry at all. Finally, the social tone and setting of the English version is lower than that of the French original, and although *Bébé* is full of characters rushing around to conceal themselves it does not contain in its stage directions the sort of traditional nineteenth-century English farce business specifically required in *Betsy* and exemplified by these two quotations:

MCMANUS. You keep my secret and I'll keep yours. [*Nudges him.*

ADOLPHUS. [*Nudging* MCMANUS *violently.*] I think I got the best of him that time.

Adolphus and his friend Dick are talking to Dawson:

ADOLPHUS. Ah, you've been a gay dog in your time.   [*Nudging him.*
DICK. A slyboots, eh?
    [*Both dig him in the ribs till he falls; they pick him up, apologizing.*

Farces in which a married man is discomfited by a sequence
of domestic contretemps, misconceived by all about him, and
everybody's antagonist in turn, until the pressures of cumulative
harassment build up to a comically explosive climax involving
the whole household, remained popular. Whether original or
adapted from French or German, their pattern was similar.
The *Pink Dominos–Forbidden Fruit* plot was also popular, but
not ubiquitous. Two examples of the former plot are *The
Snowball* (1879) and *The Arabian Nights* (1887), both by Sydney
Grundy. In *The Snowball*, Felix Featherstone, resolved to
teach his wife a lesson for going to see *Pink Dominos* without
his knowledge, writes her a note signed 'Pink Dominos'
appointing a rendezvous. The wife discovers his plot, and,
equally determined to chastise him for going to the same play
on the same evening without *her*, manages it so that he believes
he has actually given the note to the maid, Penelope. Terrified
of his wife finding out, he tries to escape from Penelope, and
when that fails attempts to bribe her into silence. She, however,
is also bribed by Mrs. Featherstone to threaten him with dis-
closure. Utterly bewildered and very frightened, Featherstone
has no idea that his wife is playing a trick on him or that
Penelope is unaware of the contents of the note. Domestic
complications multiply, and from all sides he is browbeaten
into a state of panic and despair. The Act II curtain finds five
people chasing him several times across the stage in order to
deliver notes to him. Ultimately all is happily resolved when he
decides to make a clean breast of it and tell the truth—a rare
occurrence in French farce. Arthur Hummingtop of *The Arabian
Nights* gets himself into just as much trouble as Featherstone.
Inspired by the example of Harun al-Rashid, he goes disguised
into the streets where he meets a pretty girl lost in the fog and
gallantly escorts her to a theatre. To his horror the girl—a
circus performer—turns up at his house the next day and will
not leave. Under the grim eye of his mother-in-law he introduces her as his niece just arrived from New York, hurries the

real niece off to a hotel, is of course suspected by his wife, and sweats his way through further twists and turns of the plot. At the Act II curtain five women faint successively upon recognizing each other or receiving damaging information; by Act III Hummingtop is the helpless victim of a situation completely out of control, a situation not only injurious to himself but also, because of his wild inventions, to everyone in the house.

To the kind of drama that presented the comic agonies of such as Felix Featherstone and Arthur Hummingtop, Shaw took the strongest exception:

To laugh without sympathy is a ruinous abuse of a noble function; and the degradation of any race may be measured by the degree of their addiction to it . . . we find people who would not join in the laughter of a crowd of peasants at the village idiot, or tolerate the public flogging or pillorying of a criminal, booking seats to shout with laughter at a farcical comedy, which is, at bottom, the same thing— namely, the deliberate indulgence of that horrible, derisive joy in humiliation and suffering which is the beastliest element in human nature.[1]

What alarmed Shaw was not farce at all, but that part of human nature which enjoys farce as a means of sadistic gratification not available in ordinary life. Certainly, physical and mental humiliation is an essential aspect of farce, and it can be found abundantly in English farce of the nineteenth century. Both the comedy of physical business and the comedy of the despairing imprisonment in unrelenting circumstance—much intensified in the farce of the last quarter of the century—can be directed to this end. Yet despite the sufferings of its protagonists and the powerful influence of late-century French farce, the English farce of the nineteenth century, taken as a whole, remains essentially innocent of malice and destructive anarchy. Its homely domesticity, its fondness for ideals, morality, and sentiment, its seemingly naïve charm, its bumbling aggression, its friendly contact with its audience—all these things effectively and cheerfully keep at bay the darker devils of farce.

[1] *The Saturday Review*, lxxxi (9 May 1896), pp. 473–4.

Harlequin in His Element. Grimaldi as the watchman. Scene iv.

V. PANTOMIMES, EXTRAVAGANZAS AND BURLESQUES

In Thomas Dibdin's *Harlequin Hoax* (1814), Columbine says that pantomime audiences

are always so very silent and attentive: now tragedies, comedies, operas, and farces are doom'd to suffer all the complicated combinations of 'Pray ask that gentleman to sit down,' 'Box keeper, where's my fourth row on the second circle?' 'Take off your hat,' and 'Keep quiet in the lobby.' But in a Pantomime, Sir, the moment the curtain goes up, if any unfortunate gentleman speaks a word, they make no reply but throw him over directly.

A more business-like point of view was that of Francis Place, who told the Select Committee on Dramatic Literature in 1832 that the financial records of Covent Garden from the season of 1810–11 to the season of 1820–1 showed that the theatre had been maintained by the success of its Christmas pantomimes, and that 'no profit was got from all their earlier performances during the eleven seasons when the concern was most prosperous'.[1] And that faithful *aficionado* of pantomime, Leigh Hunt, could declare in 1817, albeit hyperbolically, that 'there is no such thing as modern comedy, tragedy, nor even farce since Mr. Colman left off writing it; but Pantomime flourishes as much as ever, and makes all parties comfortable . . .. there is something *real* in Pantomime: there is animal spirit in it'.[2]

Pantomime continued to be popular well beyond the Regency into the reigns of Victoria and Edward VII (and, indeed, up to the present day), its nature and appeal evolving and changing over such a long period. In the course of the nineteenth century it was joined as an eccentric, fantastic, and often lavish entertainment by extravaganza and burlesque. As will appear, these

---

[1] *Report from the Select Committee on Dramatic Literature* (1832), p. 206. Times had not changed. The Prompter in Henry Fielding's satire against pantomime, *Tumble-Down Dick* (1736), tells an indignant author that the pantomime arranger 'brings more Money to the House, than all the Poets put together'.

[2] *The Examiner*, 15 January 1817.

three forms of nineteenth-century theatre are specifically related in ways that make obvious their inclusion in the same chapter. More generally, all of them are, both in historical fact and dramatic spirit, holiday theatre. The Christmas pantomime, the Easter or Christmas burlesque or extravaganza—whatever the season or genre the audience saw the embodiment in theatrical art of varying combinations of high spirits, whim, absurdity, grotesquerie, iconoclasm, fairy-tale, scenic splendour, topsy-turveydom, and nightmare. Much nineteenth-century theatre was light entertainment. Pantomime, extravaganza, and burlesque comprised a great deal of it, attained heights of popularity, and then suffered severely in the esteem of critic–historians (including contemporaries), who, if they had to write about what to them was the miserable degradation of nineteenth-century drama, were certainly not going to descend to the darkest depths of popular theatre.

Of these three dramatic types of light entertainment, panto-mime was the most genuinely popular, in both senses of the word, since it drew audiences throughout the nineteenth century, and entertained all classes, appealing to the patrons of working and lower-middle-class theatres as much as it did to more socially elevated audiences. Extravaganza and burlesque were almost entirely aimed at the relatively educated and the middle class.

Early nineteenth-century pantomime directly descended, not only from the traditions of *commedia dell' arte* as they had evolved for centuries, but also from the distinctively English pantomime of the eighteenth century, an amalgam of serious scenes from classical and modern legend or fable with un-related harlequinade episodes depicting the love of Harlequin and Columbine, their unsuccessful pursuit by the parent or guardian figure, Pantaloon, and his assistants, and the tricks and transformations wrought along the way by the magic powers of Harlequin's bat.[1] This pattern had changed little from the years of John Rich's pantomimes at Covent Garden and Garrick's at Drury Lane, except that after Sheridan's *Robinson Crusoe* (1781) the harlequinade scenes constituted the

---

[1] English pantomime of the period 1806–36 has been the subject of a compre-hensive and detailed study, David Mayer's *Harlequin in His Element* (1969), to which I am directly indebted.

second and greater part instead of being interwoven with the serious and refined scenes. They were also directly related to what became known as the 'opening' (the first part) by the transformation of the principal characters in that opening—the young lovers, the parent or guardian and his servant, the rival suitor—into the regular personages of the harlequinade: Harlequin, Columbine, Pantaloon, Clown, and sometimes Lover. At the same time the supernatural being effecting the transformation awarded Harlequin his wonder-working bat, which, slapped upon scenery, floor, or object, gave the cue for a transformation whose purpose was to hinder pursuit or bewilder, frighten, and torment the pursuers; this ritual existed in England from the earliest days of eighteenth-century pantomime.

Thus the nineteenth century inherited a fairly stable pantomime form, which developed over the years until the accession of Victoria but did not alter its basic structure. The introductory part, or opening—much shorter than the harlequinade until the 1830s—took its subject-matter, as before, from folk story, fairytale, nursery-rhyme, mythology, history, or exotic literature; and presented, usually in rhymed couplets or blank verse, the basic plot of authoritarian father or guardian—king, squire, magician, &c.—set on frustrating the desire of his beautiful daughter or ward to marry the young man of her choice, offering her instead to a foolish or elderly and often wealthy suitor. To prevent this happening, a benevolent spirit or fairy intervenes, takes the young lovers under her protection (the good spirit is commonly female), transforms them into Harlequin and Columbine for their better safety, gives Harlequin his magic bat, sometimes allotting him a task or quest so that he prove his worth, transforms the other characters (sometimes a rival and evil spirit undertakes this part of the transformation) into Pantaloon, Clown, and Lover, and condemns them for their sins to comic pursuit of Harlequin and Columbine. Then follow the largely dumb-show antics of the harlequinade, in sharp contrast to the spoken, elevated, and often scenically resplendent opening. After many scenes of chase, trickery, and literally knockabout low comedy, Harlequin somehow loses his magic bat to Pantaloon and is deprived of his power. This occurs in a 'dark' scene: a dismal cave, grotto, or ruin. The supernatural being intervenes again, unites the lovers, and reconciles them with their pursuers. The pantomime then ends with a choral finale celebrating love and happiness, set in a spectacular scene representing a temple or palace, the dwelling-place of the benevolent fairy. Orchestral accompaniment was extensive—there are, for instance, sixty-seven music cues in the manuscript of Thomas Dibdin's *Harlequin and Humpo* (1812)—and comic and pathetic songs, dances, displays of skill such as rope-dancing, and scenic dioramas interrupted the course of the harlequinade. Altogether such a pantomime ran for an hour or two without intermission, making up the second half of a bill whose first half was endured with some impatience by audiences eager for the pantomime. At the major theatres pantomimes were offered at Christmas and Easter (early in the century, in November as well); at the minor at Easter and midsummer. Not until the 1840s did pantomime become, as it was to remain, Christmas fare only.

While the great Clown, Joseph Grimaldi, dominated the harlequinade of Covent Garden and Sadler's Wells between 1806 and his retirement in 1823, Clown rather than Harlequin was the most prominent character. The latter lost the ascendant position and comic attributes he possessed in the eighteenth century and became a dancer, a *poseur*, a magic-worker. In *Harlequin Hoax* is the dictum that 'Harlequin is the worst part in a Pantomime—a thing of shreds and patches'. Of course comedy originated from Harlequin's tricks and transformations, but these arose from scenic mechanisms and were no part of Harlequin himself. On the other hand Clown was a creator of anarchy, an inventor of schemes, a ludicrous victim of his own plots and Harlequin's pranks, a comic original with—especially in the hands of Grimaldi—a richly developed comic character:

The Clown is a delightful fellow to tickle our self-love with. He is very stupid, mischievous, gluttonous, and cowardly, none of which, of course, any of us are, especially the first; and as in these respects, we feel a lofty advantage over him, so he occasionally aspires to our level by a sort of glimmering cunning and jocoseness, of which he thinks so prodigiously himself as to give us a still more delightful notion of our superiority. When he shakes his shoulders therefore at the dullest trick in the world, we laugh with equal enjoyment; when he pilfers from the cake-man, and looks the most outrageous lies in the latter's face, we love the profligate wag who so unambitiously amuses us at another's expense; and when he trips up his poor old master, whose face comes on the ground like a block of wood, we shout with rapture to see the lesser stupid overturn the greater.[1]

After the retirement of Grimaldi and the lack of an immediate successor of his quality and comic ingenuity, the harlequinade portion of the pantomime gradually lost favour in the eyes of the audience. Openings lengthened until they comprised half the pantomime and more; scenic elements became more spectacular and important; and the harlequinade began the long decline from which it never emerged. However, such events did not affect the popularity of Regency pantomime, and their full consequences belong to a later point of chronological narration. Leigh Hunt succinctly stated the appeal of this pantomime:

The three general pleasures of a Pantomime are its bustle, its variety, and its sudden changes. We have already described the increasing vivacity of the music. The stage is never empty or still; either Pantaloon is hobbling about, or somebody is falling flat, or somebody else is receiving an ingenious thump on the face, or the Clown is jolting himself with jaunty dislocations, or Colombine is skimming across like a frightened pigeon, or Harlequin is quivering hither and thither, or gliding out of a window, or slapping something into a metamorphosis. But a Pantomime, at present, is also the best medium of dramatic satire. Our farces and comedies spoil the effect of their ridicule by the dull mistakes of the author; but the absence of dialogue in the Pantomime saves him this contradiction, and leaves the spectators, according to their several powers, to imagine what supplement they have to the mute caricature before them.[2]

Pantomime audiences were offered two things for the price of one, so to speak: the formality, relative refinement and solemnity, romantic illusion, scenic splendour, idealized love, and ordered progression of the opening were complemented by the fast-paced, extravagant low comedy of a world of ideal disorder and chaos. The governing spirits of the Regency harlequinade were misrule and anarchy: the freedom to commit amusing capital crimes and set law and authority at nought was bestowed abundantly upon Harlequin and Clown. Thus the harlequinade was, like melodrama, psychologically escapist, offering audiences a release for sadistic impulses toward cheating, tricking, larceny, cruelty, wanton destruction, violence, and rebellion. Melodrama, however, idealized morality, revered the aged parent, rewarded virtue and punished vice; pantomime satisfied different desires and did the exact opposite. The same audiences enjoyed both genres, and both found common ground in a general hostility toward constituted and inherited authority. In melodrama this was largely a matter of class conflict, but in pantomime the same hostility manifested itself in vicious treatment of an oppressive father-figure, Pantaloon, and his watchman or policeman surrogate. Yet pantomime audiences, like melodrama audiences, could eat their cake and have it too. No amount of mischance, natural disaster, villainy, crime, and bloodshed could thwart the course of true love, virtue, and justice in melodrama; in pantomime, Harlequin and Columbine were always united at the end and their pursuers frustrated. Furthermore, the brutality and savagery of harlequinade assaults and killings, as in the animated cartoons of today with their ritualized and endless pursuit, cruelty, and violence, were merely and hugely laughable. Thus the often turbulent, grim, repressive, and brutal world of Regency London was comically inverted by the trick mirrors of the harlequinade, which satirically and crazily reflected that real world and simultaneously laughed at it.

This pantomime world was of the city, not the country. The number of rural scenes in the eighteenth-century harlequinade was considerably reduced when Grimaldi—a London Clown, born, bred, and trained—and his colleagues were on the stage. Not surprisingly, therefore, this kind of pantomime dramatized, though confusedly and undiscriminatingly, aspects of contemporary life such as changes in fashion, technological development and new inventions, economic questions, the war against France, and a wide range of topical social matters, a few significant, most trivial and ephemeral. What is immediately striking about the social context of the harlequinade is the extent to which *goods* (from a profusion of *shops*), *things*, and *objects* motivate the characters and determine the nature of the comedy. In Thomas Dibdin's *Harlequin and Mother Goose* (1806) a live duck flies out of a pie about to be consumed by Pantaloon and Clown; the chair on which Clown is seated suddenly ascends into the air, terrifying him; Clown is caught by a steel trap, and a spring gun instantly fires and alarms Pantaloon; Clown and Pantaloon are frightened by the two figures beating the time on St. Dunstan's clock, which Harlequin has caused to descend; Clown's hand is caught in a letter-box which Harlequin has changed to the mouth of a lion; a sideboard becomes a beehive stand and the bees swarm around Pantaloon and Clown, who run off bellowing. In *Harlequin and Humpo* Clown is rolled off-stage wrapped round a carriage wheel; Harlequin changes a coach into a balloon that rises and carries off Clown, Pantaloon, and Lover; Clown successively and rapidly consumes a jelly, a tart, a sausage, and a plum-cake, each in a mouthful; Harlequin makes the animated figures on a Dutch clock come to life and assault Clown and Pantaloon; Pantaloon and Lover forcibly administer a series of medicinal draughts to Clown, who '*swells prodigiously*'; Clown becomes the pendulum of a clock; a tele-scope changes to a gun that shoots Clown, who refuses medical aid and instead steals and eats dumplings from a pastry-cook's; a box suddenly encloses Clown, who is carried off roaring.

Episodes of this sort occur in every pantomime of this period, and years later Clown and Pantaloon were suffering in the same way. A reviewer commented on one scene from the harlequinade of *The Castle of Otranto* (1840):

The fun consists in the gradual progress made from a well-furnished room to bare walls, under the influence of Harlequin's wand, to the great annoyance of the two lodgers. Chair after chair slips through the wall or floor, fire-irons find their way up the chimney, candles whirl round when wanted to light a cigar, window-curtains dissolve to nought, sofas and tables take their departure, the chimney orna-ments fling themselves at the clown, and the huge looking-glass falls on his head with fearful smash, leaving him standing in melan-choly astonishment in the empty frame.[1]

In nineteenth-century farce man is initially responsible for his own absurd predicament, although chance and an implacable universe drive him inexorably thereafter over the edge of comic catastrophe. In the Regency harlequinade man's plight is often created by the transformation, misbehaviour, and relentless hostility of objects and mechanical devices: things are not what

[1] *The Times*, 28 December 1840.

they seem to be, or rather they are, but then they change frighteningly into something else. Nothing can be relied on; the very ground itself dissolves under the feet of the helpless characters. Such comedy is almost cosmic in its implications; audiences were really laughing at the yawning gulfs in man's own life. As is usual in extreme forms of comic theatre, a terrible seriousness underlies the jollity and 'animal spirit' of pantomime that Leigh Hunt so much admired.

By the 1830s several writers considered that pantomime was declining. Charles Rice said of *Harlequin and Old Gammer Gurton* (1836) that 'there is none of that poignant satire which used formerly to characterize this species of entertainment'.[1] Hunt complained at length:

It is agreed on all hands that Pantomimes are not what they were. The story with which they used to set out, and which used to form merely a brief excuse for putting the Harlequinade in motion, now forms a considerable part of the performance; an innovation which we should hail with pleasure if it were always in such good taste as in some instances, but which is rarely apt to be so, and is followed by a set of tricks and transformations equally stinted and wanting in fancy, and a total departure from the old and genuine Harlequin plot, which consisted in the run-away vivacities of a couple of lovers full of youth and spirits, the eternal hobbling after them of the decrepid Pantaloon, and the broad gluttony, selfishness, and mischief of his servant the Clown, all tending to one point. The Clown retains something of his character still, but the rest has become a mere mass of gratuitous absurdity without object. There is no real action going on. Sometimes none at all. Columbine takes her rest; Harlequin dances at his leisure; the parties, instead of pursuing one another, often join with one accord in a mysterious truce; and Pantaloon, though at Covent-Garden he has fallen into the hands of one who ought to represent him best, has become as active as Harlequin, and without any shadow of pretence for not overtaking him. The Clown talks too much, without saying anything to the purpose. At least he says very little to the purpose. He does not enter into the true humour of the Clown, which is to be merely sensual and selfish in ordinary, and never to speak, except at some rich and rare interval, when an overwhelming sensation forces the words out of his mouth;— better if one word, or a monosyllable. When Grimaldi used to say,

---

[1] *The London Theatre in the Eighteen-Thirties*, ed. A. C. Sprague and Bertram Shuttleworth (1950), p. 11.

'Don't!' to some fellow putting him to a horrible torture; or 'Nice!' when eating gingerbread; or 'Nice moon!' after sentimentally contemplating the moonlight, the necessity with which he was delivered of his exclamation was made apparent to everybody and contained a world of concentration. We have nothing of this now. The sayings are old and reiterated, and the occasions gratuitous. Pantomime used formerly to be the representative of the Old Comedy, and gave us some good Aristophanic satire on the events of the day. It attempts this but sparely now, and but seldom does it well. The contrivers appear to be worn out, and the managers stingy of their money. Even the slaps on the face are not what they used to be, nor the boltings through flap-doors in the walls. . . .

In short, Pantomimes seem to have become partakers of the serious spirit of the age, and to be waiting for the settlement of certain great questions and heavy national accounts, to know when they are to laugh and be merry again.[1]

The pantomime that Hunt was reviewing, *Hop O' My Thumb and His Brothers*, had eight scenes in its opening, twelve in the harlequinade. Two years later the opening of *Old Mother Hubbard and Her Dog* (1833) contained nine scenes, the harlequinade only eight. The managers of the major theatres were emphasizing scenic spectacle. *The Times* noted that the 1826 pantomimes at Drury Lane and Covent Garden had cost £1,000 each.[2] For Drury Lane's *Harlequin and the Flying Chest* (1823) Clarkson Stanfield painted a diorama of Plymouth Harbour, the new breakwater, a vessel in distress during a storm which then clears away, a rainbow, an Indiaman aground, and a general view of Plymouth. This diorama, which interrupted the harlequinade, was 272 feet in length and alone cost £1,380.[3] Scenic splendour was also increased in the opening, which flourished as the harlequinade correspondingly declined. Such a development did not antagonize everybody. Henry Crabb Robinson, for instance, seemed to enjoy anything in pantomime but the harlequinade. Of *Harlequin and Friar Bacon* (1821) he wrote that 'the scenery is beautiful and the buffoonery shorter than usual. Indeed, scene painting is now carried to a degree of excellence quite delightful.'[4] After seeing *Harlequin and the Talking Bird, the Singing Tree, and the Golden Waters* (1824) he

---

[1] *The Tatler*, 28 December 1831.   [2] *The Times*, 1 January 1827.
[3] *The Theatrical Observer*, 29 December 1823.
[4] *The London Theatre 1811–1866*, ed. Eluned Brown (1966), p. 96.

entered in his diary: 'Saw the new Pantomime which beautiful scenery rendered amusing.' *Harlequin and the Dragon of Wantley* (1824) was 'a fatiguing exhibition though with beautiful scenery';[1] *Harlequin and Number Nip* (1827) was 'one of the most splendid I ever saw . . . the comic part not excellent but luckily short—Slackrope dancing the most astonishing I ever beheld'.[2] Thus pantomime, for one reason or another, maintained much of its former popularity, although it had no Grimaldi. It also had no rival holiday entertainment, at least not until extravaganza's arrival in force in the 1830s.

After attending an evening of farce and extravaganza at the Olympic in 1833, Henry Crabb Robinson commented that 'these petites pieces are all that is left of the Theatre that is endurable'.[3] The extravaganza he saw was J. R. Planché's *High, Low, Jack, and the Game*, the first he had written for Madame Vestris's management to be entitled an 'extravaganza'. It was in part a burlesque—an ingredient of all extravaganza— in the manner of Henry Fielding's *The Tragedy of Tragedies, or The Life and Death of Tom Thumb the Great*. All characters are cards and dressed accordingly; they all speak blank verse. The Queen of Hearts is the object of the affections of her captor, the King of Spades, as well as of the treacherous Knave of Hearts, responsible for the defeat of the Hearts by the Spades and the death of the King of Hearts, whose Ombre, or Ghost, appears to his consort and the frightened monarch of Spades. The Queen is rescued by the King of Clubs at the head of an army of Clubs and Hearts, and the play concludes with a dance of victors and vanquished alike. Lively, ingenious, sprinkled with puns and songs from popular airs and operas set to new lyrics, full of allusions to current card games, whimsical and fantastic, yet homely and common in touch, *High, Low, Jack, and the Game* is typical of the general style and character of Planché extravaganza, though unusual in conception.

One can afford to dwell almost entirely upon Planché in outlining the development of extravaganza, since for a generation he dominated the genre and, in collaboration with Charles Dance, virtually invented his style of it in the English theatre. The term 'extravaganza' had in the first thirty years of the

---

[1] *The London Theatre, 1811–1866*, p. 110.   [2] Ibid., p. 120.
[3] Ibid., p. 138.

century been applied to pantomimes, burlesques, and otherwise unclassifiable entertainments. Planché defined it as 'distinguishing the whimsical treatment of a poetical subject from
the broad caricature of a tragedy, which was correctly described
as a burlesque'.[1] Because of the various licensing laws governing
the minor theatres in the 1830s, the early Olympic extravaganzas were called 'burlettas', a word whose vagueness of
meaning legally permitted the performance under that name
of a wide variety of drama, except legitimate comedy and
tragedy, outside the patent theatres. Even *High, Low, Jack,
and the Game* had 'burletta' added to its title-page.[2] After
Planché moved with Vestris and Mathews to Covent Garden
in 1839, there was no need to keep the old term, and following
the passage of the Theatre Regulation Bill in 1843 and the
freedom of all theatres to play what they wanted (subject only
to the Examiner of Plays), the convenient 'burletta' was un-
necessary. Planché's classical extravaganzas were derived from
burlesques of classical legend traditional on the English stage—
Fielding's are notable examples—and the fairy-tale extravaganzas from his earlier visits to Paris and enjoyment of the
folies féeries, themselves dramatized from the seventeenth- and
eighteenth-century fairy stories of Charles Perrault, Madame
d'Aulnoy, and others.

Early in 1831 Planché and Dance opened the Vestris management of the Olympic with *Olympic Revels* and followed it with
four successive Christmas pieces of the same kind: *Olympic
Devils* (1831), *The Paphian Bower* (1832), *The Deep Deep Sea*
(1833), and *Telemachus* (1834). Dance collaborated with Planché

---

[1] *Recollections and Reflections*, rev. edn. (1901), p. 268.

[2] *Telemachus* (1834) is the only one of Planché's Olympic pieces in the collected
edition of his *Extravaganzas* to be entitled an 'extravaganza' without qualification.
There was much controversy over the definition of 'burletta'. Even the Lord
Chamberlain's office seemed uncertain, and several definitions were offered in
testimony before the 1832 Select Committee. Planché himself believed that
'burletta' comprehended 'dramas containing not less than five pieces of vocal
music in each act, and which were also, with one or two exceptions, not to be found
in the *repertoire* of the patent houses'. (*The Extravaganzas of J. R. Planché* (1879),
ii. 23.) In *The Drama's Levée* (1838), Drama asks what plays are performed at the
Olympic:

PRAISE. Burlettas only.

DRAMA.   What on earth are those?

CENSURE. Nobody ever knew that I could find.

on his first fairy extravaganza, *Riquet with the Tuft* (1836). Except for *Blue Beard* (1837), also with Dance, Planché was sole author of the remaining Olympic, Covent Garden, and Lyceum extravaganzas.[1] When Vestris and Mathews undertook their Covent Garden management, Planché assumed the job of supplying them with Easter pieces. Between 1842 and 1847 he wrote mostly for the Haymarket, and when Vestris and Mathews resumed management at the Lyceum contributed a series of Christmas and Easter extravaganzas.[2] After 1853 and the demise of this management Planché wrote only four more extravaganzas, notably *The Yellow Dwarf and the King of the Gold Mines* (1854) and *The Discreet Princess* (1855) for Frederick Robson and the Olympic. By the time of his Covent Garden work, Planché was well into the writing of fairy extravaganzas and produced only five more classical plays.

The classical extravaganzas followed English theatrical custom in domesticating gods and goddesses and depicting their low-life behaviour. *Olympic Revels*, for instance, shows Jupiter and the other gods playing whist. Juno is jealous of Vulcan's new creation, Pandora, so Pandora is given to the comic Prometheus and opens her box despite an injunction not to; 'FIENDS *of every description issue from it tumultuously.*' Jupiter and his court arrive to pass judgement, but Hope emerges last from the box and all is forgiven. The settings are Mount Olympus and a street on Earth. There are numerous songs with new lyrics to music from operas and established airs: Juno ticks off Jupiter to 'Judy Callaghan'; the gods sing a chorus to 'The Roast Beef of Old England'; and Prometheus expresses alarm at the opening of the box to the tune of 'Bonnie Laddie, High-

---

[1] 'Sole author' in a way that no pantomime 'arranger' could possibly be. Arrangers wrote openings, songs, and choruses, and in part devised the business of the harlequinade. Here, however, they were assisted and even displaced by performers and technicians. Clowns like Grimaldi created their own comic material, and machinists developed trick-work appropriate to Harlequin's magic. Because of his prestige, Planché probably had unusual authority in the writing and production of an extravaganza. In 1876 John Hollingshead declared that 'it is worse than useless for an untried writer to suggest an "Oriental extravaganza" to a manager, as pieces of that description are almost written on stage, in consultation with manager, actors, scene-painters, costumiers, and musical directors'. (*The Era Almanack* (1876), p. 92.)

[2] Of the forty-three extravaganzas and revues in the collected edition, twenty-five were written for three Vestris managements—a remarkable collaboration extending over twenty-three years.

land Laddie'. *Olympic Devils*, livelier than its predecessor, with cleverer lyrics and dialogue, and more elaborate scenically, is set in Pluto's palace, at the gates of Hell, and in the temple of Bacchus. The story is that of Orpheus and Euridice. Orpheus' musical ability is represented by his defeating Pluto's music master, Signor Tweedledee, in a violin contest. (These were the days of Paganini's sensational English appearances.) The Temple of Bacchus disintegrates and its columns and statues waltz to Orpheus' 'Voulez-vous danser'. Charon sings 'Begone, dull care' in a quartet with the three heads of Cerberus. In the first scene Pluto and his friends drink after dinner from flaming goblets while their ladies, including the Fates and Furies, urge them to leave the table and partake of coffee. Both pieces contain a fair number of the puns that flowed so readily and with such fatal facility from the pens of later extravaganza and burlesque writers. Prometheus, for example, is identified in the dramatis personae of *Olympic Revels* as an 'eminent *Man*-ufacturer'; Minos describes Atropos in *Olympic Devils* as a daughter of '*shear* necessity'.

These two plays set the pattern for Planché's remaining classical extravaganzas, of which the most interesting is *The Golden Fleece* (1845), an adaptation of Euripides' *Medea*. Planché was inspired to write *The Golden Fleece* by an *Antigone* at Covent Garden (from the German, with music by Mendelssohn) 'after the Greek manner', with a raised stage and chorus. His plot is generally that of Euripides, with the omission of a tragic ending. Instead, Medea and her two children fly off, to the finale of 'Post Horn Galop', in a chariot drawn by two dragons. Charles Mathews represented the entire Greek chorus on a stage 'constructed after the approved fashion of the re-vived Greek Theatre', and in his role introduced the play to the audience, sang explanatory songs *solus* and a duet with Medea, called on Jason to save his children, and led off the finale— a thoroughly ingenious and wittily conceived role, and one of Mathews's most famous parts.[1]

Planché's use of a single-character chorus in *The Golden Fleece*

---

[1] Planché's Medea was Vestris; in 1856 Robson's tragic–burlesque performance of the role in Robert Brough's *Medea* caused a sensation. Because of its partly tragic conception of Medea and her suffering, Brough's burlesque has little of Planché's wit, elegance, and fantasy; it is a much darker play.

is an example of a theatricalist technique that can be found—to digress briefly—in other extravaganzas and burlesques. In *The Sphinx* (1849), by Robert and William Brough, Mercury as Chorus hurriedly interrupts a senate meeting, informs the audience of the background, points out the King of Thebes, falls into the language of a circus showman in introducing his 'monster' the Sphinx, advises king and senate on a course of action, predicts plot developments, complains of the author's being unclassical when the male Sphinx falls in love with Jocasta, persuades Oedipus to act, and saves the Sphinx from suicide after Oedipus answers the riddle. In William Brough's *Perseus and Andromeda* (1861), Minerva is the chorus, and as the Spirit of Extravaganza (in a *'pantomimic style of dress'*) in the last scene, explains the necessity of a happy ending:

> But in the character I now assume, I
> Can't bear an ending tragical and gloomy.
> Extravaganza seeks but harmless mirth.

A chorus was employed not only in classical pieces; in *Rasselas* (1862), also by William Brough, Dr. Johnson is Chorus. He comments on the action as it unfolds, speaks of himself as a man 'p'raps too fond of trying by jocosity / To compensate for want of ponderosity'. But he walks out on the play before it ends, indignant because he no longer recognizes his own work. The comic convention of Chorus which Planché appears to have initiated in extravaganza and burlesque was part of a wider interaction in nineteenth-century theatre between actor and audience and a full comic awareness on the part of the author that his characters exist in a play whose mechanism can be amusingly revealed to the audience.[1]

---

[1] Such an awareness, for instance, exists in nineteenth-century farce. In extravaganza it was not confined to the use of a chorus. Danae in *Perseus and Andromeda* abuses her husband's dinner guests for possessing 'silly supers' supercilious airs'. The guests, played of course by supers, react angrily. In William Brough's *Prince Amabel* (1862) the fairy tells the Prince, 'I am a fairy', and he replies: 'So I should have guessed / By the amount of gauze in which you're dressed.' The tyrant Turko enters with his 'army' behind him offstage and commands:

> So, let the foremost rank stand at the wing.
> An old stage trick—the audience by those means
> May think we've hundreds more behind the scenes.

The device of a character who comments upon situation, action, and theatrical convention was also extensively used in another dramatic form, of which Planché said that 'with very few exceptions, I believe I have been the sole contributor of this peculiar species of entertainment to the English stage'.[1] This was the revue, which Planché borrowed from the French *pièce de circonstance* and adapted in the form of a loosely structured one-act play in bouncing rhymed pentameters, with songs remarking on matters of immediate topical interest, usually theatrical. A narrator, often an allegorical or symbolic figure, would call up in turn significant theatrical and social events from the past season, represented also by symbolic personages or by actual characters from the plays passing in review. This method enabled Planché himself to make appropriate comments through the observers of such scenes.

The first play of this kind was *Success* (1825). Fashion's daughter Success is wooed by the hits of the past season, portrayed by characters like Zamiel (*Der Freischutz*), Paul Pry (*Paul Pry*), two monkeys (*Jocko, or The Brazilian Monkey*), and Long Tom Coffin (*The Pilot*). The newspapers of London are summoned to aid her in her choice and of course cannot agree. Fashion's conclusion, as he speaks of Success, is an accurate summation of public taste in 1825:

> Still must she lead her usual vagrant life,
> More like a fickle mistress than a wife.
> Now flirt with this and now with t'other fellow,
> Now love a monkey, now a Punchinello;
> Now for Rossini, now for Weber burn,
> And even Shakespeare may be borne in turn.
> Feel for each novelty a tender passion
> And change as often as her Father Fashion.

The only such piece Planché wrote for Vestris and Mathews was *The Drama's Levée* (1838), which opens on a scene representing 'the British stage in a deplorable condition. The DRAMA is discovered in a languishing state upon it, surrounded by the different Theatres'. Wearied and distracted by disputes between her two sons, Legitimate and Illegitimate, the Drama, at the

---

[1] *Extravaganzas*, i. 14.

urging of Praise and Censure, revisits her realm to see if there has been any improvement. Drury Lane, Covent Garden, the St. James's and other theatres present their successes of the past season, including the Gnome Fly, an acrobat who walked on the ceiling. Appropriately, the Drama favours the Olympic, and the play ends with a tribute to Vestris before the beginning of her American tour.

Planché's next efforts in the same vein were *The Drama at Home* (1844) and *The New Planet* (1847), both written for Webster's Haymarket management. The former, whose first scene shows a desert and '*the Ruins of the Temple of the* DRAMA' is an entertaining but pessimistic examination of the state of the theatre after the Theatre Regulation Act of 1843 and the use of Covent Garden in 1844 for Promenade Concerts. Puff shows the despairing Drama visions of entertainment at Drury Lane and Covent Garden, and then takes her to the Haymarket, where a series of characters from plays performed after the abolition of the patent monopolies is followed by a procession representative of currently popular London exhibitions—the Ojibway Indians, General Tom Thumb, the Centrifugal Railway, Madame Tussaud, the Industrious Fleas, &c. Nominally at home in the Haymarket, the Drama nonetheless comments sadly:

> I see no rising drama worth the name,
> And now the law is surely not to blame.

The immediate stimulus of *The New Planet*, described as a 'Classical, Astronomical, Quizzical, Polytechnical, Experimental, Operatical, Pantomimical Extravaganza', was the discovery of Neptune. The planets visit Earth to see what is going on in London, and are taken sightseeing by Mercury, who plays Harlequin and reveals the sights by striking the scenes with his wand. Among these sights are the Polytechnical Institution, the Egyptian Hall, the Mysterious Lady, the Ethiopian Serenaders, and scenes from opera and ballet. The play is full of references to the latest popular sensations (including Van Amburgh's lions at Drury Lane) and scientific discoveries.

Probably the best of these revues is *The Camp at the Olympic* (1853), written to inaugurate the Wigans's management of that theatre. Fancy is summoned to their aid in the search for a piece with which to open; the scene then changes to the *'Camp of the Combined British Dramatic Forces'*. Appearing in review before the Wigans, each claiming merit and superiority and the right to the first play, are—in the costume of characters from appropriate dramatic works—Tragedy, Comedy, Burlesque, English Opera, Ballet, Melodrama, Pantomime, Hippodrama, and Spectacle. The purpose of *The Camp at the Olympic* was to ingratiate the Wigans with their first audiences, but nevertheless a great deal of information on dramatic trends and taste in 1853 is conveyed by graceful rhyming couplets, lively songs, modest spectacle, and much theatrical colour.

A similar piece of the same date is *Mr. Buckstone's Ascent of Mount Parnassus*, which opened Buckstone's tenancy of the Haymarket. The play was cast as a travesty of Albert Smith's immensely popular travelogue-entertainment *The Ascent of Mont Blanc*, then still running. Accordingly, Buckstone, like the Wigans depicted as frantically searching for a play with which to begin his management, is first visited by the Spirit of Fashion, with whom an interesting discussion ensues concerning fashionable patronage of theatre (and the lack of it), and is then taken by Fortune to see what she has 'crowned with special favour'. In addition to Smith as the Spirit of Mont Blanc, Buckstone sees the Spirit of the Corsican Brothers, who, as the ghost in that play, shows him a tableau of the duel scene and imitates Charles Kean. The Spirit of Drury Lane reveals the scene of the Australian diggings in Charles Reade's *Gold*, and other such Spirits follow him, including six Uncle Toms representing six of the many versions of *Uncle Tom's Cabin* recently dramatized in London. Finally Buckstone ascends Parnassus by means of a panorama; the nine muses meet him at the Castalian Spring, and he promises Apollo and the Haymarket audience to 'learn the highest ways / To those fine arts which may the Drama raise'.

Planché wrote two more revues for Buckstone, *Mr. Buckstone's Voyage Round the Globe* (1854)—mostly concerned with the current rage for exhibitions—and *The New Haymarket Spring Meeting* (1855), in which the City of London is visited by Westminster and her two daughters Belgravia and Tyburnia. The piece comments on the theatre, successful plays, new building, social habits, and the Crimean War. Westminster and Time urge London to progress and reforms, and Westminster tells her:

> Instead of up the Thames alone swan-hopping,
> Help me to keep it clean from Kew to Wapping;
> Release the poor from pestilential sties,
> Think of their rooms more than your companies.

Imitators followed Planché into the revue field,[1] but as in extravaganza he completely dominated a genre that he popularized on the English stage. The value of dramatic revues is not so much their undoubted vigour, ingenuity, and sense of fun, but the great amount of topical comment on drama and theatre imparted in such an entertaining manner. Each one, although of necessity flattering to the particular management producing it, is essentially a review of the past theatrical season in the form of staged and symbolic illustrations of that season. Taken collectively, they constitute a lively and absorbing report on the state of the contemporary drama.

Engaging and theatrically engrossing as Planché's classical extravaganzas and revues are, they are not his most significant achievement in the extravaganza form. This distinction belongs to the fairy extravaganzas, which stretch in time from *Riquet in the Tuft* (1836) to *Young and Handsome* (1856); twenty-two altogether, if *Blue Beard* (1839), a nursery-tale adaptation but not a fairy play, is excluded and *The Seven Champions of Christendom* (1849), a vaguely political allegory in fairy-tale form, is included.

Planché declared that 'it had been the custom of my predecessors, in dramatizing fairy tales of almost every description, to lay the scene in Oriental regions, probably considering that more splendour could be introduced in the *mise en scène*; and as they were usually treated seriously, the general theatrical opinion that there was "no fun under a turban" was not an argument against it'.[2] He was referring to pantomime openings

---

[1] Two imitations are Albert Smith's *The Alhambra* (1851) and J. S. Coyne's *Buckstone at Home* (1863). The former represents Mrs. Keeley at the Princess's desperately searching for a new Easter piece. Aided by fairies who were in London for the Great Exhibition, she sends the magician Asmodeus to Spain by diorama and balloon for a subject. The latter shows Buckstone pondering his latest Haymarket novelty and viewing a succession of characters from the most recent theatrical successes.   [2] *Extravaganzas*, ii. 107–8.

and spectacle plays; indeed, although Planché acknowledged his source in the *folie feérie*, he was also indebted to the English pantomime. In fact, the fairy extravaganza is essentially a pantomime with the harlequinade removed and the comedy and magic tricks transferred to the opening. The supernaturalism and the intervention of benevolent and malevolent spirits remained more or less what it was, and the grand transformation—of scenery and not of characters—concluded the piece as before: a spectacular scene representing joy and happiness revealed to the audience when the fairy waves her wand. Lesser transformations equivalent to the mechanical and scenic legerdemain of the harlequinade also remained, detached from the comic business of the harlequinade characters. However, what happens to characters because of this scenic trickery is much the same as what happens to Clown and Pantaloon when they suffer the effects of Harlequin's magic powers. In *The Sleeping Beauty in the Wood* (1840), the Prince approaches the impenetrable wood surrounding the castle in which the Princess sleeps; the wood '*changes to a deep blue*' and opens to let him through—as if the Prince were Harlequin himself. But when the comic Larry O'Log tries to follow him, '*briars and thorns rise in his path.* . . . *The trees close upon him and beat him with their branches*'. In *The Bee and the Orange Tree* (1845), '*the* PRINCE *is changed into an Orange Tree, covered with fruit and blossom, and in a finely sculptured vase.* . . . *A Hive rises round* AMY *and encloses her.*' The ogre Ravagio sits down beneath the tree and the bees attack him; as Clown used to do in an identical situation, he '*runs off roaring and fighting with the Bees*'. The transformation of the Dame's cottage in *The Good Woman in the Wood* (1852) from a poor, lowly dwelling to '*a pavilion formed entirely of roses*' is a pantomime change, and the wicked king inside the cottage is treated in the same way as Clown and Pantaloon, who are merged in the common fairy-extravaganza character of the unpleasant but simultaneously comic father and tyrant. The King sits on the bed and '*the roses change to thorns*'; he pulls the bell-rope, which '*changes to one of nettles*' and stings him; he sinks into a chair that '*changes to one of thistles*'. The Princess of *Once Upon a Time There Were Two Kings* (1853) saves herself from approaching villains by touching a nosegay of magic gilliflowers: '*Her dress changes to that of a peasant.*

Part of the bank changes to a Cow—a milking pail and stool rise near her.'
More elaborate transformations and settings also abound, and were also developments of pantomime and spectacle staging. A conventional concluding pantomime transformation begins the last scene of *Riquet in the Tuft*, and a more elaborate one ends *The Sleeping Beauty in the Wood.* The first act of *Once Upon a Time There Were Two Kings* ends when the Fairy Amazona waves her wand—benevolent spirits in extravaganza possessed the powers of their sisters in pantomime in addition to the magic of Harlequin—and the scene changes from a willow glen to '*Seaweed Hall, the marine abode of* AQUA MARINA. *Grand Ballet by* CORALINA *and* SEA NYMPHS.' The opening scene of *The Golden Branch* (1847) is identical in setting with the first scene of many a mid-century pantomime: '*Spirit vaults beneath the Enchanter's Castle.* MANDRAGORA, *the Sorceress, discovered brewing mischief, assisted by* BLUERUINO *and other* ILLICIT SPIRITS. HUMGUFFIN, *the Enchanter, rises.'* The nasty potential of this scene is of course negated by the good Fairy Pastorella, who effects the final transformation from these gloomy vaults to the '*Golden Gardens and Fairy Tree of Entertaining Knowledge*';[1] the contrast in light, beauty, and moral nature between the realms of good and evil was an essential part of contemporary pantomime, and in Regency pantomime the benevolent spirit changes the 'dark' scene, where Harlequin and Columbine are endangered, to the realms of love, bliss, harmony, joy, or whatever was thought relevant to a happy and scenically attractive ending. The increasing emphasis on spectacle in extravaganza production had been apparent for many years; this emphasis was also a part of pantomime. Stage settings and transformations in both genres became richer and more ostentatiously ornamented. The Valley of Violets and the

---

[1] Planché noted in his preface to the play that 'the scenes in Arcadia, designed from *chef d'œuvres* of Watteau, presented a succession of *tableaux* certainly never previously equalled on the English stage . . . and gave a *cachet* to the reputation of the new management of the Lyceum for the production of spectacular drama . . . the *mise en scène* of *The Golden Branch* is imperatively required to be of so elaborate and costly a description that it has less chance of a revival than any other of my Extravaganzas'. (*Extravaganzas*, iii. 184.) Henry Morley thought that the concluding scene of *Once Upon a Time There Were Two Kings* was perhaps 'the crowning triumph of the theatre so far as mere spectacle is concerned'. (*The Examiner*, 31 December 1853.)

Castle of Flowers are two scenes in *Young and Handsome*; the castle is located '*in the centre of a lake, and composed entirely of flowers*', and the final transformation is from the Dragon's Den to an Illuminated Porcelain Pavilion. Previously the fairy Princess had changed the hovel of the shepherd Alidor '*to a beautiful pavilion formed entirely of flowers, jessamine and orange flowers being predominant*'. A few moments later '*she waves her wand,* ALIDOR's *dress changes to one of amber satin and silver; his hat, which he had flung on a bank at entering, becomes one of jonquils and blue hyacinths; his crook turns to a gold one, richly ornamented with jewels, and his scrip, hung upon a branch, is beautifully embroidered and suspended by a wreath of roses*'. Alidor is not changed to Harlequin, but the mechanics of the change are the same, and its ornate nature is an extension of the ritualistic changes of person in pantomime to the closely related and increasingly decorative extravaganza.

The curious combination in Regency pantomime of elaborated fantasy and comic nightmare is paralleled in fairy extravaganza by a mixture of the same kind of fantasy, even richer and more dream-like in texture, with homespun down-to-earth domesticity. The two would seem mutually destructive, or at least mutually incompatible. In fact they coexist harmoniously, complement each other perfectly, and are much better integrated than the disparate elements of pantomime. And as very real components of terror and destruction in the Regency harlequinade are rendered harmless and mirthful by accompanying comic business, so too in fairy extravaganza is any potential for fear or horror inherent in the wide variety of evil spirits, sorcerers, demons, tyrants, and their threats to the innocent and heroic nullified by the domestic, ordinary, and topical comic contexts in which these threats occur. The juxtaposition of the serious and mythological with the lesser domesticities of daily life is the principal method of classical burlesque; Fielding, Planché, and other dramatists used it repeatedly. The juxtaposition of the fantastic and the domestic, the comic and the fearful, the old legend and the topical triviality, is subtler and rather more complex.

This aspect—and it is a striking feature of fairy extravaganza—can be illustrated by several examples. In *The Golden Branch* Prince Peerless encounters Princess Dumpy in an

Arcadian landscape just after a dance of shepherds and shep-
herdesses:

PRINCE. Too lovely maid, ah! wherefore dost thou fly me?
PRINCESS. Sweet shepherd, if you please, don't come a-nigh me.
PRINCE. What from her Corydon can Phillis fear?
PRINCESS. Making herself too cheap, and him too dear!
　　Besides, no longer aught I here to stay.
　　'The curfew sounds the knell of parting day,
　　The lowing herds wind slowly o'er the lea',
　　And there are yet no lodgings found for me.
PRINCE. I have a lodging in Lamb's Conduit Street,
　　Genteelly furnished, small, but very neat.
　　To occupy it, if you'll but consent,
　　I'll never ask you for a farthing's rent.
PRINCESS. Lodge at a bachelor's! You don't expect
　　I should do anything so incorrect.

A little later the Captain of the Guards courts the Princess's
maid:

QUIVER. To Amaryllis love compels my way,
　　My grazing sheep up Gray's Inn Lane may stray.
SUIVANTA. You'll lose a lamb while you are following me.
QUIVER. I'm a lost mutton since I gazed on thee.

A duet follows that includes this verse sung by Quiver:

　　　　My cottage shall be thine,
　　　　At Shepherd's Bush 'tis found
　　　　With kitchen garden, paddock green,
　　　　No end of pleasure ground.

Thus pastoral myth combines with topographical reality and
a humbly domestic frame of reference to produce a pleasant,
homely fantasy whose principals are, simultaneously, enchanted
prince and princess wooing in a fairyland Arcadia and simple
Londoners out courting, possibly in Bloomsbury, in the year
1847. The result may seem endearingly naïve, but it is really
precisely calculated and achieved with much creative ingenuity
on the author's part.

The topical allusion also serves to fix fantasy firmly to the earth—to contemporary London, in fact—and as the above examples demonstrate, the twinning of romantic dream and topical reference, delicately but familiarly and often jocosely expressed, creates an odd but charming unity of style. Such a frame of reference can also neutralize menace as well as domesticate fantasy. An instance is the quintet concluding the fourth scene of *Beauty and the Beast* (1841), when Beauty is on her way to apparently certain death at the hands of the Beast:

> To death, per omnibus, poor Beauty goes,
> And all because her pa just plucked a rose,
> Mild as the moon, when a cream-cheese she resembles,
> And sweet as sugar-plums, Birch's best.[1]

Similarly, this kind of antithetical comedy invalidates danger and despair, and makes them instead pleasurable and amusing. This negation can be achieved by the comic aspects of the wicked king, giant, or evil enchanter himself; such a one is King Bruin of *The Good Woman in the Wood*, the Irish Ogre in *Puss in Boots* (1837), or Haridan, the Desert Fairy in *The Yellow Dwarf and the King of the Gold Mines* (1854). Exceptional are the Yellow Dwarf himself and Prince Richcraft in *The Discreet Princess* (1855), both of them capable of genuine evil and cruelty and yet both also grotesquely comic and even pathetic. The sinister Dwarf and the revengeful, bloodthirsty Richcraft were played by Robson, whose pathetic and tragic powers in the characters of extravaganza and burlesque impressed audiences as extraordinary.[2] Thus these two plays are darker in tone than Planché's other extravaganzas; fear and horror become almost—but not quite—a stage reality.

Even the fear of death is comic on the extravaganza stage,

---

[1] To remark upon or at least refer to current affairs was common in pantomime, extravaganza, and burlesque. Morley praised *Once Upon a Time There Were Two Kings* for the relative lack of such comment: 'He has abstained almost wholly, and might as well have abstained altogether, from political allusions, for there is no connection between corn-laws, foreign wars, cab-strikes, and fairyland. . . . Allusions to current events are the life of a pantomime; but they are the death of a fairy spectacle, presented in good, earnest, fairy style.' (*The Examiner*, 31 December 1853.)

[2] Planché himself said of Robson as the Yellow Dwarf that 'so powerful was his personation of the cunning, the malignity, the passion and despair of the monster, that he elevated Extravaganza into Tragedy'. (*Extravaganzas*, v. 37.)

and its comic aspects are not mingled with the genuine though momentary terror at the heart of the same fear in the harlequinade. Princess Sabra in *The Seven Champions of Christendom*, bound to a stake and awaiting the devouring dragon, declares:

> Was ever Princess in so sad a scrape?
> Were I unbound, I'm bound not to escape.
> Come quickly, death, put up poor Sabra's hatchment,
> Victim of this unfortunate attachment.

Furthermore, the dragon is hardly the dreadful monster of legend; he enters '*dancing a hornpipe; he has his tail under his arm, and uses an eye-glass*'. Similarly, Andromeda in *The Deep Deep Sea* asks for a pint of porter as, chained to a rock, she awaits the sea-serpent; Finfin in *The Good Woman in the Wood*, trapped by the magic of the evil Abaddun, admonishes his would-be rescuer:

> Take warning by the rash step we have taken,
> Nor by a rasher think to save our bacon.

A pun, indeed, serves just as well as an incongruous response to deflate a threatening or serious situation. Princess Desiderata of *The Prince of Happy Land* (1851), shot by an arrow while changed into a fawn, exclaims,

> Whatever fears may shake my woman's frame,
> I've been a deer, and trust me I'll die game!

Beauty pleads with the Beast to let her return briefly to her sick father:

BEAUTY. My pa will die, and you will be the cause;
  My fate is in your hands.
BEAST. Ah! [*He looks at her and remains silent.*]
BEAUTY. [*Looking at his hands.*] Awful *pause*!

When characters both good and evil have to die or be killed, they are almost immediately revived to participate in a jolly finale; in extravaganza death does indeed lose his sting and the grave's victory is entirely temporary.

Planché's last extravaganza was *Orpheus in the Haymarket* (1865), an opera-bouffe adaptation of Offenbach. He had already dramatized the legend of Orpheus and Eurydice in *Olympic Devils*, and objected to the Offenbach treatment, not because of the 'utter subversion of the classical story' but because of 'the unmeaning buffoonery forced upon it'.[1] Planché was referring to Offenbach, but his remark could have applied equally well to the burlesque and extravaganza then popular on the West End stage. In the same year as *Orpheus in the Haymarket* was performed Robert Reece's *Prometheus*, entitled an 'extravaganza', a strongly burlesque treatment of the classical story. Prometheus' comic mother, Outis, drinks heavily; Minerva tells Mercury, 'Take an umbrella, Merky, it looks showery.' It was a sign of the times. Planché's graceful, delicate, witty, and tasteful pieces were not favoured in the 1860s; the public preferred the stronger flavour of burlesque. Reviewing these developments in 1879, Tom Taylor commented, in referring to the heyday of Planché's extravaganzas:

The nigger invasion had not then taken by storm the strongholds of dance and song; breakdowns and music-hall choruses, with bone and banjo accompaniment, were unknown. I have seen these creeping up and on, till now, with their attendant deluge of pun for pun's sake and slang *à tout propos*, they have flooded our comic stage and drowned out, alike, grace, and point, sweet song, and witty dialogue. Planché was then the Lord and Master of Burlesque . . . combining in one entertainment pretty story, humorous action, pointed and graceful dialogue, sweet music, beautiful scenery, and tasteful costumes, as no man ever before or since combined them.[2]

In 1880 Palgrave Simpson lamented similarly:

Eminently successful and highly prized as these vivacious and witty effusions were, illustrated by the prettiest and most graceful melodies in vogue at the period, they ceased in time, even during the author's life, to maintain a hold on public favour. They grew to be old-fashioned. The graceful extravaganza was gradually elbowed off the stage by the modern burlesque, in which pun was set aside for jingle

---

[1] *Extravaganzas*, v. 234.

[2] 'Some Personal Reminiscences of Alfred Wigan', *The Theatre* (January 1879), pp. 413–14. Actually the minstrel show was influencing extravaganza by the mid-forties, especially with its songs. The Virginia Minstrels visited London in 1843, and the Ethiopian Serenaders made a considerable impact in their first London appearance in 1846—they are referred to in *The New Planet*—and after that the minstrel tide rolled irresistibly through the world of English light entertainment.

of words or distortion of syllables; 'breakdowns' became a necessary ingredient to catch the public fancy; and music-hall songs were substituted for popular Italian airs.[1]

Although the taste for Planché's style of extravaganza had declined, he nonetheless exercised a considerable influence on writers who followed him. He taught them skilful plotting and a harmonious combination of imaginative situation, pleasing verse, wit, and light burlesque. As the characteristics of the Olympic's *petites comédies* of the 1830s, which Planché himself wrote, emerged once again in the delicacy, restraint, and comic lightness of touch of Robertson's comedies of the sixties, so too were the lessons of Planché's extravaganzas absorbed by W. S. Gilbert in his fairy comedies of the seventies and comic operas.[2] As with the development of all drama in the nineteenth century, the story of pantomime, extravaganza, and burlesque is one of continuous evolution and the reworking of inherited traditions and modes of dramatic writing.

From the point of view of definition, it is not easy to distinguish between extravaganza and burlesque. However, problems of definition are so common in dealing with nineteenth-century drama that one should not worry about them; better to indicate characteristics, similarities, and differences rather than frame imprecise definitions of little value. Certainly there is an element of burlesque in all extravaganzas, achieved in large part by the very coexistence, so fundamental to extravaganza, of the domestic and contemporary milieu with the fairy-tale, classical legend, or historical event dramatized. In Planché such burlesque is restrained and never overwhelms the spirit of the original story. By the 1860s, however, plays labelled 'extravaganza' tended to be what the public understood as burlesque; they were undoubtedly 'extravagant', and the terms 'extravaganza' and 'burlesque' were used interchangeably.

What this understanding was is best expressed by reference to the contemporary use of 'burlesque'. In John Halford's

---

[1] 'James Robinson Planché', *The Theatre* (August 1880), pp. 97–8.

[2] In reviewing Gilbert's *The Palace of Truth* in 1870, Dutton Cook noted that Gilbert had 'aimed at the dignity of comedy, notwithstanding the basis of enchantment upon which his fable rests. The work more nearly approaches the early extravaganzas of Mr. Planché—when he depended little upon musical or scenical assistance—than any later achievements of the stage.' (*Nights at the Play* (1883), p. 92.)

Faust and Marguerite (1853)—a burlesque of Gounod, though called an extravaganza in the author's preface—the Manager rejects Clown's offer of fairy stories as dramatic subjects:

> I know their virtues, friend—but beg to say,
> This house is not exactly in that way;
> We're open to the lively and grotesque
> But see them in their newest form—'Burlesque'.
> I want a Parodist who will and can Sir
> Come down at once with an Extravaganza.

'Lively' and 'grotesque' are key words here; 'absurd' is also appropriate, for the absurd is much stronger in the later burlesque than in the earlier extravaganza. Planché was disturbed by 'the rage for mere absurdity which my extravaganzas so unintentionally and unhappily gave rise to'.[1] English audiences had always loved the absurd on stage, and never more so than in the nineteenth century: one only has to think of the immense popularity of such widely diverse forms as the Regency harlequinade, the farce, and the Gilbert and Sullivan opera; Burlesque made one more. Criticizing Wilkie Collins's *The Red Vial* (1858), Henry Morley decided that 'the fatal defect . . . is that it makes no allowance for the good or bad habit that an English audience has of looking out for something upon which to feed its appetite for the absurd'.[2] *The Red Vial* is a melodrama—another form whose basic absurdity was essential to its nature—but the point could have been just as well made of a burlesque.

Other writers were more specific about the character of burlesque. At the conclusion of Gilbert's parody of *Norma, The Pretty Druidess* (1869), Norma comes forward to address the audience:

> . . . the piece is common-place, grotesque,
> A solemn folly—a proscribed burlesque!
> So for burlesque I plead. Forgive our rhymes;
> Forgive the jokes you've heard five thousand times;
> Forgive each breakdown, cellar-flap, and clog,
> Our low-bred songs—our slangy dialogue;
> And, above all—oh, ye with double barrel—
> Forgive the scantiness of our apparel!

---

[1] *Recollections and Reflections*, p. 351.   [2] *The Examiner*, 16 October 1858.

Chudleigh Dunscombe, the objectionable young toff of Robertson's comedy *M.P.* (1870), says that only burlesque is to the taste of the present day, and explains to his inquiring father that 'it's an entertainment crammed full of fun and singing, and dancing, and tumbling, and parodies on popular songs, and—it is written in verse'. Indeed, Dunscombe wishes to become a burlesque actor and play the part of Venus. Robertson's description of the Burlesque Actress in *The Illustrated Times* reveals much about burlesque itself:

She can sing the most difficult of Donizetti's languid, loving melodies, as well as the inimitable Mackney's 'Oh, Rosa, how I lub you! Coodle cum!' She can warble a drawing-room ballad of the 'Daylight of the Soul' or 'Eyes melting in Gloom' school, or whistle 'When I was a-walking in Wiggleton Wale' with the shrillness and correctness of a Whitechapel bird-catcher. She is as faultless on the piano as on the bones. She can waltz, polk, dance a *pas seul* or a sailor's hornpipe, La Sylphide, or the Genu-*wine* Transatlantic Cape Cod Skedaddle, with equal grace and spirit; and as for acting, she can declaim à la Phelps or Fechter; is serious, droll; and must play farce, tragedy, opera, comedy, melodrama, pantomime, ballet, change her costume, fight a combat, make love, poison herself, die, and take one encore for a song and another for a dance, in the short space of ten minutes.[1]

Much of this energy and peculiar *mélange* of style is evident in early nineteenth-century burlesques, but these did not possess the same character as the burlesques of the 1850s and the 1860s. At the beginning of the century they were specifically intended, in the traditions of English burlesques like *The Rehearsal, Chrononhotonthologos*, and *The Critic*, as parodies of particular methods and conventions of dramatic writing and staging. Thus W. B. Rhodes's *Bombastes Furioso* (1810) is in the manner of Fielding's *The Tragedy of Tragedies*, replete with heroic similes, a 'tragedy' depicting high personages of state involved in trivial and ludicrous matters speaking ridiculously 'elevated' verse. Bombastes, King Artaxominous' brave general,

---

[1] T. E. Pemberton, *The Life and Writings of T. W. Robertson* (1893), p. 120. In another passage, on burlesque itself, Robertson observed that 'it is these broad and over-palpable jocularities that hit modern audiences hardest. Smart writing, keen satire, and hard raps at social abuses, though they look well in print and are admired of critics and *habitués*, fail to elicit the loud roars of laughter that follow an ingeniously audacious pun, or a happy paraphrase or parody.' (Ibid., p. 113.)

enters with his army (*'one Drummer, one Fifer, and two Soldiers, all very materially differing in size'*) and addresses them:

> Meet me this ev'ning at the Barley-Mow;
> I'll bring your pay, you see I'm busy now:
> Begone, brave army, and don't kick up a row.

Bombastes finds out that his king also seeks the favours of his beloved Distaffina; the discovery is made as Bombastes salutes her tenderly:

> O let me greet thee with a loving kiss—
> Hell and the devil! Say who's hat is this?

Bombastes and Artaxominous fight; the latter is slain. Bombastes is then killed by the king's minister Fusbos, but both dead men revive to join in a merry finale with Fusbos and Distaffina. Weakly imitative of *Bombastes Furioso* is Planché's first play, *Amoroso, King of Little Britain* (1818); like *The Tragedy of Tragedies*, which then still held the stage, it ends in a general massacre. George Daniel's *Doctor Bolus* (1818), which ends similarly, is in turn a feeble imitation of *Amoroso*. The mock-heroic burlesque tradition of which Fielding's play is the finest example was by this time quite exhausted.

Rehearsal-burlesque in the mode of *The Rehearsal*, *The Critic*, or Fielding's Haymarket pieces of the 1730s exists in the nineteenth century, but it is neither significant nor satirically unified, although many plays, like Planché's revues, are set in theatres and begin with discussions between a Manager and other characters. However, the intention of parodying literary styles and theatrical devices was fulfilled in other ways. A discussion between the Manager and Bathos opens George Colman the Younger's *The Quadrupeds of Quedlinburgh* (1811); the best things in it are all taken from *The Rovers*, by George Canning, John Hookham Frere, and George Ellis, published in 1798 in *The Anti-Jacobin*, but not performed. *The Rovers* cleverly parodies the sentiment, morality, and plot devices of Kotzebue, Goethe, and Schiller; Colman's play merely adds a concluding battle fought by soldiers *'on basket Horses'*—a travesty of the equestrianized *Timour the Tartar* by Matthew Gregory Lewis, performed in its new version at Covent Garden shortly before *The Quadrupeds of Quedlinburgh.*[1] The rage for spectacular displays of horsemanship on stage was also parodied in Charles Dibdin's *Harlequin and Bluebeard* (1811), in which the Genius of Burlesque transforms the main characters of Colman's newly equestrianized spectacle–melodrama *Blue-Beard* into the harlequinade stereotypes.[2]

Of all the objects of parody aimed at by nineteenth-century burlesque,[3] melodrama was by far the most popular. Melodramatic conventions, moralities, character stereotypes, stage business, and rhetorical style all attracted the attention of burlesque authors. Their target was a large one: melodrama so dominated the nineteenth-century theatre and was so popular with all classes of audience that the satirical shafts aimed at it were unfelt pinpricks in the hide of a Brobdingnagian. Not until the second half of the century did burlesque affect melodrama destructively, and even then its authors had such an obvious affection for melodrama that they often wrote it themselves. An early example of such affection is Thomas Dibdin's *Boni-facio and Bridgetina* (1808).[4] Dibdin clearly intended to burlesque Gothic melodrama, since his settings—hermitage, Gothic chamber, windmill, robbers' cave—properly belong to it, as do such characters as the rightful heir disguised as a hermit and the band of brigands. However, despite attempts at burlesque that included a comic ghost and a garrulous hermit longing to talk of his mysterious past to anyone who will listen, Dibdin— who wrote scores of melodramas—clearly revelled in the elements of real melodrama at his disposal. At the climax, for instance, after a burlesque combat between Jack Bologna (a noted Harlequin) and Grimaldi, 'the music then assumes the real character of stage business; parties of robbers in miniature, with

[1] Henry Crabb Robinson saw Colman's play, and remarked in his diary that 'burlesque is a cheap mode of producing laughter and soon fatigues'—a sentiment that was to be extensively repeated and elaborated fifty years later. (*The London Theatre 1811–1866*, p. 38.)

[2] Pantomime was also quite capable of burlesquing itself. The opening of *Broad Grins, or Harlequin Mag and Harlequin Tag* (1815) shows a pantomime in rehearsal, casting problems, and the inept performance both of pantomimists and mechanical tricks. Thomas Dibdin's *Harlequin Hoax* (1814), while not a pantomime, is in part a satirical piece concerned with the rehearsal of a pantomime.

[3] These objects are detailed in W. Davenport Adams's *A Book of Burlesque* (1891), the only substantial nineteenth-century survey of theatrical burlesque.

[4] Subtitled 'A New Grand Comick, Tragick, Operatick, Pantomimick, Melo-dramatick Extravaganza'.

lights, are seen to issue from the distant forest—musick and shouts grow louder—a party of robbers come on the stage and force the mill, which is also set on fire'. Likewise, Dibdin's burlesque of *Don Giovanni* (1817) contains a *'furious mock combat'* between Don Giovanni's men and the watch, with *'several imitations of Broad-sword Combats of two, three, and four'*. The title of Dibdin's *Melodrama Mad!* (1819) suggests burlesque, but instead the play is a spoof on the siege of Troy, with elaborate battles, processions, and stage effects quite unconnected with the conventions of classical burlesque and no doubt meant to be enjoyed for their own sake. Much better is *The Earls of Hammersmith* (1811), by Dennis Lawler and John Poole, in which the tyrant Bluster, who keeps Lord Simple in chains in the Gothic vault and intends to wed Lady Simple, is overthrown by a rebellion led by the virtuous Sir Walter Wisehead and forced into the ghost of a post-chaise drawn by the ghosts of four horses and accompanied by the ghosts of two postilions; the chaise promptly sinks into the nether regions. *The Earls of Hammersmith* contains parody as admirable as this:

> *Thunder—Ghost of a Footman in livery rises and presents a note—* SIR WALTER *reads.*
> 'The ghost of the Dowager Countess of Hammersmith presents her compliments to Sir Walter Wisehead.' [*Thunder—Ghosts of the* DOWAGER *and* BETTY, *her maid, holding her train,* [*rise*]. . . . *The Footman gives scroll—*] 'Wed not Lady Margaret, she is your grandmother!'

This last revelation leads Sir Walter to a tempestuous and heartbroken scene with Lady Margaret, which he concludes with a passionate farewell:

LADY MARGARET. Adieu!
SIR WALTER. My love, my soul, my life—my grandmother!
> [*They embrace.*

The play parodies melodramatic situations and acting style as well as melodramatic conventions, as in the following instance:

> [LADY SIMPLE *and* SIR WALTER *start at seeing each other.*
> LADY SIMPLE. [*Aside.*] Is it possible?
> SIR WALTER. [*Aside.*] What is this?
> LADY SIMPLE. [*Aside.*] Can it be? Yes. No!

SIR WALTER. [*Aside.*] No. Yes!

LADY SIMPLE. [*Aside.*] Is it my son I see, or is it another?

SIR WALTER. [*Aside.*] Oh, yes!

LADY SIMPLE. [*Aside.*] Oh, no!

SIR WALTER. [*Aside.*] It is, it is my mother. [*Embracing—bawls in her ear.*] Be secret, we're observed.

LADY SIMPLE. [*Bawling.*] I will.[1]

Clever, satirically pointed, and energetic, written in sprightly rhyming couplets and lyrics to traditional airs, *The Earls of Hammersmith* owes some debt to eighteenth-century burlesques like *The Tragedy of Tragedies* and *Chrononhotonthologos*, but is much more contemporary in burlesque spirit than *Bombastes Furioso* or *Amoroso*. It is one of the best burlesques of the first half of the nineteenth century.

Among the favourite means of playwrights burlesquing melodrama was ridicule of the villain, a towering figure and therefore easy to shoot at. Such ridicule, however, is usually gentle and friendly. The traditional villain of Byron's *Ali Baba, or The Thirty-Nine Thieves* (1863) is advised that 'vulgar violence is on the wane', and that he should update his style, dress elegantly, start fraudulent joint-stock companies, swindle widows, and do all the things a modern villain is supposed to do. He replies:

> Bother! that's not of villainy my notion;
> Give me the tangled wood or stormy ocean—
> A knife—dark lantern—lots of horrid things,
> With lightning every minute at the wings;
> A pistol, big enough for any crime,
> Which never goes off at the proper time;
> Deep rumbling, grumbling music on the drums—
> A chord wherever one observes 'She comes',
> An opening chorus, about 'Glorious wine',
> A broadsword combat every sixteenth line;
> Guttural vows of direst vengeance wreaking,
> And thunder always when one isn't speaking.

---

[1] The stage-struck Pippo in H. J. Byron's burlesque *The Maid and the Magpie* (1858) is a great admirer of melodramatic acting, whose specifics he discusses at some length. Such acting is burlesqued in William Dimond's farce *Stage Struck* (1837), particularly in the reunion of hero and heroine after painful separation, a scene including the stage direction '*they approach each other by sudden starts, embrace, then faint away alternately, supporting and reviving each other by turns*'.

A rather less positive burlesque villain is Gruffangrimio, the king's scheming but confused prime minister in William Brough's extravaganza, *Prince Amabel* (1862). Gruffangrimio vows a characteristically uncertain revenge on his monarch:

> Tremble, proud tyrant! Here I vengeance vow.
> It shall o'ertake thee—though I don't know how.
> A day of reckoning is at hand! Till then
> My vengeance sleeps—though I can't say till when;
> But I'll a deed perform—although I've not
> At present the remotest notion what—
> Which in the dust shall lay your pride so high.
> Tremble then, tyrant—though I don't know why.
> What then? 'Tis not for men like me to care for
> The how, the when, the what, the why, the wherefore.

The joyful contemplation of desperate crime was of course an integral part of melodramatic villainy; its thorough execution, although usually bungled, was no less desirable. The villain of T. E. Pemberton's burlesque *Gentle Gertrude, or Doomed, Drugged, and Drowned at Datchet* (1881) prepares to murder his sleeping victim: '*Enter* GILES *with a sword, a blunderbuss, and a large pistol; these he places on a table, and going off again returns with a small cannon, a long Richelieu sword, and a huge dagger.*'

Apart from obviously enjoying what they were doing and satirically manipulating the characteristics and conventions of melodrama for the pleasure of their middle-class audiences, it is doubtful if burlesque authors had a clearly defined purpose or artistic aim in view—although the Author in Byron's revue *1863, or The Sensations of the Past Season* claims one:

> Burlesque is like the winnowing machine:
> It simply blows away the husks, you know;
> The goodly corn is not moved by the blow.
> What arrant rubbish of the clap-trap school
> Has vanished—thanks to pungent ridicule;
> What stock stage customs, nigh to bursting goaded,
> With so much blowing up have now exploded.
> Had our light writers done no good save this,
> Their doggrel efforts scarce had been amiss.

It is even more doubtful whether burlesque was solely responsible for such changes, which affected the style rather than the fundamental character of melodrama. Of the acting style in particular, Clement Scott commented in 1880 that 'the old days of mouthing and ranting—penny plain and twopence coloured—are over, burlesque has killed them, and if they were to arise they would be hooted down'.[1] The number of burlesques of melodrama falls off sharply late in the century. Perhaps it was felt that victory had been won; perhaps dramatists realized that nothing they could write would better the self-parody of, for instance, the Drury Lane autumn dramas of the eighties and nineties. The more sophisticated and theatrically cynical part of the middle-class audience could happily enjoy themselves at these performances (as they did) rather than require a special form of burlesque entertainment parodying melodrama.

Essentially good-natured and affectionate toward its originals though burlesque of melodrama was, nevertheless it was eventually destructive. By the beginning of the twentieth century a substantial and influential portion of the middle-class audience could no longer take the traditional conventions and situations of melodrama seriously. The cumulative effect of so much burlesque, so much genial contempt for the sacred articles of melodramatic faith, must have been a factor in the decline of melodrama. Such burlesque reflected the advanced views of the iconoclast and educated audiences in the process of disbelief.

This process, however, gathered momentum only after 1850. Earlier, there had been general burlesque of the kind already indicated; popular melodramas were also specifically burlesqued. From at least Isaac Pocock's *The Maid and the Magpie* (1815)—not to mention the even earlier burlesques of equestrian melodrama—almost every really successful melodrama, opera, and 'drama' was spiritedly and usually promptly burlesqued. These burlesques are so numerous that exemplification and analysis would be both wearisome and repetitive, but two instances, with a generation between them, can be given for the sake of illustrating the style and working mechanisms of such burlesque. These are Frederick Cooper's *Blackeyed Sukey, or All in the Dumps* (1829) and *The Miller and His Men* (1860), by Byron and Francis Talfourd. The former, a burlesque of Jerrold's *Black-Eyed Susan*, which had appeared six months earlier, is

---

[1] *The Theatre* (September 1880), p. 176.

located in Billingsgate, a green-grocer's shop, the King's Bench prison, and a watch-house—all 'low' settings suited to this type of burlesque. William, a 'decayed Waterman', is in prison for non-payment of rent. Sukey (Susan) tries to keep the grocery and fruiterer's business going. Jerrold's Gnatbrain is transformed to Doughy, a muffin-man, and Captain Crosstree into Muzzy, a parish beadle. Hatchet, Raker, Doggrass, and Jacob Twig are merged into Gripe and Bite, tax-collector and bailiff. The court martial becomes a hearing before Dozey, a constable. William is sentenced to the black hole (a punishment cell) before a revived Muzzy appears. The piece is in blank verse with songs, a few puns, and several extended parodies of Shakespearean speeches, especially from *Hamlet*. The general plot of the original is approximately adhered to and several of its incidents reproduced. *The Miller and His Men*, subtitled 'A Burlesque Mealy-Drama', preserves the settings, characters, and plot (simplified) of the original, except that nobody is killed; the play concludes with '*a faint inocuous [sic] explosion . . . supposed to blow the Characters up into the air*' and a finale to the currently popular tune of 'Skidamalink'. There are a great number of puns and a fairly precise parody of every character and important situation or sentiment of the original, as well as of several of the original stage pictures and attitudes. Characters dance off, individually or together, at the end of almost every scene. The flavour of the writing is best conveyed by quotation. The gloomy Kelmar speaks after the millers' opening chorus happily declares their desperate villainy:[1]

> Last Spring my fortune fell, and I lost all;
> In fact, to me, it proved both Spring and fall.
> I was the tumbler in that fall upset——
> That Spring and fall embraced my summerset.
> The year in fact's played leap year with my woe;
> Would it might jump to a conclusion so.

---

[1] Gilbert's parody of Balfe's opera *The Bohemian Girl*, *The Merry Zingara, or The Tipsy Gipsy and the Pipsy Wipsy* (1868), opens with a chorus that also glances at the robbers' chorus (and others like it) closing the first act of *The Miller and His Men*; the stage direction is '*Retainers discovered about stage drinking tea, with the air of robbers carousing. Attendants carrying trays of muffins, water-cresses, &c.*' To 'Sound now the trumpet fearlessly' from *Il Puritani* they sing 'Brown now the crumpet fearlessly . . . Toast now the tea-cake peerlessly'.

A little later, the villains Riber and Golotz enter to '*melodramatic music*':

RIBER. Confusion!

GOLOTZ. Ditto!

RIBER. Foiled!

GOLOTZ. Destruction!

RIBER. True!

GOLOTZ. Cuss everything!

RIBER. I quite agree with you.
Claudine, we to her father's hut have track'd.

GOLOTZ. Then 'tis *an 'ut* must presently be *cracked*.

RIBER. Stay, here's a chink. [*Going to window.*

GOLOTZ. So humble is the cot
I fear it is the only *chink* they've got.

RIBER. The man I *loathe there*!

GOLOTZ. Ha, hallo *there*!

RIBER. *Lo, there*!
I see *Lothair*!

GOLOTZ. Then we had best not go there! [*They retreat from cottage.*

RIBER. On his return he dies! Confusion!

GOLOTZ. True!

RIBER. This night he meets his doom!

GOLOTZ. He do, he do!

The standard burlesque treatment of a play, of heroic or classical legend, or of past history was to reduce character and situation to the level of domestic life, the humbler the better, and violently juxtapose them with the topography, social life, and supposed comic eccentricity of modern London. *Blackeyed Sukey* is an instance of this treatment; Lester Buckingham's *Virginius* (1859), a burlesque of Sheridan Knowles's tragedy, is another. The villain Appius is Lord Mayor of London and wants Virginia for his cook; she is therefore forcibly apprenticed to his kitchen. Buckingham wrote another parody of Knowles, *William Tell* (1857). Here Tell's son rows with his mother and reads Chartist pamphlets; the tyrant Gessler keeps the Crystal Palace closed on a Sunday.

Such burlesques, and others less closely related to the original subjects, were almost purely theatrical in appeal. Even the most popular of them can make difficult reading today. F. C. Burnand's *The Latest Edition of Black-Eyed Susan* (1866), for example, was one of the most successful burlesques of the century and ran for 400 nights.[1] Virtually unreadable now, it was played with great dash and spirit. There are numerous songs and dances, including a trio and dance for Doggrass, Hatchet, and Raker (the *'dance generally characteristic of villainy'*), a double hornpipe for William and Susan, followed by an Irish jig for five characters, followed by a *'naval dance with flags'* by Sailors and Girls. Crosstree, William, and Susan sing a trio to the music-hall hit 'Champagne Charlie is my name', and the admirals presiding over the court martial sing 'He's a jolly bad fellow'. A description of one of the high spots gives some impression of the theatrical vitality of the performance:

The quintette of 'Pretty Seeusan' was inimitably sung by them, all dancing the while, and never for an instant quiet any one of them, except for the second when all had to listen to Patty Oliver's nightingale trill, which, leading from the verse to the refrain, literally brought down the house in thunders of applause. Then the dancing and chorus were resumed, the movement faster and faster, until Danvers, as Dame Hatley, after bounding about like an irresponsible indiarubber rag doll, or a puppet in a fantoccini show, and after responding to half a dozen encores, which roused the quintette to fresh exertions, sank exhausted. . . . It was a roughly and very readily written burlesque, with jingling rhymes of indifferent merit, but it was dramatic, and it was acted with such energetic earnestness by all the principals as I have rarely seen equalled in all the representations of this class of piece.[2]

Burnand's *Ixion* (1863) is another example of a burlesque execrated by critics but much admired by contemporary audiences. Vulgar, vigorous, disrespectful toward the gods and the classical legend, full of atrocious puns (and some good ones) and clever topical references, *Ixion* too was an eminently theatrical piece. Augustin Filon, who saw the first production,

---

[1] Burnand said that Shepherd, the manager of the Surrey, was not interested in the play because the Surrey audience would not understand it and would dislike a burlesque of *Black-Eyed Susan*. (*Records and Reminiscences*, 4th edn. (1905), p. 292.) [2] Ibid., pp. 301–2.

read it thirty-five years later—'a singularly dismal undertaking'. But this was not being fair:

To form any just impression of the piece, you must try to picture to yourself the little theatre (The Royalty) . . . the pervading odour of the *poudre de riz*, the *flanflans* of the orchestra, the quivering of the gasaliers and of the dazzling electric light, the diamonds, the gleaming white shoulders and the soft silk tights, the superabundance of animal life and high spirits which seem almost to glow like kindling firewood.[1]

H. Barton Baker remembered burlesque at the Strand Theatre, where it flourished under the Swanborough management from 1858 to about 1870, and how difficult it was to withstand its appeal:

There certainly was a 'go', an excitement about burlesque at the Strand in those days that was never approached by any other house. The enjoyment of the performers was really, or apparently, so intense that the wild ecstatic breakdown into which they broke at the end of almost every scene seemed perfectly spontaneous; it was a frantic outburst of irrepressible animal spirits, and they seemed to have no more control over their legs than the audience over their applause. You might call it rubbish, buffoonery, vulgarity, anything you liked, but your temperament must have been abnormally phlegmatic if you could resist the influence of that riotous mirth and not be carried away by it.[2]

Such was the character and style of burlesque at the height of its popularity in the 1860s: a compound of music hall, minstrel show, extravaganza, legs and limelight, puns, topical songs, and gaudy irreverence—the lightest, frothiest, most loved and most detested of Victorian light entertainments.

This kind of burlesque developed largely from extravaganza, as indicated above; its methods were basically those of extravaganza with the burlesque element heightened. Principal boys acted in extravaganza and pantomime well before the 1860s, and Madame Vestris as Don Giovanni in W. T. Moncrieff's extravaganza *Giovanni in London* (1817) displayed a shapely figure and beautiful legs that created the theatrical sensation of the century. It is interesting to note techniques

---

[1] *The English Stage* (1897), p. 95.
[2] *History of the London Stage*, 2nd edn. (1904), p. 448.

that characterized almost every burlesque. The dance inevitably following a song and concluding a scene is one of them. Planché said of a piece of business that ended the first scene of *The Fair One with the Golden Locks* (1843) that 'someone having suggested at the rehearsal that the King, Court, and Guards should dance off, the idea was adopted, and has since become general in burlesques in similar situations'.[1] In Byron's *The Maid and the Magpie* (1858) a dance was introduced following a duet by Pippo and Isaac. Marie Wilton, whose Pippo was the talk of London, recalled that 'it was a novel thing at that time to introduce a dance after a song or duet, and this one became the rage, as well as the *pièce de resistance* of all the hurdy-gurdies and barrel-organs of the day. Encore followed encore every night, and from that time till now no singing has been complete in a burlesque without a dance to follow.'[2] It was also in this piece that John Hollingshead taught Marie Wilton a minstrel dance, the Squash Hollow Hornpipe, which was successfully introduced; Hollingshead claimed that 'this was the first of the series of dances which became known as "cellar-flap breakdowns" '.[3] The minstrel show affected extravaganza from the 1840s—witness Prospero playing the bones in *The Enchanted Isle*—and even earlier the 'Jim Crow' song and dance swept London when Thomas Rice appeared in 1836 and 1837; he had imitators for years afterwards. The lively, eccentric, and sometimes grotesque dances of the minstrels were imported wholesale on to the extravaganza and burlesque stage, and a deluge of hit minstrel tunes had appropriate new lyrics written for them. By the 1860s the music-hall influence was also strong, and to the traditional popular airs, opera arias and choruses, and minstrel songs were added the current music-hall favourites. Nonsense refrains like 'Whack fol lol lol; whack fol lol lol; whack fol lol lay' and 'Fol de fol diddle dum day' had been common for generations, but the burlesque of the sixties, taking some of these refrains from minstrel songs and the music hall,

---

[1] *Extravaganzas*, ii. 241.
[2] *Mr. and Mrs. Bancroft On and Off the Stage*, 4th edn. (1888), i. 79.
[3] *My Lifetime* (1895), i. 140. A breakdown was a kind of extraordinarily lively shuffle, with vigorous and often grotesque arm and body movements; burlesque performers in turn or together would dance it, especially at the end of scenes. A cellar-flap breakdown was danced on virtually the same spot, without mobility.

achieved heights of infantilism in this style. Gilbert, of all people, happily indulged in such refrains. In *Dulcamara* (1866) the audience was offered

> If you say nay I can only say
> Skid-a-ma-link and a doodah day,
> Boodle, oodley, umshebay,
> And a hunky dorum, doodle day.

This is followed by chorus refrains of 'Oh, tootle-tum, tootle-tum tay', and 'Oodley oodley umpty oo'; the finale of *The Merry Zingara* (1868) informs the audience that 'It's a tiddly, widdly, popply wopply / Pickly, ickly sing!' Which they must have been pleased to know.

The popularity of burlesque was supplemented in the 1870s by a taste for opera-bouffe. Offenbach's *Orpheé aux Enfers* had already been turned by Planché into *Orpheus in the Haymarket* (1865), and *La Grande Duchesse de Gerolstein* appeared at Covent Garden in 1867, adapted by Charles Kenney. *Ching-Chow-Hi* (1865), William Brough's adaptation of Offenbach's *Ba-ta-clan*, was performed by the German Reeds. Hervé's *Chilperic* was done at the Lyceum in 1870, and between 1869 and 1871 Hollingshead produced at the Gaiety English versions of several more Offenbach operas: *La Princesse de Trébizonde, Trombalcazar, Barbe-Bleue, Les Deux Aveugles, La Belle Hélène,* and *La Grande Duchesse de Gerolstein*. *La Périchole* was given at least four productions in the 1870s at various London theatres, and other Offenbach operas were also performed. The fact that the Gaiety, in the seventies and eighties London's centre for burlesque, was responsible for Offenbach adaptations indicates that Hollingshead found that opera-bouffe fitted comfortably into his burlesque-oriented repertory. Native English opera-bouffe was also written: Burnand claimed to have started it with *Windsor Castle* (1865) at the Strand and to have replaced (more accurately, complemented) that theatre's burlesque repertory by English opera-bouffe with original music. Gilbert's *Thespis* (1871), with Sullivan's music, was an opera-bouffe with classical burlesque content appropriate to the Gaiety, where it was first performed, and it was Gilbert and Sullivan who emerged from the ruck of native opera-bouffe and light opera librettists and composers in the seventies to go on to their later triumphs. Such progress, as he deemed it, delighted William Archer, who reviewed the situation in 1886:

A few years ago we used never to be without two, three, or even more French operettas running simultaneously at as many theatres, while the 'sacred lamp of burlesque' was assiduously tended at the Gaiety, and flared intermittently in several minor fanes. Now, to parody an often quoted saying, opera-bouffe spells ruin and burlesque bankruptcy. . . . No doubt there is still, and will always be while the present constitution of society maintains itself, a special public for mere 'leg-pieces', but the general public seems, for the moment at any rate, to have turned its back upon the flesh-pots of Egypt. . . . The supply of French opera-bouffe, both as regards quantity and quality, has notably declined, so that even if the demand had been as strong as ever, there would have been difficulty in meeting it; and, on the other hand, there has been a fall in the demand owing to powerful native competition in the shape of those most popular entertainments of the day, the Gilbert–Sullivan operettas. Here, at last, is matter for almost unmixed rejoicing. The victory of Gilbertian extravaganza over opera-bouffe as adapted for the London market, is the victory of literary and musical grace and humour over rampant vulgarity and meretricious jingle.[1]

Archer was not so certain regarding the causes of the decline of burlesque, but he suggested that the burlesque audience had divided, the lower half patronizing the music halls, and the upper the three-act farce.

By the 1870s, indeed, music-hall personalities such as Kate Vaughan, Constance Gilchrist, and Phyllis Broughton were appearing on the stage of the Gaiety, and burlesque was moving further in the direction of musical comedy, although retaining many familiar characteristics. A good example of this type of part burlesque, part opera-bouffe is Alfred Thompson's *Aladdin II* (1870). It has few puns, considerable delicacy, charm and grace, and lavish Japanese costumes and settings.[2] The subject was a traditional one of pantomime, and the play resembles a

---

[1] *About the Theatre* (1886), pp. 20–1.

[2] Thompson also designed costumes for Gaiety burlesque. Hollingshead noted that his designs were essentially French and a little too detailed, 'but for delicate and harmonious combinations of colour, mostly half-tints, he was quite unrivalled. . . . The old coarse costume combinations—strong reds, strong greens, strong blues, and strong yellows—were doomed from the hour that Alfred Thompson's dresses appeared before the footlights.' (*Gaiety Chronicles* (1898), p. 43.)

pantomime opening, with a principal boy (Nellie Farren) as Aladdin, a Genie of the Lamp, and a substantial low comedy role for J. L. Toole. In 1880 Hollingshead inaugurated a period of three-act burlesques with Robert Reece's *The Forty Thieves*. Eight more followed, some based upon familiar pantomime themes, before Hollingshead relinquished management in 1886. He described Reece's *Aladdin* (1881) as 'a favourable specimen of the new school of burlesque, in which artistic dancing is substituted for the cellar-flap breakdown, in which the music is carefully selected, and executed in a way worthy of comic opera, and in which gracefully designed costumes take the place of the old red, green, and blue abominations'.[1] Three-act burlesque survived for a few years at the Gaiety under George Edwardes, but the retirement of Nellie Farren in 1891 and the death of Fred Leslie in 1892 deprived him of his two great burlesque stars. This loss, combined with a declining public taste for burlesque and a demand for greater musical originality and quality, impelled Edwardes to choose musical comedy as the form in which his theatre would excel; the first of these distinctive musical comedies—complete, of course, with the Gaiety Girls, already an established institution—were *In Town* (1892) and *The Shop Girl* (1894). Increasing refinement of middle-class taste had finally driven burlesque into the arms of musical comedy, just as, conversely, an alteration and coarsening of the same taste had, years before, driven Planché's graceful extravaganzas out of favour and welcomed the bouncing energy of the comparatively cruder mid-century burlesque.

Such refinement of taste was not the property of audiences who viewed those pantomimes which competed with Planché's extravaganzas as holiday entertainment in the thirties, forties, and fifties. They were audiences more interested in the comic and scenic material of the opening than in the tumultuous, anarchistic harlequinade that so delighted the earlier, Regency audiences. And as the years went by, pantomime became more and more an exclusively Christmas and family entertainment catering for children, who formed an ever-increasing part of the audience. The Regency pantomime was not thought of as children's entertainment—although children went—and such a development naturally affected the content of pantomime: it

---

[1] *My Lifetime*, ii. 154.

grew simpler, less satiric, less cruel, more obvious comically and scenically, more ostentatiously moral and even instructional —in a word, less adult.

The lengthening of the opening, and shortening of the harlequinade have already been noted. By the 1840s the former was often longer than the latter; after 1850 the number of scenes in the harlequinade rarely exceeds six, and by the late 1860s and 1870s drops to four and three, with an opening at least twice the length. The development of the opening also meant a much longer entertainment altogether; from an afterpiece of an hour or two early in the century, pantomime by the end of it was the sole item on a bill that took between three and five hours to perform. Together with the emphasis on the first part went a gradual detachment from it of the harlequinade and its personnel. Since the opening became self-contained, a complete dramatic story in itself, there was no need for its characters to expiate their sins or play the game of flight and pursuit in the harlequinade, which therefore grew to be a disconnected set of comic episodes tagged arbitrarily on to the end of a play that was over. Furthermore, although the characters of the opening were still changed into Harlequin, Columbine, Pantaloon, and Clown, the actors who played in the harlequinade were not necessarily the same as the principals in the opening. For instance, in J. M. Morton's *Harlequin Blue Beard* (1854) the actors of Selim and Ibrahim reappear as Harlequin and Pantaloon, but Columbine and Clown are played by new performers. In the same author's *Aladdin and the Wonderful Lamp* (1856) Aladdin and the Princess are changed to Harlequin and Columbine, but different performers are substituted. In E. L. Blanchard's *Hop O' My Thumb and His Eleven Brothers* (1864) the harlequinade company is entirely separated from the actors of the opening, and this separation was established practice for the rest of the century. This pantomime also possesses two sets of harlequinade artists, one appearing in the first two scenes and the other in the last two. Sometimes the two groups alternated scenes; sometimes they played together in one of the scenes. This development may have been the idea of Blanchard himself. If so, he did not stop there: his *Peter Wilkins* (1860) contains three Clowns. Additional and superfluous characters like Harlequinas and Sprites are also common in mid-Victorian harlequinades.

The decline of the harlequinade and the elevation in importance of the opening tilted the dramatic balance toward the latter and led to significant changes in its character. Rhyming couplets slowly replaced the dumb-show components of the earlier opening, and speech was extended to the previously almost speechless harlequinade; after 1850 Clown was often accused of talking too much.[1] One of the most striking changes in the nature of the opening was the transference of comic business from the harlequinade into what had usually been a fairly refined and sometimes solemn preface to subsequent hilarity. It was not long before the harlequinade was being accused of humourlessness—an accusation that would have made Grimaldi turn dismally in his grave. As if in compensation the mid-century opening was loaded with comic business, which was often, as in contemporary farce, associated with the preparation, serving, and eating of food—a common association since the earliest days of Grimaldi's Clown but now generally extended to almost all characters in the opening. Kitchen scenes abounded. The plot of Blanchard's *Harlequin Hudibras* (1852) is almost entirely advanced by low comedy; one example is the scene in the Great Kitchen of Boscobel Manor House, in which *'utensils of the usual grotesque pantomime size are scattered about the Scene'*. Eating the joint and drinking the wine provide opportunities for much comic business. Similarly, in *Harlequin Blue Beard* cooks and scullions enter Blue Beard's kitchen with *'various sorts of fish, poultry, joints of meat, hams, large cabbages, carrots, turnips, &c.'* A turtle knocks a fat cook into a large fish kettle; Blue Beard enters and the turtle *'waddles between his legs and throws him down—all run to help him up; a fight takes place between them, ending in* BLUE BEARD *running for the red-hot poker and applying it to the* COOK, *who runs screaming off'*. (An interesting example, incidentally, of a character in an opening appropriating a piece of comic business—the use of the red-hot poker—traditionally and specifically the property of Clown.)

---

[1] Clown developed in other directions besides garrulity. An unidentified critic writing in 1861, in addition to protesting that 'what Clown *says* conduces as frequently to the success of the scene as what he *does*', described him as not the awkward, lumpish Clown of old but 'an accomplished dancer, a wonderful exciting acrobat—not infrequently a performer on various musical instruments and the possessor of a troop of highly trained dogs and monkeys'. (Quoted in A. E. Wilson, *Pantomime Pageant* (1946), p. 52.)

A moment later Blue Beard blows himself up with all the food—with only amusing results; as formerly in the harlequinade violence and disaster end merely in comic discomfiture. Even evil spirits were not exempt from this kind of domestic comic business. Earlier in the same pantomime the demon Rustifusti and his imps drink punch, 'RUSTIFUSTI *keeping them in order with sundry knocks on the head—great rubbing of stomachs'*. Such low comedy was not confined to kitchens, food, and eating. In *Aladdin and the Wonderful Lamp* the sorcerer orders his assistant to fetch the dictionary:

KASRAC *in attempting to get the huge dictionary down from the shelf pulls it down on his head, and is again floored—after great difficulty he takes up the dictionary and pitches it up to* ABANAZOR, *knocking him off his stool on to the stage.* KASRAC, *dreadfully alarmed, runs and helps him up. As soon as he is on his legs the* TOM CAT *runs between them, throwing him forward on his nose.* ABANAZOR *indignant seizes his wand and makes a blow at the* CAT *which* KASRAC *receives.* CAT *leaps on the table, scattering the bottles, conjuring apparatus in all directions, and makes his escape—bottles &c. are picked up by the* IMP PAGES.

Kasrac, who becomes Clown in the harlequinade, is a mute in the opening, in which for all intents and purposes he is also Clown. The opening of *Aladdin and the Wonderful Lamp* is really a highly physical farce with the conventional magic and scenic elements of pantomime added. However, very few nineteenth-century farces contained the excess of physical business essential to so many Victorian pantomime openings.[1] As for acting, the pantomime opening was, like farce, the domain of the low comedian.

The continuing emphasis on low comedy in the opening was matched by a moral emphasis that remained a distinguishing feature of Victorian pantomime for some years. Implicit in the Regency pantomime was a conflict between the forces of love, freedom, and happiness (and thus goodness), as manifested in the alliance between Harlequin, Columbine, and the benevolent spirit, and the forces of persecution and intolerance in the pursuing duo—or trio, with Lover—of Pantaloon and Clown,

---

[1] But not all. Many are virtually without low comedy and possessed of considerable charm and grace. E. L. Blanchard, for example, frequently wrote this kind of opening.

occasionally aided by a malevolent spirit. The opening sometimes depicted a clash between supernatural goodness and supernatural evil. However, the moral issues of such a conflict were by no means clearly defined. Harlequin could be a morally ambivalent character, and Clown's rapacity and continuous criminal activity endeared him to rather than alienated him from audience sympathy and affection.

In mid-century, moral boundaries in pantomime were much more sharply demarcated, probably for the edification of the increasing number of children in the audience, and a fixed moral pattern became apparent in the opening, in both characterization and scenic effect. Many pantomimes of this period begin with a gloomy scene in the realm of the evil spirit and his henchmen, followed by a sharply contrasting scene set in the bright dominion of the good fairy, who sets herself against the evil spirit and resolves to frustrate his work. Sometimes it is the other way around. Whatever the order, the good fairy takes the hero and heroine under her protection, and the evil spirit determines to do as much harm to them as he can. In the Regency pantomime this point was reached in the transformation scene; that is, at the moment when the principal characters of the opening were changed into their harlequinade equivalents. But the primacy of the opening meant that the plot had to be developed and concluded within it, and not finished in the harlequinade. A moral confrontation of this kind was obviously and often elaborately expressed. Thus in the anonymous *Harlequin and King Pepin, or Valentine and Orson* (1843) the first scene is 'The Abode of Idleness'; Industry emerges from a beehive and the scene changes from dismal and ruined countryside to the 'Fairy Abode of Industry', busy and fruitful farmland. Industry and Idleness dispute about education; the former sponsors Valentine and the latter Orson. J. M. Morton and Nelson Lee use the same idea and scenic detail in *Harlequin Hogarth* (1851): Ignorance and Idleness contest with Industry and Knowledge over Hogarth's two apprentices. The plot is worked out through moral contrast as well as comic business. In Frank Green's *Harlequin Beauty and the Beast* (1877) Ignorance and his attendant demons (Mischief, Hatred, Folly, Malice, Envy, and Stupidity) pit themselves against Knowledge and her subordinates Progress, Intelligence, and Perseverance. It is

Ignorance who transforms the Prince into the Beast. Morton's *Harlequin Blue Beard*, with the same preponderance of low comedy as *Harlequin Hogarth*, contains consecutive scenes laid in 'The Caverns of Gloom, near the Slough of Despond, in the Regions of Despair' and 'The Crystal Fountains and Enchanted Gardens, the Summer Residence of the Good Fairy'. Its subtitle is explicitly moral: *The Good Fairy Triumphant over the Demon of Discord*. Naturally, the Demon aids Blue Beard and the Fairy his victim, Fatima.[1] The first scene of Lee's *Harlequin Blackbeard* (1864) is 'The Abode of King Night and Ruins of an Ancient Castle'; the second is the 'Haunt of Queen Sunlight'. Blackbeard is assisted by King Night and five sprites including Stab-i'-the-dark and Black Despair. Byron also made striking scenic use of such a moral contrast in *Robinson Crusoe* (1860). In Lee's *Harlequin and O'Donoghue* (1850) the hag Mischief calls up the evil spirit Poteen and numerous horrendously named attendant demons. Poteen gets the hero drunk, but he is saved from suicide by the mysterious immortal, O'Donoghue, who addresses him sternly:

> Desist! nor madly seek the drunkard's end;
> And if you wish sincerely to amend,
> Your fault may be forgiv'n, of that be sure,
> If you will stick but to the water cure.

The first scene description of Lee's *Harlequin Alfred the Great* (1850) is entirely characteristic of the initial 'demon' scene, a scene hearkening back to the penultimate 'dark' scene of the Regency harlequinade. The setting is 'The Gulph of Despair':

The Stage represents a black and dismal Cavern, running into perspective until it is lost in utter darkness. Loud thunder, with heavy rain, is heard. Shrieks and all kinds of horrid noises fill the air, as the ground opens, and DESPAIR *ascends, seated on a Throne fantastically formed of all such things as may be supposed to lead to despair, such as dice-boxes, dice, bottles, &c. &c.*

Among the characteristics of this demon scene one writer mentioned 'the hideous glare of the green-eyed devils, the

---

[1] The malignity of the Demon is somewhat tempered by his fondness for punch and his tendency to utter, in moments of stress, remarks like 'Oh crikey! Here's a pretty go.' Such demons were often partly comic and sometimes rather domestic. Authors and audiences saw nothing incongruous in this; despair and darkness had also been easily and comically domesticated in Victorian farce and extravaganza.

occasional rolling of thunder, and clashing of cymbals in the orchestra, the frequent operations of the traps of divers kinds, the presence of red fire, and an atmosphere strongly savouring of brimstone'.[1]

The expression of morality through scenic and mechanical devices points to another marked feature of mid-century pantomime, the increasing tendency—as in other forms of contemporary drama—to scenic elaboration and spectacle. Planché's complaints about what happened to extravaganza after the scene painter William Beverley's success with the transformation scene of *The Island of Jewels* in 1849 are well known, but perhaps they can be repeated here:

The *last* scene became the *first* in the estimation of the management. The most complicated machinery, the most costly materials, were annually put into requisition, until their bacon was so buttered that it was impossible to save it. As to me, I was positively painted out. Nothing was considered *brilliant* but the last scene. Dutch metal was in the ascendant. It was no longer even painting; it was upholstery. Mrs. Charles Mathews herself informed me that she had paid between £60 and £70 for gold tissue for the dresses of the supernumeraries alone, who were discovered in attitudes in the last scene of 'Once Upon a Time There Were Two Kings'.[2]

When *The Invisible Prince* (1846) was revived in 1859, Planché had to add a verse to the finale apologizing for the absence of a transformation scene. He was also aware of the influence upon pantomime of extravaganza's transformation scene, a development of the ultimate transformation in Regency pantomime when the dark scene was changed to the effulgent realm of bliss, love, or happiness by a wave of the benevolent spirit's wand. In turn, the richness and scenic splendour of the mid-century extravaganza transformation influenced the old pantomime transformation scene—in its full magnificence now terminating the opening rather than the harlequinade—to take the same scenic direction.

In 1840 *The Times* complained that 'the adventures of the four characters of pantomime are no longer the staple commodity of the piece. They rather act as the thread to connect a number of works by scenic painters and mechanics which have

---

1 Leopold Wagner, *The Pantomimes and All About Them* (1882), p. 28.
2 *Recollections and Reflections*, p. 338.

little to do with their own vicissitudes.' Clown, especially, 'is but an unimportant personage, and amid admiration for mechanical ingenuity and dioramic painting his existence is nearly forgotten'.[1] The English harlequinade had often been interrupted by speciality acts, and from the 1820s by dioramas also. Tableaux dependent upon mechanical contrivance were also popular and grew more elaborate with improvements in stage technology. Audiences had always enjoyed stage processions, and these were fitted into pantomime as well as other kinds of drama. Few such interpolations were related to pantomime content; they were rather to be enjoyed as displays in their own right and for apt topical reference, when this was relevant. For instance, the harlequinade of Nelson Lee's *Harlequin and Mother Red Cap* (1839) stops dead to accommodate several scenes, painted by William Telbin, illustrative of the 'Beauties of Ireland, Gem of the Sea', for no better reason than Columbine's desire to see them. The same harlequinade also contains a performance by the Kamschatkian Brothers, the 'Flying Devils of the Rope', and concludes with a chivalric pageant. A dioramic ride by Guy to the Enchanted Castle adorns *Guy, Earl of Warwick* (1841) by J. M. Morton; the final scenes of the harlequinade are a view of the 'Railroad from New Cross',[2] Woolwich Dockyard, and the launching of the H.M.S. *Trafalgar* of 120 guns. Patriotic and naval references are plentiful. The harlequinade of *Harlequin and King Pepin* ends with 'Nelson's Last Victory', which includes the 'Advance of the British Fleet Led by the Royal Sovereign', the 'Battle and Death of the Hero', and a 'Grand Allegorical Tableau' with a view of the just-completed Nelson's Monument in Trafalgar Square. Blanchard's *Harlequin and the World of Flowers* (1852) at the Surrey makes the usual transition from scenes of pure fantasy in the opening—'The Glittering Regions of the Silver Star', 'The

[1] *The Times*, 28 December 1840.

[2] Pantomimes and extravaganzas were very aware of the railway age and the industrial scene. Factories, warehouses, docks, and railway stations appear in pantomime scenes. An anonymous *Harlequin and the Steam King* (1845) is concerned with trains, railway shops, and railway speculation. Blanchard wrote *The Birth of the Steam Engine, or Harlequin Locomotive* (1846). Planché's extravaganza *The Bee and the Orange Tree* (1845) is full of railway references and lauds progress in the form of railway building; the good fairy even arrives at the crucial moment by '*Fairy Atmospheric Down train*', complete with a '*State Carriage of the Directors*' and fairy guards.

Lake of Water Lilies by Sunset', 'The Valley of Bluebells'—to the matter-of-fact London shop and street scenes of the harlequinade, with a final 'Surrey Tribute to England's Hero' in the form of 'A Grand Pictorial Illustration in Remembrance of Britain's Duke' (Wellington had died three months before). In the opening of *Harlequin Alfred the Great* Hope patriotically prophesies the might of the British navy with lines referring to Alfred:

> For who will dare her Hearts of Oak to meet
> When changed by him into an English Fleet?

Alfred then *'holds up both his hands. All the Oak Trees change into Ships, as the band plays "Rule Britannia".'* It would not have troubled the audience that at another point in the opening Alfred and his supporters enter *'as Ethiopian Serenaders. Their disguise merely consists of a black dress coat, with enormously long tails, white wristbands a good way up their arms, high white collars, black masks down to the mouth, and woolly skull caps.'* To their own accompaniment of banjo, concertina, and bones they sing to the tune of 'Zip Coon' a song beginning 'Alfred de Great, he was a larned skoler'. The harlequinade of Blanchard's *Grimalkin the Great* (1868) has negro dances and a negro vocalist, as well as the Albanian Minstrels and other non-harlequinade matter: a troupe of performing dogs, a ballet ('The Girls of the Period'), and a final scene on the deck of a man-of-war manned by '300 Children and the Infant Drummer Master Vokins'. This scene depicts preparations for a voyage, an inspection by the Duke of Edinburgh, rifle drill, cutlass exercises, a battle with the enemy, and a hornpipe by 'sixty Able-Bodied Young British Tars'. In contrast, Blanchard's opening is unusually refined and delicate for the time.

Pantomime authors or 'arrangers', as they were known earlier, never had complete control over the harlequinade, which after 1850 became more and more a matter for the artist who played Clown; it was he who devised and rehearsed comic business, determined the sequence of scenes, and in consultation with the machinists developed trick-work. Harlequin or a ballet master (often the Harlequin) would supervise the dancing. The opening was also more of a collaboration between dramatist, manager, scene painter, machinist, and gasman than the literary responsibility of a sole author. The degree of the author's responsibility largely depended on his stature in the theatre, but such collaboration had always been a feature of pantomime writing and production. In the second half of the century, as spectacle, low comedy, and music-hall importations increasingly dominated the opening, the role of the dramatist diminished even further. Gilbert described the pantomime author's function in the 1860s:

He writes simply to order, and his dialogue is framed upon the principle of telling as much as possible in the very fewest words. He is ready to bring in a 'front scene' wherever it may be wanted, and to find an excuse at the last moment for the introduction of any novelty in the shape of an 'effect' which any ingenious person may think fit to submit to the notice of the manager. From a literary point of view his work is hardly worth criticism, but he ought, nevertheless, to possess many important qualifications if it is to be properly done. It is not at all necessary that he should be familiar with the guiding rules of prosody or rhyme; nor is it required of him that he shall be a punster, or even a neat hand at a parody; but he must be quick at weaving a tale that shall involve a great many 'breeches parts.' He must be intimately acquainted with the details of stage mechanism and of the general resources of the theatre for which he is writing. He must know all the catchy songs of the day, and he must exercise a judicious discrimination in selecting them. He must set aside anything in the shape of parental pride in his work, and he must be prepared to see it cut up and hacked about by the stage-manager without caring to expostulate. He must 'write up' this part and cut down that part at a moment's notice; and if one song won't do, he must be able to extemporize another at the prompter's table; in short, he must be prepared to give himself up, body and soul, for the time being, to manager, orchestra leader, ballet-master, stage-manager, scenic artist, machinist, costumier, and property-master—to do everything that he is told to do by all or any of these functionaries, and, finally, to be prepared to find his story characterized in the leading journals as of the usual incomprehensible description, and his dialogue as even inferior to the ordinary run of such productions.[1]

---

[1] 'Thumbnail Studies: Getting Up a Pantomime', *London Society*, xiii (January 1868), pp. 56–7. Wagner remembered a provincial pantomime performance of *The Yellow Dwarf* 'in the course of which were discovered "Tyler's Silver Band" in oriental costume, playing *Come back to Erin* on the terrace of King Rambo's Palace on the banks of the Ganges! Thus, we have proof how a too energetic manager utilises his libretto, merely as a peg upon which to hang all the heterogeneous talent engaged together.' (*The Pantomimes and All About Them*, p. 11.)

Gilbert's low opinion of the importance of the pantomime author doubtless arose from his collaboration with Charles Millward on Astley's pantomime for 1866, *Hush-a-Bye Baby*, and the slipshod production of his own *Harlequin Cock Robin and Jenny Wren* at the Lyceum in 1867. Earlier, however, he had penned an acidic Bab Ballad which gives a vivid though cruel picture of mid-Victorian pantomime. Three verses are as follows:

> Seedy sprites forever vaulting, seedy metre ever halting,
> Men of 'property' cobalting eighteen-penny devil's face:
> And the foolish culmination in a weary 'transformation,'
> Whose complete elaboration takes a twenty minutes' space!
>
> Then the green and crimson fire, and the women hung on wire
> Rising higher, rising higher—oh, their bony, baggy knees!
> And the never-failing 'rally,' and the fine old crusted sally,
> And the 'Ladies of the Bally,' and the fays who sniff and sneeze!
>
> All the stockings gone in ladders—then the sausages and bladders,
> And the chromes, and greens, and madders, that I've seen five thousand times;
> And the glitter, gauze, and spangle, and the clown turned in the mangle,
> And the everlasting jangle of the mutilated rhymes.[1]

Yet Gilbert was as ambivalent about pantomime as melodrama; not only did he write in both genres, but they also influenced his later work. *The Fairy's Dilemma* (1904), based on a complete misunderstanding between the Demon Alcohol and the Fairy Rosebud, is in fact the best satire on pantomime written.

Whatever the playwright's role, there is no doubt that after 1850 he had to take into account the popularity of burlesque, which strongly influenced the pantomime opening. Before this, of course, as already noted, pantomime had influenced the development of extravaganza and vice versa. The more one studies pantomime, extravaganza, and burlesque, the more one realizes how closely the three are interrelated. They shared the same plots, the same twinning of the fantastic and the topical–domestic, the same puns, the same rhyming doggerel, the same mode of high-spirited extravagance, and the same

---

[1] 'Pantomimic Presentiments', *Fun*, 2 December 1865.

stamp of holiday entertainment. The terms 'extravaganza' and 'burlesque' were often interchangeable in contemporary usage, and by the early 1850s Henry Morley was referring to the pantomime opening as the 'introductory burlesque'. With some exceptions the development of the opening in the second half of the century was towards an indissoluble if not always comfortable marriage between burlesque and scenic spectacle. The once healthy harlequinade continued to sicken and became only an irrelevant appendage of four, three, and two scenes—occasionally being dispensed with altogether—to a lengthy and supremely dominant opening.

Outside the West End, however, the traditions of the harlequinade were preserved longer, even until the end of the century. It must again be remembered that the middle-class West End theatre, although it was the mainstream of theatrical development in the nineteenth century and of prime importance, was not the only stream; the provinces and London urban areas outside the West End preserved a vigorous and often independent theatrical life of their own, till the breakdown of the local stock company and the reliance of theatres outside the West End upon the touring company put an end to any such independence and any native dramatic flavouring. The five pantomimes discussed here were first performed in West End theatres—Drury Lane, Covent Gardem, and the Princess's—but this is not a selection justly indicative of the variety and strength of pantomime elsewhere in Britain. Leopold Wagner noted in 1882 that Leeds, Manchester, Liverpool, Birmingham, Leicester, Sheffield, Bradford, Edinburgh, Glasgow, and Dublin were the most important provincial centres for pantomime (Manchester had three theatres performing Christmas pantomimes), and praised the quality of the Brighton pantomime.[1]

As late as 1882 Wagner also recorded pantomimes the previous Christmas at nine London theatres outside the West End: the Britannia, the Surrey, the Standard, the Grecian, the Victoria, Astley's (which had offered pantomimes on horseback), the Elephant and Castle, the Crystal Palace, and the Alexandra.[2]

---

[1] *The Pantomimes and All About Them*, pp. 32–3.
[2] Ibid., pp. 28–30. Shaw enjoyed himself thoroughly at the Britannia pantomime of 1897, and his account of the performance and the audience, in *The Saturday Review*, lxxxv (9 April 1898), is well worth reading.

The East End theatres in particular had their own loyal neighbourhood audiences from the working and lower middle class,
and their own distinctive pantomime traditions. Long after
West End theatres had all but abolished the harlequinade the
Britannia kept its own; the Grecian under the management of
the Conquests from 1851 to 1879 specialized in scripts (as did
the Britannia) that did not use the conventional fairy-tales.
George Conquest, one of the greatest of all pantomimists, a
superb acrobat, dancer, mime, and costume designer, appeared
in bizarre, macabre, demon- and monster-filled pantomimes
with titles like *Harlequin Rik-Rak* (1867), in which he played a
gigantic gnome who became a turnip and then a monkey, *The
Wood Demon* (1873), with him as a withered tree, a giant, and
an animated pear, *Spitz-Spitze the Spider Crab* (1875), *The Grim
Goblin* (1876)—in which he played an octopus and a gigantic
ape as well as the goblin—*Hokee-Pokee, the Fiend of the Fungus
Forest* (1878), and *Harlequin Rokoko, the Rock Fiend* (1879).[1] In
Hokee-Pokee Conquest appeared as a porcupine and a huge
vampire bat with glaring eyes; in *Harlequin Rokoko* a monstrous
toad carved in rock that comes horribly to life. In these pantomimes George Conquest and his son made extensive and danger-
ous use of traps, springs, trapezes, and counterweights for
thrilling extended combats and chases in which they leaped,
flew, and hurtled wildly around and mostly above the stage.
Weird, grotesque, haunted, surpassingly fantastic, and brilliantly
executed, the Christmas entertainments of George Conquest
were not merely extraordinary but unique in the annals of
pantomime.

Further west than the Grecian, Britannia, and Standard,
pantomime to most theatregoers meant Drury Lane, which
dominated English pantomime in the last twenty years of the
nineteenth century. *The Theatre* commented in 1882 that Drury
Lane's manager, Augustus Harris, 'enjoys what is really a
monopoly at Christmas-time. We do not select theatres for
special reasons at pantomime-time. We go to Drury as a matter
of course, and to as many more houses as the pocket or inclination will allow.'[2] The following year it declared that 'a
Drury Lane pantomime is an English institution. We can no

---

[1] All these pantomimes were written by Conquest and Henry Spry.
[2] *The Theatre* (February 1882), p. 103.

more do without it than roast beef, plum-pudding, and mince pies.'[1] Harris mounted his Christmas pantomimes with the same attention to lavish spectacle and grandiose production that marked his autumn dramas, and in so doing spent a great deal of money. However, he took in considerably more than he put out: despite the occasional box-office failure, pantomime was a lucrative business, not only for Harris but also for other pantomime producers. This was as true for Victorian managers as it was for the manager of Covent Garden early in the century. In 'Getting Up a Pantomime' Gilbert referred to his Manager as

[one] who probably looks upon the pantomime he is about to produce as the only source of important profit that the year will bring him. Its duty is to recoup him for the losses attendant upon two or three trashy sensation plays, a feeble comedy, and a heavy Shakesperian revival; and if he only spends money enough upon its production, and particularly upon advertising it, he will probably find it will do all this, and leave him with a comfortable balance in hand on its withdrawal.[2]

Gilbert's view was acidulous but correct. Many managements stayed in business for the rest of the year only through the profits of the Christmas pantomime; if these profits did not materialize, bankruptcy often did. In a very real sense, then, pantomime served the interests of the new and revived drama by providing it with regular subsidies. Expensive though the annual production of pantomime was, it remained both lucrative and financially essential.

Drury Lane pantomime continued to appeal to adults, most obviously through the shapely transvestism of the principal boy and the presence of music-hall stars, but its attractions seem to have been mainly aimed at children, or, at least, at children and adults in family parties. References to children in the audience, to the necessity of pleasing them, and to their real or alleged loyalty to Drury Lane abound in the texts.[3] The structure and

---

[1] Ibid. (January 1883), p. 13. [2] *London Society* (January 1868), p. 55.
[3] Shaw noted that when it came to the boxes and stalls at Drury Lane the manager 'caters for the children alone'. (*The Saturday Review*, lxxxv (1 January 1898).) Max Beerbohm complained that pantomimes were presenting idealized, prettified, Kate Greenaway versions of children on stage, which appealed more to adults than children, who did not want such versions of themselves, nor refinement, nor graceful dancing, nor pretty songs. What they wanted was 'a show with plenty of monsters, demons, noise, and buffoonery. These things are to be found

content of this pantomime have been adjusted appropriately. Verse and dialogue are simpler (though not plots and scenic effects), the general tone more child-like. Traditional opening scenes contrasting the gloomy haunts of evil with the radiant realms of the good fairy have been largely but not entirely abandoned. For instance, *Puss in Boots* (1887), by Blanchard and Harris, opens in the 'Den of the Demon Lawyer'; Love and the Demon Lawyer contest for victory. *Mother Goose* (1902), by J. Hickory Wood and Arthur Collins, opens in 'The Ruined Belfry', whose resident demon and the Fairy Heartsease take sides over the future conduct of Mother Goose. Indeed, the conventional struggle between good and evil spirits remained embedded in pantomime structure. In Blanchard's *Cinderella* (1883) the benevolent Electra vanquishes Ignoramus just before the transformation scene, a transition from 'The Home of Malice and Darkness' to 'The House of Love and Light'. In *Dick Whittington* (1894), by Harris, Cecil Raleigh, and Henry Hamilton, the King of the Cats takes Dick under his protection, and the King of the Rats, who makes the usual demonic entrances through traps, resolves to destroy him.

In place of the conventional initial scene there was sometimes a scene assigning the origins of the pantomime to the world of children. The first scene of *Babes in the Wood* (1897), by Collins and Arthur Sturgess, is laid in the Nursery and possesses a chorus of Nurses. An attempt by the Spirits of Indigestion and Castigation to ruin the children's Christmas and prevent them from seeing the Drury Lane pantomime is foiled by the Spirit of Youth. The opening scene of *Cinderella* (1895), by Harris, Sturgess, and Raleigh, is set at a station in Toyland:

General business of toys. Enter TOY KING. *A practicable railway signal drops at back and a prolonged whistle is heard far away.*

TOY KING. [*Going up back and looking down line.*]

At last they come, my children home return;
They're tired, sleepy, and for rest they yearn.
Poor little toys! At end of every day,
From earth they come, and leave their business—play!

at Drury Lane, but there, alas! unpleasantly overlaid with didactic processions, allegorical ballets, and all the rest of it.' (*The Saturday Review*, lxxxviii (30 December 1899).)

[*March Grotesque. The whistle sounds nearer and the rattle of a train is heard.* T O Y K I N G *steps back as train rushes on. The doors fly open and the toys alight. Business of a Railway Station. Some of the toys carry black bags, others evening papers; some yawn and stretch themselves, others fumble for tickets, etc. There is a great slamming of doors and confusion. Some toys are obviously damaged.*

G U A R D. [*Ringing bell.*] Change here! Noah's Ark! Toy Land! Stand back there!

The Spirit of Pantomime, seeking a subject for his annual entertainment, also alights from the train, and confers with the Toy King.

The 1895 *Cinderella* was one of four pantomimes with this title performed at Drury Lane between 1878 and 1905, and during this period many a *Cinderella* was also seen at other London theatres. After 1850 authors turned more and more to the popular fairy stories for pantomime subject-matter; in 1882 Wagner estimated that only about twenty-five such stories and rhymes were used in all Christmas pantomimes.[1] Such limitation of choice continued into the twentieth century: of the hundred pantomimes staged in Britain in 1933, there were eighteen of *The Babes in the Wood*, seventeen of *Cinderella*, twelve of *Dick Whittington*, eight of *Robinson Crusoe*, and seven of *Jack and the Beanstalk*.[2] Ingenious managers or authors, not satisfied with a single subject, conflated two or three traditional stories, thereby arousing critical wrath and confusing many children. Well above the average level is *The Sleeping Beauty and the Beast* (1900), by Wood and Collins; less successful is the muddled *Little Bo-Peep, Little Red Riding Hood, and Hop O' My Thumb*, by Harris and Wilton Jones, the Drury Lane pantomime for 1892. Not content with using these three sources, the authors of the latter add many more nursery-rhyme and fairy-tale characters, some of whom play important parts. The Dame, for example, is the Mary who had a little lamb, and Red Riding Hood finds matrimonial happiness with Little Boy Blue.

Augustus Harris, who governed Drury Lane from 1879 to 1896, did not produce a pantomime outside the standard range of fairy-tales and nursery-rhymes. Yet versions of the same tale

---

[1] *The Pantomimes and All About Them*, p. 49.
[2] A. E. Wilson, *Christmas Pantomime* (1934), p. 249.

were quite different from one another, and Harris continued the custom of cramming his nominal subject with any relevant or irrelevant material that attracted him—plots, characters, jokes, songs, processions, masks, banners, animals, ballets, dances, topical references, acrobatics, and gorgeously painted scenes. Over all aspects of these immensely elaborate and complex productions Harris ruled with absolute authority, an authority that extended to the script as well; he was no respecter of dramatists, even established ones. Blanchard complained sadly and repeatedly of Harris's alterations. He found the 'smooth and pointed lines' of his *Robinson Crusoe* (1881) 'turned into ragged prose and arrant nonsense'.[1] 'For the . . . grossly interpolated book I am in no way responsible . . . hardly anything done as I intended, or spoken as I had written',[2] he said of *Sinbad the Sailor* (1882); and of *Aladdin* (1885), 'the panto. not at all following the text I have written'.[3] *The Forty Thieves* (1886) caused Blanchard more pain: 'Oh, what a mass of miserable nonsense I have heard this night, spoken in the pantomime ascribed to me, and with which I took some pains!'[4] Harris doubtless thought Blanchard's scripts old-fashioned, and had no hesitation in reworking them and turning them over to his comics for a generous infusion of gags. The manager treated all pantomimes submitted in the same ruthless manner, as one contemporary noted:

When the pantomime was written he went over it most laboriously with a view to its improvement, and passed it to one of the principal managers for further revision. This done, he took another turn at it, until what with his cuts, additions, and interlineations, in all sorts of coloured inks, the manuscript was a mystery to all but the learned in the craft. Dramas were also treated in the same way, but not to such an extent. The anguish of the susceptible author was something excruciating.[5]

Such rough treatment of a script was the practice not only of Harris. Joe Graham, who from 1898 produced thirteen panto-

[1] *The Life and Reminiscences of E. L. Blanchard*, ed. Clement Scott and Cecil Howard (1891), ii. 528.
[2] Ibid. ii. 542.   [3] Ibid. ii. 578.
[4] Ibid. ii. 597.
[5] Geneviève Ward and Richard Whiteing, *Both Sides of the Curtain* (1918), pp. 241–2.

mimes at the Prince of Wales's, Birmingham, described his own dealings with dramatists:

> Although . . . one may lay down the lines on which the pantomime is to be played, Custom exacts that some more or less known accepted playwright shall father the production. Having arranged with the scribe you think best suited to the task, you furnish him with a list of the artistes engaged, describe their characteristics, say what special qualities you wish in each case to be featured, furnish him with a detailed scenario setting forth the effects you wish to introduce by his thoughtful co-operation with your scenic artists; and then, when at long last the completed script comes along, you will probably find that two-thirds of it is composed of patriarchal padding which has to be promptly jettisoned and the entire scheme rebuilt with the assistance of your principal comedians.[1]

Under managers like Harris, a pantomime author (or librettist, as he was perhaps more fittingly called) was a man of little authorial individuality and less status. But that, as we have seen, was always more or less the case.

The presence of music-hall singers and comedians is one of the more notable characteristics of Drury Lane pantomime late in the century. Harris did not initiate this practice, which was common by the seventies, but he followed it to the extent that the principal parts of many pantomimes were filled by stars from the halls: for example, *Robinson Crusoe* (1893), by Harris and Harry Nicholls, contained Dan Leno, Herbert Campbell, Little Tich, Ada Blanche, and Marie Lloyd. Naturally stars introduced their own usually irrelevant speciality songs, acts, and comic business from the music-hall stage, and commanded very high salaries, especially the low comedians. A substantial proportion of the adult audience went to pantomime to see such artistes, but conservatives complained that they degraded pantomime. E. L. Blanchard was just as upset over the music-hall 'invasion', as it was termed, as over the treatment accorded his scripts. 'The music-hall element crushing out the rest, and the good old fairy tales never to be again illustrated as they

---

[1] *An Old Stock-Actor's Memories* (1930), pp. 163–4. Additions, interpolations, and revisions by low comedians were common. The comedian Harry Randall recalled that he would introduce scenes and episodes of his own devising into the pantomimes he was playing in at the Grand, Islington, in the nineties. (*Harry Randall, Old Time Comedian* (1930), p. 68.) Harry Nicholls, collaborator with Harris on several pantomimes, was also a principal comedian at Drury Lane.

should be'—thus he disapproved of his *Sinbad the Sailor*, 'a very dreary music-hall entertainment'.[1] Among other causes of irritation, 'the gagging of the music-hall people' wearied him in *Aladdin*.[2] It was also objected that music-hall art was expelling from the stage the traditional arts of pantomime; one critic preferred the older school, 'where the success depended almost entirely, if not quite, on thoroughly good genuine pantomime business, where there was very little talk and a great deal of action. Nowadays there is very little action and a very great deal too much talk.'[3] For this plethora of 'talk' the music-hall comedians were partly responsible. Even before Harris took over the management of Drury Lane, complaints of this kind were widespread; W. Davenport Adams asked that there should be 'a minimum of topical allusions, an absence of vulgar ditties, and no interruption at the hands of "specialties"', and that 'legitimate artists, rather than music-hall "stars"' should be engaged.[4]

Topical allusions, which many years previously Henry Morley had considered the life of a pantomime, continued to be as popular in the Harris pantomimes as they were in Morley's time or in Grimaldi's. A note in the published *Jack and the Beanstalk* (1889), by Harris and Nicholls, says that 'this Libretto is subject to alterations from time to time for the introduction of topical allusions'. They were introduced wherever possible: the King in *Jack and the Beanstalk* is a 'Johnnie'— a dandy-about-town of the eighties and nineties—and dressed like one; in the 1883 *Cinderella* one scene is laid in the Junior Johnnies Club, whose membership includes the Prince, '*over-dressed as a* MASHER'. He sings a song about how to dress and behave 'If you a Johnnie want to be'. Other 'mashers' (generally synonymous with 'Johnnies' and 'chappies') enter and sing, rather charmingly:

> Chappies are we!
> Chappies are we!
> Say, shall we split, boys,
> A Soda and B?

---

[1] *The Life and Reminiscences of E. L. Blanchard*, ii. 541.
[2] Ibid. ii. 578.
[3] W. Yardley, 'A Chat about the London Pantomimes', *The Theatre* (February 1881), p. 92.
[4] 'A Plea for Pantomime', *The Theatre* (February 1879), p. 27.

In the *Cinderella* of 1895 the heroine rides to the ball in an electric motorcar; automobiles also make an appearance—baffling and enraging the principals—in *The Sleeping Beauty and the Beast* and the 1902 *Mother Goose*; in the latter Mother Goose and her son Jack sail over Gooseland in an airship, and the Demon's Palace of Fantasy is specifically and completely Art Nouveau. Personalities and current events were frequently alluded to, and pantomimes remained as patriotic as ever. In 1897 Ada Blanche appeared as the Kaiser in *Babes in the Wood* and sang an anti-Kaiser number. In 1899 the death of the giant Blunderbore in *Jack and the Beanstalk*, by Collins and Arthur Sturgess, is equated with a hoped-for British triumph in the Boer War, and British soldiers march victoriously over his body.[1]

Patriotic spectacle was only part of the larger spectacle of Drury Lane pantomime. In lavishing money and care on his openings—the harlequinade was reduced to two perfunctory scenes—Harris was especially fond of enormously elaborate and lengthy processions. Requiring hundreds of supers, these were richly and prodigally costumed and inserted on the slightest textual excuse, or none at all. Invited to the ball with Cinderella's family in the 1883 version are the Heroes of Nursery Rhymes and Fairy Stories. The Giant of the 1889 *Jack and the Beanstalk* holds in his power all Shakespeare's heroines; Jack frees them at the request of Oberon (also a character, along with Titania and Puck). Naturally there follows a procession of Shakespeare's Characters, 106 in all, emerging from huge tomes in the Giant's library; another procession, in no way connected with the text, is of forty-four Gods and Goddesses, with a huge retinue of priests and attendants. A procession of twenty-nine nursery-rhyme and fairy-tale characters adorns *Little Bo-Peep, Little Red Riding Hood, and Hop O' My Thumb*, as well as another procession of twenty-one popular sports. The opening of the 1893 *Robinson Crusoe* concludes with a 'Grand Procession of Kings and Queens of England from William I to H.I.M. Queen Victoria', and bears no relation whatever to the preceding scenes. The Lord Mayor's Show in full array passes majestically

---

[1] A vivid recreation of this pantomime from the point of view of a child in the audience is offered by W. MacQueen-Pope in *Carriages at Eleven* (1947), pp. 94–100.

across the stage in the 1894 *Dick Whittington*. Such pageantry
may have irritated critics demanding a return to the simpler
joys of an earlier pantomime, but they dazzled appreciative and
gasping audiences with the glitter and massed movement of a
stage alive with silk, satin, silver, and gold; armour, bells, flags,
and shields; lilies, poppies, buttercups, and bluebells; a ballet
of roses, an underwater ballet of fishes, a dance of Japanese
dolls. Processions, pageants, ballets, aerial and acrobatic displays, shimmering and splendid transformation scenes—anything
conducing to magnificent spectacle in the most abundant and
variegated colour fascinated Harris, filled his pantomimes, and
swelled his profits.

In providing his patrons with a gorgeous show, Harris was
only doing more lavishly what most pantomime producers had
done to the limit of their means for a hundred years past. In
other respects, too, in characterization, songs, dances, fantasy,
rhyming verse, interpolated speciality acts, and comic business,
Drury Lane Christmas entertainment at the end of the century
maintained and elaborated pantomime traditions rather than
offered significant innovations. To take just one instance, low
comedy domesticated and made topical the royal, the fantastic,
and the supernatural as it had always done, particularly in the
traditionally comic uses of cooking and eating. Kitchen scenes
remained popular. The Giant in the 1889 *Jack and the Beanstalk*
is a less fearsome being than he might have been, despite his
nasty eating habits, when he appears in his own kitchen in a
dressing-gown, with a cigarette and a newspaper. The Babes in
the 1897 *Babes in the Wood* eat a comic meal in their kitchen,
and of course the copper explodes. The King and Dame Trot
in the 1889 *Jack and the Beanstalk* eat a comic meal on the
rooftops; later there is a comic wedding breakfast. The harlequinade, attenuated though it was, continued to make grotesquely comic uses of food.

Although still respecting and employing much of its traditional heritage, pantomime had been evolving since the days of
Grimaldi. The end result of such evolution, as in all other
forms of nineteenth-century drama, is fully meaningful only
in so far as one understands the processes that produced it, and
pantomime itself cannot be considered in isolation. One of the
purposes of this section has been to show the close relation-

ships existing between pantomime, extravaganza, and burlesque, the influence of one genre upon another, the varied uses of common material and stage techniques. It should also be obvious that no complete impression of these forms can be obtained from printed text or manuscript. Full appreciation must embody recognition of the richly diverse, comically eccentric, and extraordinarily vigorous life they lived on the stages of countless nineteenth-century theatres.

SELECTED BIBLIOGRAPHY OF
NINETEENTH-CENTURY DRAMA
AND THEATRE 1970-9

IN comparison to the produce of other fields of critical endeavour, the amount of comment on English nineteenth-century drama and theatre emerging over the last ten years could hardly be described as vast, but it is respectable, and far greater in quantity and quality than that of the previous decade. I am not including in this list everything that came out, but have chosen what seems useful for a reasonably comprehensive selection from the ten years following the publication of the first volumes of *English Plays of the Nineteenth Century*.

There are three bibliographies as such; one is *English Drama and Theatre 1800–1900: A Guide to Information Sources*, ed. Leonard W. Conolly and J. P. Wearing (1978). The bulk of this guide concerns the drama rather than the theatre; 110 dramatists are listed, with collected works, principal acted plays, unacted plays, biographies, and critical studies included in their entries. Much smaller sections relate to theatres, acting and management, contemporary history and criticism, and modern history and criticism. Like all omnibus bibliographies it has gaps, but it is valuable for the range and sheer quantity of its entries. The revision of R. W. Lowe by James F. Arnott and John W. Robinson, *English Theatrical Literature 1559–1900* (1970) includes only contemporary items and contains a great deal of nineteenth-century matter. For some years it has been an essential research tool, although even here significant material is omitted. Not really a bibliography in the literary sense of the word but nevertheless an important listing of primary sources is Diana Howard, *London Theatres and Music Halls 1850–1950* (1970). The first and greater part is a directory of theatres, music halls, and pleasure gardens in the period chosen, with attached bibliographies, and the second a list of relevant official records and publications, newspapers, and periodicals, as well as a brief but helpful account of libraries and collections containing theatrical material, almost all in London.

As yet there is no calendar of performances for the London stage in the nineteenth century, but at least the 1890s are covered in J. P.

Wearing, *The London Stage 1890–1899: A Calendar of Plays and Players*, 2 v. (1976); it is arranged chronologically rather than by theatre.

Three collections of articles are *Gilbert and Sullivan*, ed. James Helyar (1971); *Nineteenth Century British Theatre*, ed. Peter Thomson and Kenneth Richards (1971); and a special issue of *Theatre Survey*, xvii (May 1976). All three collections owe their material to conferences. The special nature of the first collection means that many articles are not of particular interest to students of nineteenth-century theatre and drama generally, but one should draw attention to Terence Rees, 'W. S. Gilbert and the London Pantomime Season of 1866' and Jane W. Stedman, 'Gilbert's Stagecraft: Little Blocks of Wood', on Gilbert's ways as a producer and his conduct of rehearsals. *Nineteenth Century British Theatre* contains thirteen articles; of particular interest are Donald Roy's examination of a provincial repertory on three different dates each separated by thirty years, 'Theatre Royal, Hull: or, The Vanishing Circuit', M. Glen Wilson's facts and figures in 'The Career of Charles Kean: A Financial Report', and Jan McDonald's account of an early but isolated experiment in Elizabethan staging, '*The Taming of the Shrew* at the Haymarket Theatre, 1844 and 1847'. Of the eight *Theatre Survey* articles, Carol Carlisle, 'Helen Faucit's Acting Style' is a careful and thoughtful analysis of the technique of one of the nineteenth century's best actresses.

Many articles in these collections are about performance rather than the drama itself, and of course the two cannot be separated in any full investigation of the period. More, in fact, has appeared on theatres and performance in the last decade than on plays, although the all-important audience has received far too little study. Two ventures in this area are Michael R. Booth, 'East End and West End: Class and Audience in Victorian London', *Theatre Research International*, ii (February 1977), and Clive Barker, 'The Audience of the Britannia Theatre, Hoxton', *Theatre Quarterly*, ix (no. 34, 1979). The former is basically theoretical, the latter full of detail and highly relevant social information; it is a good example of the methodology of audience research and of the problems of how to interpret a mass of disparate material about audiences. A very different sort of audience from the East End workman was Queen Victoria, but she was just as enthusiastic. The story of her theatrical visits and tastes is gracefully told in George Rowell, *Queen Victoria Goes to the Theatre* (1978).

General studies of the period usually and properly combine theatre and drama. A standard survey is George Rowell, *The Victorian Theatre 1792–1914* (1978). First published in 1956, it has been reissued with a new chapter and an extended bibliography. Another survey is the

Revels History of Drama in English, vi, 1750–1880 (1975). The dates are awkward, but there are substantial contributions on the social and literary context (Michael R. Booth), on theatres and actors (Frederick and Lise-Lone Marker), and on plays and dramatists (Robertson Davies). This last takes up half the book, and though critically perceptive suffers from a decade-by-decade approach. A shorter and technically informative section on theatre architecture and scenery (Richard Southern) rounds out a useful survey of a field that is not often broadly approached.

Both Richard Southern, *The Victorian Theatre* (1970) and Victor Glasstone, *Victorian and Edwardian Theatres* (1975) are pictorial surveys and contain valuable iconographic material. The focus of the latter is almost entirely architectural, with several splendid colour plates; the former also includes staging techniques. Each has interesting illustrations of audiences.

Of the works concentrating on particular periods, Joseph Donohue, *Theatre in the Age of Kean* (1975) goes from the 1790s to about 1830 and discusses plays as well as acting, theatres, audiences, and critics. It, too, is a survey but possesses few of the faults of that kind of writing; the criticism is thorough and perspicuous if biased toward conventional literary standards of judgment. John Stokes, *Resistible Theatres* (1972) looks at the end of the century rather than the beginning and is an illuminating analysis of the aesthetic movement, the theatrical work of the designer–archaeologist E. W. Godwin, and the painter–producer–experimenter with lighting Hubert von Herkomer; there is also a chapter on the Independent Theatre. These should be known better than they are; that they are known in recent criticism is because of this book.

Acting has received little sustained attention, although actor-managers have been the subject of several studies. Michael Baker, *The Rise of the Victorian Actor* (1978) examines the social origins and familial connections of the actor and their relationship to his career; the slow professionalization of acting, working conditions, and the social position of the actress form the material for other chapters. Michael R. Booth, 'Going on Stage' in *The Mind and Art of Victorian England*, ed. Joseph L. Altholz (1976) is an account of the various ways in which nineteenth-century actors obtained positions on the stage and the workload they carried once there.

As for actors and managers themselves, Richard Findlater, *Joe Grimaldi* (1978) is the second edition of a book published in 1955, now with some new material. Mostly biography, it also offers an acute analysis of Grimaldi's stage art. Another book by Findlater, *The Player Queens* (1976), includes Sarah Siddons and Ellen Terry among its histories; although there is really no new material here the story of each actress's life and art is competently encapsulated within the space of a single chapter. Roger Manvell, *Sarah Siddons* (1970) is a full-scale study, and, like all these studies, stronger on biography than on acting technique. The career of an important actor-manager is well documented in Christopher Murray, *Robert William Elliston* (1975). Elliston's great contemporary is the subject of another biography, Raymund Fitzsimmons, *Edmund Kean* (1976), which retreads familiar paths.

Perhaps the most scholarly study of an actor-manager is Jane Williamson, *Charles Kemble* (1970). Also partly biographical in emphasis is William W. Appleton, *Madame Vestris and the London Stage* (1974), superior in organization and documentation to Clifford John Williams, *Madame Vestris* (1973). As important a manager as Vestris is Samuel Phelps, too much neglected in favour of Macready and Charles Kean. Shirley S. Allen, *Samuel Phelps and Sadler's Wells Theatre* (1971) tries to restore the balance and remains the only substantial modern study of Phelps. His Shakespearean acting is considered as well as his management and production methods. A later actor-manager, Charles Wyndham, is the subject of an interesting chapter by George Rowell in *The Theatrical Manager in England and America*, ed. Joseph Donohue (1971), and Frances Donaldson includes the Bancrofts, Irving, Alexander, and Forbes-Robertson in *The Actor Managers* (1970), a handy but popular book drawing largely on secondary material. A very specific article by Alan Hughes, 'The Lyceum Staff: A Victorian Theatrical Organisation', *Theatre Notebook*, xviii (no. 1, 1974) precisely informs us of the administrative arrangements and distribution of specialist personnel in a large company; detailed information of this kind usefully supplements more general and sometimes superficial accounts of nineteenth-century theatrical companies.

Two vital books for an understanding of production and staging methods are Terence Rees, *Theatre Lighting in the Age of Gas* (1978) and J. P. Moynet, *French Theatrical Production in the Nineteenth Century*, ed. Allan S. Jackson and M. Glen Wilson (1976). The former explains the highly technical business of the development and practical application of gas, limelight, and electric light in terms perfectly comprehensible to the most non-technical layman; the explanation is aided by numerous and well-chosen illustrations. The latter is Moynet's *L'envers du théâtre* (1875) translated into English and supplemented by other contemporary material. Although Moynet was concerned with the elaborate production methods of the Parisian stage and especially the Paris Opera, many of the mechanical and scenic techniques were also used in England. Between them, these two books provide a wealth of fascinating and essential information on how the nineteenth-century stage actually worked. Two articles which deal with the widely prevalent pictorial, archaeological, and spectacular style of production are by Michael R. Booth: 'Shakespeare as Spectacle and History; the Victorian Period', *Theatre Research International*, i (February 1976) and 'Spectacle as Production Style on the Victorian Stage', *Theatre Quarterly*, viii (no. 32, 1979). The first article also treats of the use of Shakespeare for the recreation and teaching of history from the stage. The function of music in the nineteenth-century theatre and the significance of the almost continuous musical accompaniment to performances of melodrama is pointed out by David Mayer, 'Nineteenth Century Theatre Music', *Theatre Notebook*, xxx (no. 3, 1976).

That melodrama is reasonably well represented in the selection of plays published since 1969 outside the volumes of *English Plays of the Nineteenth Century*. It is unfortunately still not possible to read widely in new editions of nineteenth-century drama, but several collections issued over the last decade have helped to remedy deficiencies. *Nineteenth Century Plays* and *Late Victorian Plays*, both edited by George Rowell and first published in 1953 and 1968 respectively, made a welcome reappearance in 1972. The former contains ten plays, the latter seven—only two of them, Pinero's *The Second Mrs. Tanqueray* and Jones's *The Liars*, actually from the nineteenth century. A selection of nine plays from the first four volumes of *English Plays of the Nineteenth Century*, with a new introduction, appears in *The Magistrate and Other Nineteenth-Century Plays*, ed. Michael R. Booth (1974). Two of these plays, *The Factory Lad* and *The Corsican Brothers*, are duplicated in *Victorian Melodramas*, ed. James L. Smith (1976), which includes Milner's *Mazeppa* and Selby's *London by Night*. The twelve selections, ranging from Holcroft's *A Tale of Mystery* to Potter's *Trilby*, in *The Golden Age of Melodrama*, ed. Michael Kilgarriff (1974) would have made a much better volume if the original texts had not regrettably been abridged by the editor. *The Hour of One*, ed. Stephen Wischusen (1975) is a specialized anthology of six Gothic melodramas from Lewis's *The Castle Spectre* to Fitzball's *The Flying Dutchman*, with a complete text of the *Tale of Mystery*. The texts are facsimiles of early acting editions, and in all three collections little or no actual editing of texts seems to have been done. All three contain short general introductions which can only be described as superficial, inadequate, and inaccurate. Quite different are the brief but excellent introductions to the five volumes of *Nineteenth-Century Shakespeare Burlesques*, introduced by Stanley

Wells (1977). The texts have not been edited, but there are thirty-three altogether from a little-known but extraordinarily vigorous and imaginative branch of nineteenth-century playwriting. Four volumes are devoted to English burlesques from John Poole to W. S. Gilbert, and the final volume to American burlesque. It is a substantial and valuable collection.

The activities of critics of the drama have not been as noticeable in the last ten years as those of anthologists or theatre historians. Only one major book has appeared: Joseph Donohue, *Dramatic Character in the English Romantic Age* (1970). This is about the late eighteenth century as much as the early nineteenth, and is the most enlightening consideration we possess of the tragedy of the period and the way in which actors, playwrights, and critics developed notions of dramatic character that were transformed into particular critical standards and literary and acting styles. Leonard W. Conolly, *The Censorship of the English Drama 1737–1824* (1976) likewise pursues his subject only to the early part of the century. An examination of this theme extended until the end of the century would be desirable, but it is best not to comment in this fashion on any area, since, although much good work has been done in nineteenth-century drama and theatre in the last ten years, so much remains that gaps in documentation and critical history are large enough to be embarrassing. A good article that fills part of this particular gap is James F. Stottlar, 'A Victorian Stage Censor: The Theory and Practice of William Bodham Donne', *Victorian Studies*, xiii (March 1970). Donne was Examiner of Plays from 1857 to 1874.

Gilbert Cross, *Next Week—East Lynne* (1977), which is concerned with domestic melodrama between 1820 and 1874, is a spotty book that makes unwarranted assumptions about both audience and performance, but contains a useful chapter on the semiology of melodrama. James L. Smith, *Melodrama* (1973) is a brief survey of the form in the Critical Idiom series; much of it is devoted to nineteenth-century melodrama. The title of Simon Trussler's helpful summary, 'A Chronology of Early Melodrama', *Theatre Quarterly*, i (no. 4, 1971) is self-explanatory; it covers the period 1764–1840. Joseph Donohue, 'Burletta and the Early Nineteenth-Century English Theatre', *Nineteenth Century Theatre Research*, i (spring 1973) is a careful perusal of the notorious problems of definition attaching to the most slippery term in the contemporary theatrical vocabulary; inevitably in the course of this examination much light is thrown on the literary and performance characteristics of burletta and its place, legally and dramatically, in the 'illegitimate' theatre. An unusual psychoanalytic approach to Victorian pantomime and the phenomena of transvestism, the dame, and the principal boy is taken by David Mayer, 'The Sexuality of Pantomime', *Theatre Quarterly*, iv (no. 13, 1974). The psychological premises may be difficult to accept, but the argument is challenging. A quite different attitude to transvestism is that of Jane W. Stedman, 'From Dame to Woman: W. S. Gilbert and Theatrical Transvestism', *Victorian Studies*, xiv (September 1970), which is concerned with a sympathetic explanation of Gilbert's use of stage tradition in his creation of the part of the older woman in the Savoy operas. George Rowell, 'Sardou on the English Stage', *Theatre Research International*, ii (October 1976) is a study of the use of the much-borrowed and much-performed Sardou in the London theatre, and contains a checklist of his plays in performance. Finally, nine-teenth-century dramatists have as usual attracted scant attention from biographers; one such biography is Richard Fawkes, *Dion Boucicault* (1979), which adequately outlines that extraordinary dramatist's life and playwriting career, but is less satisfactory on the contribution of Boucicault to the theatre of his time.

INDEX

acting style: drama, ix-x, 2-3, 18-21, 32, 34, 37, 215; comedy, 67, 72, 87, 94-5, 100; farce, 67, 137-8; burlesque and extravaganza, 182
Adams, W. Davenport, 178n, 208
Adelphi Theatre, 27, 35, 86-7, 114, 127f
Ainsworth, Harrison, 44
Aladdin (1881), 190; (1885), 206, 208
Aladdin II, 189-90
Aladdin and the Wonderful Lamp, 191, 193
Alarming Sacrifice, An, 116, 129-30, 137
Albery, James, 34, 89n, 97-8, 141
Alexandra Theatre, 201
Alhambra, The, 166n
Ali Baba, or the Thirty-Nine Thieves, 180
All That Glitters Is Not Gold, 85
Alma Mater, 79
Amoroso, King of Little Britain, 177, 180
Anne Blake, 18
Arabian Nights, The, 146-7
Archer, William, 47f, 189
Area Belle, The, 132
Ariane, 47
Arms and the Man, 102
Arnold, Matthew, 33n
Arnold, Samuel, 1
Ascent of Mont Blanc, The, 165
Astley's, 27, 200f
audiences, viii, 3, 33-4, 36, 55-6, 71, 103, 111-12, 114, 149f, 202, 214, taste, 68-9, 87, 103, 112, 133
d'Aulnoy, Madame, 159

Ba-ta-clan, 188
Babes in the Wood, 204f, 209f
Baillie, Joanna, 9-10
Baker, H. Barton, 96, 186
Bal Masqué, 38
Bancroft, Squire, 32, 34, 94, 96n, 101n
Bancroft, Mrs, 41, 92n
Bancrofts, 3, 32f, 52, 88, 92, 94f, 97, 216
Bannister, John, 68
Barbe-Bleue, 188
Barker, Harley Granville-, xi, 506
Barney the Baron, 130
Barrett, Wilson, 34n
Bayly, T. H., 71, 119
Beauty and the Beast, 171
Bébé, 144f
Becket, 43
Bedford, Paul, 87, 127-8
Bee and the Orange Tree, The, 167, 197n
Beerbohm, Max, 48, 203n
Beggar of Bethnal Green, The, 73ff, 79
Bell, Archibald, 1
Belle Hélène, La, 188
Ben the Boatswain, 26
Benefit of the Doubt, The, 51, 104, 106, 107-8
Bernard, W. B., 1, 117
Bertram, 11-12, 14
Betsy, 144-6
Beulah Spa, The, 71, 85
Beverley, William, 196
Binks the Bagman, 128, 133
Birth, 94
Birth of the Steam Engine, or Harlequin Locomotive, 197n